ABRAHAM JOSHUA HESCHEL

Abraham Joshua Heschel

A Life of Radical Amazement

JULIAN E. ZELIZER

Yale

UNIVERSITY

PRESS

New Haven and London

Frontispiece: Dr. Martin Luther King Jr. (*fourth from right*); Ralph Bunche, undersecretary of the United Nations; Rabbi Abraham Joshua Heschel; and Rev. Fred Shuttlesworth begin the march to the state capitol in Montgomery from Selma, Alabama, on March 21, 1965. AP Photo.

Jewish Lives® is a registered trademark of the Leon D. Black Foundation.

Yale University Press books may be purchased in quantity for educational, business, or promotional use. For information, please e-mail sales.press@yale.edu (U.S. office) or sales@yaleup.co.uk (U.K. office).

Set in Janson type by Integrated Publishing Solutions.
Printed in the United States of America.

Library of Congress Control Number: 2021935606
ISBN 978-0-300-23321-6 (hardcover : alk. paper)

A catalogue record for this book is available from the British Library.

This paper meets the requirements of ANSI/NISO Z39.48-1992
(Permanence of Paper).

10 9 8 7 6 5 4 3 2 1

This book is dedicated to the late Nathan Zelizer and his son Gerald, my grandfather and father, who both taught me what it means to live a Jewish life and showed me the central role that rabbis play in our historic community.

Justice, Justice, Shall You Pursue

—Deuteronomy

CONTENTS

ACKNOWLEDGMENTS

THIS BOOK HAS BEEN a labor of love. Coming from a family of rabbis, with a grandfather and father who were both part of the Jewish Theological Seminary and the Conservative movement in Heschel's lifetime, I have found it fascinating to explore the world of American Jewish life.

I would like to thank numerous people who made the book possible. Most importantly, Steven Zipperstein has been an enthusiastic supporter from the start. He saw early on how my work on the 1960s, particularly the civil rights and anti-war movements, created a match to write this book. He has been an ideal series editor, reading numerous drafts of the manuscript, each time offering smart and specific comments so that it could improve. Thanks also to his coeditor Anita Shapira. Ileene Smith signed the book and Heather Gold provided editorial guidance. Eva Skewes and Joyce Ippolito moved the manuscript through the production process. Lawrence Kenney did a terrific job

copyediting. Zev Mishell, a student at Princeton, assisted me with the final proofreading.

Samuel Freedman and Kevin Kruse were all extremely helpful as I developed the project. My friend Rabbi Elliot Cosgrove was supportive from the start and offered useful suggestions. Eric Alterman, Hasia Diner, Jaacob Dweck, Dov Weinryb Grohsgal, Jan Gross, Shai Held, Nicole Hemmer, Michael Kazin, and Daniel Rodgers read through drafts of chapters or the manuscript, providing insightful comments. The conversations and presentations at the Johns Hopkins University and Intellectual History Conference were helpful. Yale University Press obtained two reader's reports that provided smart guidance in the last round of edits. Douglas Grant helped me to fact check the final manuscript. Finally, thanks to Susannah Heschel, who generously spent several hours with me to discuss her father and was extraordinarily gracious with her time.

At Duke University, Elizabeth Dunn and all of the archivists were superb as they helped guide me through the exceptionally good Heschel collection. I would also like to thank the librarians, including Samantha Bowser and Jerry Schwarzbard, at the Jewish Theological Seminary, who were accommodating so that I could use the papers of Edward Kaplan and Sam Dresner at a time when they were in the middle of moving facilities. Dana Herman at the American Jewish Archives assisted me with their material.

The New-York Historical Society was a perfect place to spend my sabbatical working on the book. Thanks to everyone at NYHS, including Michael Ryan for creating such an intellectually enriching home. President Louise Mirrer was enthusiastic about the book and generously offered me a fellowship. Pam Schafler, chair of the NYHS Board of Trustees, has introduced me to some of the most interesting people in New York City. Sid Lapidus and Michael Weisberg generously made the fellowship possible. Besides granting me the precious time that

I needed to complete work on this manuscript, they have been friends and supporters throughout.

Princeton University remains an oasis of intellectual thought in an era of toxic political discourse. My colleagues and students continue to nurture my understanding of the questions that we must be asking as scholars and citizens.

My family has been terrific throughout the course of this project. Our kids, Abigail, Sophia, Nathan, and Claire, have been an ongoing inspiration with their love of Judaism. They fill our home with unyielding spirit. My father and grandfather have been models for the virtues of the Jewish life, while my mother is always encouraging and proud.

My wife, Meg Jacobs, continues to be the bedrock of our family and the love of a lifetime. From the moment I considered writing this book, she has been an endless source of enthusiasm, believing that I can do this and encouraging me to take the challenge. She read the proposal and the manuscript with extraordinary care, helping me to see how I could connect this Jewish life to broader narratives of American history. She could perceive exactly where better topic sentences were needed and how to add a little drama. Besides her immense intellectual talents, our partnership is the foundation for everything else. Together, we have built magnificent Jewish homes that were the only places I could write this book with this special meaning.

I completed the final draft of this book while living in Sag Harbor, New York, in the middle of the devastating Covid-19 pandemic and mass protests that unfolded after a policeman murdered a Black man named George Floyd. It wasn't surprising that in the wake of growing activism demanding racial justice that took place after Floyd's death, the former chancellor of the Jewish Theological Seminary, Arnold Eisen, released a statement that ended by quoting Heschel. "Rabbi Abraham Joshua Heschel reminded us pointedly," Eisen wrote, "that 'morally speaking, there is no limit to the concern one must

feel for the suffering of human beings, that indifference to evil is worse than evil itself, that in a free society, some are guilty but all are responsible.' "[1]

As people in the United States struggled to survive one of the worst public health disasters ever and respond to the effects of institutional racism, all the while witnessing the growing strength of right-wing extremism in national politics, Heschel's battles for social justice became more inspiring to this author than ever before. My hope is that this book can play a small role in promoting his ideas in the public conversation as we attempt to rebuild our broken society.

Heschel

There is an evil which most of us condone and are
even guilty of, *indifference to evil*. We remain neutral,
impartial, and not easily moved by the wrongs done
unto other people. Indifference to evil is more
insidious than evil itself; it is more universal, more
contagious, more dangerous. A silent justification, it
makes possible an evil erupting as an expression
becoming the rule and being in turn accepted.

—Abraham Joshua Heschel (1966)

A STUNNING IMAGE taken during a march from Selma to
Montgomery on 21 March 1965 is among the most iconic of the
civil rights era. Rabbi Abraham Joshua Heschel, with his long
white beard and overflowing curly hair, walks arm in arm with
prominent civil rights activists. Bearing a proud smile, he marches
in solidarity next to a more solemn looking Reverend Fred Shut-
tlesworth to his left and former United Nations Under-Secretary
General for Special Political Affairs and Nobel Peace Prize win-

ner Ralph Bunche on his right. A nun on the other end of the front line, who is holding civil rights activist John Lewis, whose skull had been fractured by Alabama state troopers a few weeks earlier during another march for voting rights, appears as if she was virtually dancing to the thrill of protest. Heschel and Martin Luther King Jr. glance toward the camera as if to signal to the photographer that they understand the historic weight of the moment. With his right hand tucked into the midsection of his dark jacket, Heschel and fellow marchers are just about to walk over the shadow of some kind of pole.[1] The clashes that took place two weeks earlier on the Edmund Pettus Bridge before this photograph was shot, when police brutally attacked protesters who were peacefully marching in support of a historic bill to protect African American voting rights, moved Heschel to accept King's invitation to fly down south. For many Jewish Americans, this black-and-white photograph is a testament to the enduring connections between religion and progressive politics. At an epic moment on the fraught streets of Selma, when brave citizens risked their lives championing civil rights, Heschel stood at the nexus of religious leaders who linked tradition, theology, and ritualistic practice to the fight against social injustice. To this day, Heschel remains a symbol of his generation's struggle to make Jewish values relevant to post–World War II America through civic action.

The photograph takes us back to a period when organized religion was booming throughout the United States. With the Cold War against communism underway, Americans rushed to join churches and synagogues. Religion proved attractive to millions who sought solace from the anxiety about nuclear war in their houses of religious worship. Suburbanization created physical space and pools of congregants to justify a breakneck speed of new church and synagogue construction. Membership in churches increased from 64.5 million in 1940 (50 percent of the population) to 114.5 million twenty years later (63 percent of

the population).[2] The nation's religious fabric was touted by political and corporate leaders, as well as in popular culture, as an essential ingredient to what distinguished a true democracy from the "godless communism" of the Soviets.[3]

During this period, there was a sizable cohort of spiritual leaders deeply involved in progressive movements that drove public policy, grassroots protest, and electoral politics. From the struggle for civil rights to the mobilization against the quagmire in Vietnam, it was common to find idealistic young college students marching side by side with older preachers. In our current era, when religious politics has become synonymous with conservative politics, we often forget the vital presence of rabbis, imams, and priests on the Left who perceived a direct connection between their theological beliefs and the struggle to achieve social and economic equality, as well as world peace. There was a robust universe of clergy and religious organizations who built on the tradition of the Social Gospel movement of the early twentieth century, when activists translated Christian ethics to mean social welfare and softening the edges of modern industrial life. After World War II, in the wake of the Holocaust, as the genocide came to be known by the 1960s, and the grave threat that democracy faced from totalitarianism, religious leaders from a broad range of denominations took to the streets to fight for social justice. Many well-known preachers and theologians—Daniel Berrigan, William Sloane Coffin, Martin Luther King Jr., and Ralph Abernathy, for example— believed that religious principle created the responsibility to stand up for basic civil and human rights.[4] They deployed a social justice discourse that differed from pragmatic liberal intellectuals who were prominent in the universities and in politics. Religious leaders such as Heschel spoke with a fiery moralistic and spiritual rhetoric—revolving around divinity, sin, redemption, God, and man—that resonated with activists who were devoting their lives to fight for a more equitable world.

In life and death, Heschel, a professor at the Jewish Theological Seminary (JTS), embodied this religious ethic. There was a strong relationship between the Jews and the Left in the United States ever since the influx of Eastern Europeans into the country after the 1880s. Jews were prominent figures in most of the major political movements that took form in the twentieth century, including unionism, early civil rights activism, communism, anarchism, civil rights, and New Deal liberalism.[5] Unlike a majority of these activists, however, Heschel was not only a Jew who decided to participate in politics. He was a religious leader and a public intellectual who dedicated his career to writing and speaking about his faith's devotion to the struggle to improve the human condition.

Given the economic deprivation, anti-Semitism, and carnage that he experienced with his family, starting as a boy in Europe, as well as his understanding of the Hebrew Prophets, when the civil rights movement took hold Heschel was primed to support African American activists. Like many of the Jews of the era, some of whom were active in politics and others who were not, Heschel espoused a worldview shaped by the trauma of the Holocaust. "I live in Auschwitz," he said. "Since Auschwitz I have only one rule of thumb for what I say: Would it be acceptable to those who were burned there?" Indeed, the Holocaust had been intensely personal for this Eastern European immigrant. All but one of the women in his birth family died in the genocide: one of his sisters (Esther) was killed in a German bombing of Poland, two of his sisters (Dvora Miriam and Gittel) died in German concentration camps, and his mother (Reizel) passed from a heart attack when German police broke into her home. Along with dozens of European Jewish refugees who entered into the intellectual networks of the United States during the World War II period, lived experience made Heschel acutely sensitive to the fragility of democracy as well as the evil that could take hold in modern society.[6]

Heschel's outlook on politics and society and his emphasis on the necessity of pursuing justice were fashioned by the discrimination and violence that Jews had suffered throughout his lifetime in Europe and the United States. Even though he rarely spoke about the Holocaust, it loomed large over everything that he did. His progressivism was born out of the kind of transnational experiences and networks—in Heschel's case, grounded in the worlds of religion and the university as well as anti-Semitism—that continually shaped American politics throughout much of the twentieth century.[7]

In Heschel's mind, and among his like-minded allies, the atrocities committed against Jews only amplified the need for spiritual religion to help rid the world of evil and ensure that such depravity did not happen again. Rather than concluding secular society posed an inevitable threat to religion, Heschel came to perceive how religion could make secular society a better place for everyone. He devoted the last decade of his life to joining a global fight for human rights for African Americans, Soviet Jews, the Vietnamese who had suffered in a proxy war between global superpowers, and other disenfranchised people. "We *affirm* the principle of separation of church and state," Heschel proclaimed in 1967. "We *reject* the separation of religion and the human situation."[8]

Nothing was inevitable about Heschel's progressive piety. The relationship between religion and politics swung many ways, including during his own lifetime. The Scopes Trial of 1925, which revolved around a man arrested for teaching his students about evolution, became a symbol to liberals of the danger that fundamentalism posed in American culture. During the early Cold War, conservative forces used religion as a bludgeon to combat liberalism. Southern preachers relied on scripture in defiance of racial integration. The Christian Anti-Communist Crusade, founded in 1953, was one of several right-wing organizations that spoke about God and Man in the name of a right-

ward crusade targeting the Left. Christian organizations in California, filled with transplants from the South, served as a vocal base of support for conservative politicians such as Governor Ronald Reagan. The evangelical minister Billy Graham amassed a large following for his sermons about how Americans needed to defend the "rugged individualism that Christ brought" into the nation. Business leaders and southern oil tycoons funded preachers in their fight against New Deal programs.[9] Senate Minority Leader Everett Dirksen (R-IL) had campaigned in 1966 for a constitutional amendment that would allow kids to pray in school. "They teach the little children sex in the schools," Dirksen complained. "They teach them about Communism. They even teach them ballet! Why not God Almighty!"[10] With regard to their response to anti-Semitism and Nazi Germany, other American Jews took very different paths forward than Heschel. The massacre of six million brethren drove President Richard Nixon's National Security Advisor and Secretary of State Henry Kissinger toward a hardheaded, realist view of international affairs.[11] The writer Lucy Schildkret Dawidowicz emerged as one of the most prominent voices of neoconservatism as a result of her own encounters with Eastern European Judaism and the Holocaust.[12]

Despite this long lineage of religious conservatism, Heschel dedicated himself to carving out space in the 1960s for those who believed in the natural connection between spirituality and progressive politics. To be a pious person came to mean, to him and his allies, mobilizing against social injustice and militarism in the lived world. With an uncanny instinct for promoting his ideas, and himself, Heschel gained prominence in several grassroots campaigns. Though other colleagues spent much more time in the trenches organizing, with Heschel's primary orientation always being that of a scholar, he left a distinct mark on movement politics. The fact that Heschel, whom civil rights activists called Father Abraham, insisted on connecting his theo-

logical traditions to the major issues of the day distinguished him from prominent colleagues who refrained from wearing religion on their sleeve. His efforts to engage non-Jewish scholars paid off handsomely when he sought admission into the leadership hierarchy of the interdenominational movements that dominated the period. Often willing to speak out against injustice when fellow religious leaders remained silent—about Vietnam, for example—he had a keen sense of the power of symbolism in words, spirituality, and direct action. He used his persona and his publications as tools for moving public opinion on unpopular issues and for providing religious support to those who were fighting power.

After his death, Heschel came to symbolize a seamless connection that some believed existed between the Jewish tradition and social activism. Americans living in the decades that followed Vietnam looked to Heschel in this way, often connecting him to the teaching of Tikkun Olam (translated by the Left since the 1960s to mean "repair the world" by ending injustice). They held him up in this light because of how he wrote about the theological and ritualistic underpinnings of Judaism, and then promoted his interpretation through real-world struggles over race and war.

To be sure, Heschel had his detractors. In personal interactions with those whom he did not know well, he could appear aloof. Critics argued that the quality of his scholarship did not stand up in rigor compared to that of other JTS scholars. His writing could be overly sentimental and excessively poetic, they said. He was a generalist in an age of specialization. His emphasis on spirituality and mysticism cut against the grain of a majority of JTS scholars who embraced a social scientific approach to understanding religion and privileged the social fabric of Jewish civilization grounded in the centrality of Jewish law. Throughout his adult life, a number of Conservative Jewish leaders accused Heschel of dismissing their work unfairly

for not exhibiting the same intensity of spirituality as his own. They suggested too that Heschel, ever in the public eye, overlooked their efforts to build strong Jewish institutions, especially the synagogues drawing in ever-larger suburban congregations. He wasn't as engaged with or understanding of secular Jews, either those living in the Diaspora or in the state of Israel.

Yet those critics missed that Heschel offered a defense of Jewish spirituality in the scientific age and the propagation of an ethically informed call to civic activism. As a rare figure who straddled the worlds of Hasidism, Conservatism Judaism, and the modern university, he conveyed in his writing the essential value of religion. Through lyrical tropes he explained the relevance of the Jewish tradition in a way that other theologians could not—so much so that to this day the work has remained an integral part of the weekly liturgical texts used by non-Orthodox Jews, with quotations from his writing sprinkled throughout in rabbinical sermons. Heschel could be effective at communicating the importance of religion to laypersons. He wrote and spoke in a poetic format, one that didn't always sit well in an age of social science but one that brought meaning to esoteric liturgical points.

While it was true that Heschel could sound dismissive of suburban pulpit rabbis, his work was not divorced from their projects. He strove to motivate the very congregants who populated places of worship and to make Judaism central in their lives through prayer and protest. "The primary task of religious thinking," he wrote, "is to rediscover the questions to which religion is an answer. Without an intellectual effort, without an understanding of the questions, Judaism and its answers are like stale bread to a sated man, like a solution without the riddle."[13] If a feeling of inspiration among laypeople is not sustained, he warned, the synagogues that Jewish leaders had built would find themselves to be barren.

Today, the conservative ascendancy, the all-consuming poli-

tics of Israel, and the convenience of contemporary life threaten Heschel's Jewish legacy, making his story more pertinent than ever before. Politically conservative religious leaders since the 1970s have drowned out almost every other spiritual voice in the public realm. Within the Jewish community, divisions over the Israeli–Palestinian conflict often turn many people away, especially young progressives, from their tradition. And religion competes with influences that pull everyone in a million directions. As the son and grandson of conservative rabbis whose lives briefly intersected with the white-bearded man featured in the Selma photograph, I found writing about Heschel to be extraordinarily meaningful. I have watched firsthand as mainstream religious denominations struggled to keep congregants, maintain institutions, sustain traditions, all at a time that virulent anti-Semitism, racism, sexism, nativism, and Islamophobia reemerged in mainstream life. Heschel, whom I grew up knowing as an image in a picture frame and the source of inspiring prayer book quotations, opened a window into a lost world of spiritual and progressive Jewish politics that became fainter during my own lifetime. In a turbulent era within a country whose history I have devoted my career to understanding, his ideas about theology, citizenship, and the place of Judaism in the world have renewed urgency. Each chapter below is organized around an important physical place in his evolution, from growing up as a rabbi's son amidst the poverty of Jewish Warsaw to becoming an internationally known figure who appeared regularly on the front pages of major newspapers alongside leaders like Martin Luther King Jr. In this book I look back at one of the most important American Jewish lives.

ABRAHAM JOSHUA HESCHEL

1

Warsaw

ABRAHAM JOSHUA HESCHEL spent an entire lifetime grappling with the complex relationship between religion and contemporary civilization. His city of origin nurtured this intense curiosity. He grew up in Warsaw, the heart of the Jewish Diaspora, where the sacred and the secular intermixed on the dark cobblestone streets. By the early 1900s, Poland, which had been divided up by Russia, Prussia, and Austria in the eighteenth century, was the hub of a robust transatlantic Jewish network.[1]

The size of the Jewish community had grown substantially since the mid-nineteenth century. Industrial growth generated jobs for those seeking economic opportunity. Jews migrated from Amsterdam as the Dutch lost their economic primacy. More Jews also secured the ability to move outside the Pale of Settlement, the territories where the Russian empire restricted them to live. Businessmen, arms merchants, and bankers moved into Warsaw.[2] They clustered around specific industries like tex-

tiles, clothing, liquor, tobacco, and artisan trades. The economy produced a range of conditions for residents, from wealthy bankers to professionals to destitute beggars, with a majority falling in the category of working poor.[3]

The Jewish community that surrounded Heschel could not be easily pigeonholed. Hasidim strolled home from their religious services, passing buildings that teemed with labor radicals plotting to bring down the tsar while Zionists mapped out the establishment of a Jewish state. Many residents of the Jewish district shed their traditional garb and abandoned religious practices as they embraced science, rationalism, and cultural assimilation. The intellectual descendants of Moses Mendelssohn, the founder of the eighteenth-century Haskalah (Jewish Enlightenment), remained committed to promoting Jewish intellectual engagement with the host culture.[4]

Secular Jews lived alongside others who proudly displayed their religious identity. The "traditional" residents were not all alike either. Some observant Jews were formal in their appearance and scholarly in orientation. They emphasized daily Torah study and structured the day around Jewish rituals. In their services, they privileged a certain level of decorum to distinguish themselves. Morning through night, they marked time by the Jewish cycle of rituals. The city's Jewish elite organized their religion around the Great Synagogue on Tlomackie Street, which opened in 1878.

Hasidim differed from their more traditional brethren in that they privileged robust and joyous prayer, not just textual study. Emerging in the eighteenth century, they constituted almost half of Eastern European Jewry by the middle of the nineteenth century, and they were prominent in the city of Warsaw by Heschel's lifetime. The rabbinic dynasties of Kotsk and Ger, of which Heschel's family was a part, adhered to custom, biblical law, and the vast body of rabbinic and mystical literature (with important distinctions between the two).[5] To be sure, at

the same time they depended on the strong financial and political backing of the city's Jewish mercantile elite, Hasidim rejected the notion that being cosmopolitan necessitated complete cultural integration.[6]

Hasidim were deeply influenced by the mysticism of the Kabbalah, believing that exuberant prayer, guided by the rebbe, could help individuals achieve a spiritual orientation toward understanding the intentions of God. Judaism could thus be lived in almost any geographic space until the final reversal of the Exile and the "End of Days" (the divine redemption) occurred. Hasidim believed that God was everywhere, even in the most mundane and material parts of life. Human beings should devote themselves to searching for that divine presence through a life of spirituality, Torah study, and morality that enabled them to see and to be in service of God.[7] To be a Jew, then, was to live a life of constant religious expression and exuberant celebration.[8] The Hasidic folklore propagated a subversive quasi-populist ethos that conveyed an appreciation for persons who didn't enjoy much material wealth but lived a pious life.[9]

Hasidim organized themselves into courts, almost all of which were headed by tsaddiks who assumed their position based on heredity. According to Hasidic belief, the tsaddik, a figure marked by singular piety and his ability to act as a spiritual leader to fellow Jews, was able to achieve a transcendent state of prayer where he became an instrument of God connecting the Divine to humankind. The tsaddik needed the material and spiritual support of his community as much as they needed him.[10] This set of beliefs had inspired in many of them a revolutionary zeal based on an optimistic feeling about the spiritual capacity of every individual human being.[11] Hasidim of different courts were easy to spot on the streets since they wore variations of distinctive dress—with subtle but crucial distinctions within the community—from head-to-toe: caps, hats, gabardines, black overcoats, trousers, socks, shoes, and white

garments with tzitzit (knotted ritual fringes). The long, curly sidelocks that hung over their ears, called peyos, instantly marked them to any passerby. They prayed at one of the three hundred synagogues in the city, two-thirds of which were Hasidic, or at one of the shtiebels, small communal halls devoted to prayer, social gatherings, and education.[12]

On 11 January 1907, Abraham Joshua Heschel was born into a distinguished rabbinic family living in the heart of this world. With six children, Abraham being the youngest, the Heschels resided in a new apartment building in the Jewish district at 40 Muranowksa Street. The short and wide street, standing between a market and a military square, was filled with tailors, shoemakers, button makers, and others sorts of artisans.[13] Heschel's parents, Moshe Mordechai (born in 1873) and Reizel, who went by Rivka, (Perlow) Heschel (born in 1874), descended from prominent rabbinical dynasties. Moshe and Rivka were married in 1890 in Minsk-Mazowiecki, where the court of Rivka's father, Rabbi Jacob Perlow, was located. Rivka's father had grown up in the home of the renowned Hasidic rebbe Rabbi Shlomo Hayim, whose court was approximately nineteen miles from Warsaw.[14] Moshe was a larger-than-life figure, descending from a long line of Hasidic rabbis and then becoming well respected in his own right.

That Moshe and Rivka came from rabbinic dynasties elevated the status of the family. According to tradition, the rebbe defined the character of all of the Jews living in his court. He served as the theological, spiritual, and political leader. During the years they lived in Minsk-Mazowiecki, Rivka had given birth to five children: Sarah Brakha, Esther Sima, Gittel, and Devorah as well as Jacob. The children were raised with a strong sense of their rabbinic heritage, which included the expectation that Jacob would be trained as a rebbe. Like many other Jews around them, the family relocated to Warsaw sometime around 1904, settling in an impoverished neighborhood where Moshe

established his court.[15] Their apartment, lined with bookcases filled with classic Jewish texts, was a place for work and family. Moshe set up a study where he met with local residents to counsel them. When Abraham was born three years after they moved to Warsaw, his parents decided to name him after his great-great-grandfather, one of the most distinguished rabbis in Hasidic history, Rebbe Avraham Yehoshua Heschel of Opatow (called Apt in Yiddish), known as the Apter Rav. Rebbe Heschel was a brilliant scholar and civic leader who spent his life in the same town in Ukraine, Medzhybizh, as the Baal Shem Tov, the founder of the Hasidic movement. He was often called the Ohev Yisrael, lover of the people of Israel.

Abraham and his siblings were impressed as they watched their father, a man of immense compassion, meet with Jews who sought spiritual and monetary assistance. Moshe would give the visitors almost everything he had, asking only for token fees, often returning as charity more than he took for his compensation. His father was so empathic that after meetings he would break down into tears and physically collapse.[16] Moshe liked to tell his children the story about the Apter Rav who was asked by other rabbis why God accepted his prayers but not theirs. He always responded, "You see, whenever some Jew comes to me and pours out his heart and tells me of his misery and suffering, I have such compassion that a little hole is created in my heart. Since I have heard and listened to a great many Jews with their problems and anguish, there are a great many holes in my heart. I'm an old Jew, and when I start to pray I take my heart and place it before God. He sees this broken heart, so many holes, so many splits, so He has compassion for my heart, and that's why He listens to me. He listens to my prayers."[17] Heschel felt a deep attachment to his namesake and the tradition he embodied, saying as an adult that "I was born in Warsaw, Poland, but my cradle stood in Medzhybizh [a small town in the province of Podolia, Ukraine], where the Baal

5

Shem Tov, founder of the Hasidic movement, lived during the last twenty years of his life. . . . Enchanted by a wealth of tradition and tales, I felt truly at home in Medzhybizh. That little town so distant from Warsaw and yet so near was the place to which my childish imagination went on many journeys."[18] The lessons from the life of the Apter Rav were reinforced by the stories that his parents shared with young Heschel about great religious leaders who had transformative powers.[19] "I was very fortunate in having lived as a child and as a young boy in an environment where there were many people I could revere," Heschel remembered, "people concerned with problems of inner life, of spirituality and integrity."[20]

Judaism was a religion built around texts, though only a small elite were able to master these. As a young man, Heschel's education revolved around the study of Torah, Mishnah, and Talmud with his father. These were the three canonical works of Judaism that together laid out law, theology, and centuries of rabbinic commentary. The Torah consisted of the five books of the Hebrew scriptures. The Mishnah was a collection of rabbinic commentary usually dated to the second century CE. The Talmud consisted of rabbinic commentary, and expansion on, the Mishnah. As a Hasid, Heschel also listened to the tales attributed to the Baal Shem Tov, that were guides to being compassionate to others and acknowledging human fallibility. Steeped in mystical Kabbalistic rituals and practice, he absorbed clever narratives that highlighted the goodness in every individual and stressed the need to act with kindness. Through Torah study, according to the lessons of the Baal Shem Tov, people could connect with God, building their character and developing the insight that was necessary to move them to devote their life toward helping others. Following the destruction of the Second Temple by the Romans in 70 CE, which had been understood as the place of a divine presence on earth, the Baal

Shem Tov stipulated that the tzaddik could be the "true dwelling place of the divine," as Heschel wrote later in his life.[21]

By the time he was eight, Heschel displayed a brilliant and inquisitive mind. He studied at a shtiebel a few doors down from his apartment. As other students were playing on the streets, Heschel analyzed important Jewish texts and prayed. Every morning he and his fellow students walked into a small, cramped room that was filled with long, wood tables and books. Physical conditions were generally unsanitary, the ventilation poor, the space overcrowded.[22] The day started at about seven o'clock in the morning with shacharit, the morning prayer service which lasted for about an hour. Prayer was followed by the study of Jewish law in small group sessions. The style of learning in the shtiebel revolved around back-and-forth questions among the boys, who spoke in a rhythmic cadence—a mnemonic technique taught by the rabbis for learning—about different portions of the text. Towels hung on the walls near the basins so that the young men could fulfill the ritual of washing their hands before each meal. Over the course of the day the students repeatedly rotated between prayer, discussion, and study. The intense atmosphere allowed minimal time for relaxation, just occasional breaks for a game of chess.[23]

Heschel worked with the other boys in his class to translate the prayer book and Torah into Yiddish, a language spoken by the vast majority of Eastern European Jews. Fluent in Hebrew, these young scholars sought to bring biblical language into their daily tongue. Gaining an understanding of how these books were integral to their spiritual lives was at the heart of the educational experience. Jewish learning was not ancillary to their "regular" studies but in fact the way through which they discovered the world. The boys were taught to understand how Jewish law and theology informed every part of their experience. Because he was so precocious, Heschel quickly moved on

to Rashi's classic commentaries as well as the code of Jewish law (the Shulchan Aruch). He thoroughly enjoyed blending his legalistic reading of the Midrash, which offered careful textual analysis based on the Torah, and spiritual Hasidic writing. Heschel was enthralled by the teachings of Jewish mysticism, which opened up his own vision about what he saw and experienced in Warsaw, pushing him to be less wedded to his rational perception of events and more open to experiencing the divine presence through deeply rooted senses. Even as the city was becoming increasingly cosmopolitan, Heschel's world revolved around ancient texts.

As a boy, the stories of the Baal Shem Tov inspired him to be caring about all Jews, regardless of their knowledge of tradition or their religious commitment, and to see humans in a compassionate light. He gleaned similar lessons from the writing of Levi Yitzchak of Berditchev, the author of the classic Kedushat Levi, who taught that the rebbe needed to serve as an intermediary between God and humans to make the world a better place. The work resonated with Heschel, who witnessed firsthand immense poverty. Jewish communities inhabited urban areas with poor conditions and low standards of living. While Warsaw offered greater prospects, most Jews lived on the margins. From the dirt to the sewage to the beggars, economic deprivation was always palpable.[24]

Most of his peers and teachers noticed how at ease the young Heschel was when grappling with complex Judaic literature. Extraordinarily proud of their child, whom they considered to be an *illui* (a prodigy and genius), his parents loved to brag to their friends about his intellectual acumen. During social gatherings at home his mother would invite Abraham into a room full of adults to show off his talents. Adults stood when he entered and listened attentively as he discussed Hebrew texts.[25]

Anti-Semitism hovered over Heschel's life. Although Warsaw's Jews had experienced a modicum of improvement under

tsarist Russia, having been granted permission to buy certain types of property and gaining seats in the Russian Duma after the Revolution of 1905, anti-Jewish violence and anti-Semitic propaganda were prevalent in Warsaw and other major cities. None of Heschel's older neighbors could forget the pogroms that had taken place against Jews between 1905 and 1906, when local citizens violently attacked them. Jews had been blamed for the economic problems facing Polish workers as well as all political turmoil; Polish inhabitants tapped into strains of anti-Semitic thought that had existed since medieval times. There had been a horrendous pogrom in Warsaw on Christmas Day in 1881 when Jews were accused of blood libel; riots targeted them and their communal institutions for three days. One thousand Jewish families suffered as their homes and businesses were destroyed. Twenty-four persons had to be hospitalized; two died. The attacks triggered a massive migration of Jews to the United States. A series of vicious attacks on Jewish workers took place throughout tsarist Russia. In Kishinev (1903), forty-nine Jews were killed; about forty were raped and wounded.[26] Anti-Semitic rhetoric and images had become commonplace as political parties positioned themselves against Jews after 1905, depicting them as a nefarious force that would ally with other groups to threaten local citizens.[27] Though the violence subsided by the time of Heschel's childhood, the memories never disappeared. There was always the real possibility of additional attacks. Heschel was physically assaulted by Polish boys who spotted him as they left church. "As a child I was frequently molested by Christian boys who called me Christ-killer and would occasionally beat me up," he later wrote.[28]

The fears were slightly mitigated by the fact that Heschel lived in a city where almost 41 percent of the population was Jewish by the 1910s, totaling over three hundred thousand (Catholics constituted about 48 percent, Protestants over 11 percent). There were hundreds of small houses of prayer scattered

on the gray cobblestone streets of the northeastern edge of the neighborhood. Thursday nights were the busiest in the neighborhood as the local residents went to and from the bustling Muranow Square market to prepare for the Sabbath. "Around the bazaar, on Muranow Square," one resident recounted, "dense clusters of peddlers gather like flies around a sweet left in the open air. They peddled in cheap candies and little toys."[29] From the time the sun went down on Friday evening to sunset on Saturday night, the Sabbath felt like a public holiday within these confines. Although Hasidim would walk by secular Jews smoking cigarettes, the streets of the Jewish neighborhood were quiet. On Friday after work, the streets cleared of commerce as men scrambled home chanting "Bless the candles!" There was a belief, Heschel recalled as an adult, that "on the way from the Synagogue the angels go with the people to their homes."[30] The merchants in the neighborhood closed their kiosks. Families celebrated the Sabbath with dinner, prayer, and song. After services ended the next morning, a majority of men returned to their homes, where they would rest before studying Talmud and Mishnah. "The festive atmosphere drove away the wretchedness of their everyday lives, and throughout the Sabbath the joy and holiness were boundless. No one dared refer to business affairs or matters dealing with one's livelihood, for doing so was considered a big sin," the coffeehouse owner Yekhezkel Kotik wrote in his memoirs.[31] Other holidays established the rhythm for the year, structuring time and influencing the public atmosphere, often turning the streets into a site of celebration. On Purim, which revolved around the story of Queen Esther's victory over Haman, who sought to destroy the Jews, there was drinking, dancing, and a carnival-like atmosphere. Outside of the Sabbath and holidays, the synagogue was always a central meeting place. Heschel recalled how he and the men in his family would spend part of every day in the building.[32]

During World War I, Warsaw's Jewish population swelled.

Between 1914 and 1918, many Jews who were displaced from rural areas in the Pale of Settlement arrived at the city. They were called Litvaks by the Hasidic Jews who feared they would accelerate the problem of secularization.

In August 1915, the conditions facing Warsaw's Jews changed when the Germans took control of the city during an offensive operation against the Russians, a major victory for the Central Powers. Russian forces withdrew. The three-year occupation brought some benefits to Heschel's community. The Germans temporarily lifted the bans that the tsar had imposed on Jewish newspapers and magazines. These freedoms allowed for an acceleration of the intellectual and literary sphere that surrounded young Heschel.

The war had a more intimate effect on Heschel's entire family. One of the victims of the Influenza Pandemic in 1916 was Heschel's forty-three-year-old father, Moshe. His death was devastating to the nine-year-old boy. Moshe had been the center of his family and the most important person in his own rabbinical training. As was custom, the family mourned for seven days after the funeral (sitting shiva). In the aftermath, Heschel's uncle took over as Abraham's rabbinic mentor.[33] The twin brother of Heschel's mother, a well-known rabbi named Rebbe Alter Israel Shimon Perlow, was among the transplants to Warsaw, along with his wife and eight children. Perlow quickly became the paternal figure to young Abraham. Only about five feet in height, the rebbe was a brilliant man who woke at around four o'clock every morning to study through the late evening. He introduced him to the Kotzker Rebbe.[34] His uncle recruited another rabbi, the distinguished genius Menachem Zemba, to assist him with Abraham's studies.

The rebbes loomed large in the minds of young Hasidic boys, as their teachings tended to shape the character and belief system of their followers. Under the tutelage of his uncle, Heschel learned about a bleaker side of Hasidic thought. The

Kotzker Rebbe stressed that Jews sought the truth and rejected the evil that was so prevalent throughout the world. The Kotzker Rebbe conveyed a sense of righteous indignation about the state of the world.[35] In contrast to the Baal Shem Tov, Kotzker expressed a pessimistic view of humankind and of the selfishness of individuals. "The world wants to be deceived," Kotzker said. According to Kotzker, people had to recognize, acknowledge, and then struggle against the evil pervading their lives before they could ever connect to God. Rejecting material possessions, and even sexuality, Kotzker believed in fighting for good. Critical of organized religious leaders, he thought that Judaism had been stultified with persons going through the motions of ritual and prayer who were not spiritually prepared to do so.

When the war ended and Warsaw officially became the capital of the newly independent Polish state in 1919, the northern section of the city remained the Jewish neighborhood. Polish independence and nationalism were layered on top of intense anti-Semitism. The Poles resented the fact that the war's victors pressured them into signing the National Minority Rights Treaty in 1919, which allowed for Jewish schools to exist and prohibited the new government from banning the Sabbath.[36] The resentment of Jews did not fade. The Polish government refused to grant Jews full citizenship.[37] Most of the new laws were ignored.[38] Anti-Semitic violence erupted in various parts of Poland in 1919 and 1920.[39] Jews, one American journalist recorded, were "boycotted, humiliated, slandered by the Poles, accused of the vilest crimes, of disloyalty, of espionage and treachery—all for the purpose of discrediting them . . . [and robbing] them even of the hope and freedom and justice in the future."[40]

The economic depression of the 1920s aggravated anti-Semitism. Jews were frequently blamed for the fact that in Warsaw there was upward of 40 percent unemployment. Jewish

communities, which were barely surviving poverty, dealt with surging anti-Semitism at the same time they tried to keep afloat financially. The Heschel family struggled. Abraham's mother sought assistance from family members and community leaders following the death of her husband. In their unheated apartment, Abraham's hands permanently swelled from chronic frostbite.[41]

Amidst these hard times, Jewish politics flourished.[42] Jews used the limited political space available to them to form organized political parties. For some, the toxic atmosphere they encountered gave Zionism stronger appeal. Theodor Herzl's arguments from the 1890s about the need for a Jewish homeland were sounding more attractive. Socialism offered another solution to Jews on the Left who believed that only through economic equality could these kinds of social tensions be alleviated. Others, including Heschel's relatives, fled to the United States or South America.

Heschel's immediate family focused on living a pious life. Abraham's bar mitzvah took place on 11 January 1920. In addition to the traditional milestone marking the maturation of a young Jewish man at his thirteenth birthday, the ceremony provided Heschel with a platform for demonstrating to the community his skill in teaching. The benches were filled with prominent rabbis, including his frail granduncle, who came to watch this prodigy wrap himself in the tefillin handed down from his maternal grandfather. They also listened to him speak words of Torah. He had been so anxious that he barely slept the night before. But the nerves washed away as Heschel delivered a magnificent drasha, a talk about a section in the Torah.[43]

Heschel loved attending the traditional third Sabbath meal that his uncle convened toward the end of each Sabbath following the afternoon prayers, called the Seudah Shelishit. The weekly celebrations attracted his entire court who came to watch him. Perlow invited Abraham to sit to his right at the head of

the table during each dinner.[44] The rebbe led the guests, who included prominent professors and physicians, in joyous song and prayer. As the sun fell, Perlow shared his sermon. For about sixty minutes, the teenage Heschel sat mesmerized, like everyone else at the table, as his uncle spoke without notes and delivered a masterful blend of textual analysis and spiritual uplift.

Heschel came of age at a time when Warsaw was becoming an international center of Jewish publishing. The number of printing presses in Warsaw blossomed. There were scientific, literary, and political publications. Eliezer Atlas, for instance, published landmark books on Jewish history. Yiddish literature and poetry, the central language of choice for Eastern and Central European Jews (over 80 percent of the Jews living in Warsaw spoke in Yiddish) proved to be a booming business.[45] There were numerous Yiddish and Hebrew daily newspapers, as well as a Polish-Jewish publication, which the community devoured like religious texts.[46] Yiddish theater flourished after the annulment of the tsarist ban on this art form in 1905.[47] There had also been an industry of Hebrew literature since the 1880s that grew out of Jewish nationalist sentiment.[48]

During these formative years, Heschel's surroundings in Warsaw created ongoing opportunities for him to encounter life outside the Hasidic world. His family did not shelter their young boy from these institutions. Heschel grew up in a religious environment open to the Jewish Enlightenment and Zionism. Members of his uncle's family read modern Hebrew literature and magazines. They believed in secular education and encouraged Heschel's interest in the world around him.[49]

The cultural vitality of the city was most evident in the coffeehouses of the Jewish Quarter. Heschel passed by these intellectual hubs on his way to the market or to study with his uncle. Yekhezkel Kotik had turned an old beat-up restaurant into one of the best gathering places, located near where the Heschels lived. The inexpensive establishment was jam-packed with small

businesspersons, clerks, teachers, Yiddish writers and journalists who spent hours drinking and eating as they discussed politics and literature. Bund leaders, who were secular Jewish socialists influential in the Russian empire until the Revolution of 1917, and Zionists, were side by side talking about news and political gatherings.[50] "People sat there for hours, reading the paper, meeting others, talking, sometimes doing everything at once, even those who had just met for the first time," one publisher recounted. "They also used to converse there about the latest literary news, the week's articles, and the manners of the writers themselves."[51]

Likewise, his education moved beyond his religious training. Rabbi Menachem Zemba ordained Abraham as a rabbi at the age of sixteen, and he continued his studies at the premier Mesivta Yeshiva, but Heschel was exposed to secular ideas in philosophy, the sciences, literature, and poetry, opening doors to his lifelong exploration of the relationship between these spheres.

Students in Poland were required to receive some kind of secular education.[52] There were more Jewish children attending state schools after Poland established universal primary education. Heschel's yeshiva offered a comprehensive program of secular studies, including mathematics and history. By the time he was fifteen years old, when he had already published articles about the Talmud in a monthly Hebrew journal, Heschel also completed some additional private secular studies through the mentorship of Fishl Schneerson, a psychiatrist with a degree from the University of Berlin who ran a clinic in Warsaw after having been a professor at the University of Kiev. Heschel met Schneerson at his uncle's Sabbath afternoon dinners. Though nervous about this kind of nonreligious education, Rivka allowed him to study with Schneerson since she understood Abraham's intellectual acumen.[53]

As they matured, some members of the Heschel family

started searching for a better life elsewhere. His cousin Gittel left for Palestine in 1925 to become involved in labor Zionism. In addition, after being ordained as a rebbe in 1923, Abraham's brother, Jacob, moved to Vienna in 1926, marrying one of his cousins and hoping to immigrate to Palestine. One of Heschel's uncles on his mother's side of the family, Rabbi Yehuda Aryeh Leib Perlow, departed to New York, where he started his own congregation in Williamsburg, Brooklyn. And a second cousin, Rabbi Nahum Mordechai Perlow, resettled in Borough Park.

Among those from Heschel's family who stayed, traditional religious life was vital. Heschel's mother's family in Vienna were members of the Agudas Yisroel political party, which formed in the 1920s to promote intensive yeshiva education for men as well as support for Jewish cultural programs. The party opposed Zionism, although they officially supported Jewish refugees settling in Palestine. Its existence demonstrated how Hasidim had become an established and traditional presence in the region.[54]

Unlike the many Hasidim who turned away from the intellectual culture of secular Warsaw, Heschel was drawn to it. His curiosity took him to the Yiddish Writers and Journalism Association on 13 Tlomackie Street. Founded in 1916, this association was at the heart of the Jewish Enlightenment; the building housed social events, adult education courses, and cultural outings. It had been created by sixty Jewish writers, poets, teachers, and journalists who came together to form a trade union. Many prominent Jewish writers, including the well-known Yiddish poets Melech Ravitch and Uri Tsevi Grinberg, made this institution their home.[55] Heschel had heard a great deal about this organization from Schneerson and from other intellectuals who were regular attendees at his uncle's Sabbath meals.

One day when he was on his way to see his uncle, Heschel walked toward the association to see what all the excitement was about. Everyone turned around when this young religious

man entered the room wearing a long black coat and black hat. The editor of the association's journal, Melech Ravitch, a poet who arrived in the city from eastern Galicia and turned his organization into a major site for Yiddish writing, recalled his feeling upon first seeing Heschel: "I raise my eyes and for a moment I am startled. In a corner by my green door stands a tall and slender young lad, in Warsaw Hasidic attire. A long, black garment, almost to the ground, scarcely showing his boots, a round hat on his head with a small, pinched peak. A severe face, though he looks at me very gently and guiltily, he also looks gruff. His eyes are black, deep, large; his skin brownish, with the first, young sprouts of a dark beard. . . . The young man knows that I am preparing a literary almanac—he has brought me some 'songs.' "[56] Intrigued by the quality of the work, Ravitch invited Heschel to submit some lines of poetry to their new journal, *Literary Pages*. He sensed Heschel's raw intellectual skill and felt that the young rabbi was deeply interested in exploring the connections between his religious upbringing and the secular world. Heschel followed up with several additional poems, all of which were published. The first came out in a 1926 anthology. Portions of the work dealt with subject matter like sensuality that were taboo in his uncle's court.

This experience, combined with the relationships he had forged during his uncle's meals and within his own family, inspired Heschel to pursue a university education. This was a significant decision for a young man considered to be a rabbinic prodigy. Fulfilling the dream would require considerable work. Universities had offered Jews only limited opportunities for admission ever since the Russians had imposed restrictions in the 1880s.[57] The "Hasidic world of Warsaw," noted his future student Rabbi Arthur Green, "was too narrow for him; he saw the small-mindedness that necessarily resulted from the tremendous effort expended to shut out the modern world."[58]

Heschel began by hiding in his room to train himself in

non-Judaic subjects. Schneerson and writers at the association put him in contact with tutors to teach him Polish and Latin. Though his mother knew what he was doing, she did not interfere, respecting his intellectual strength as well as his promise to be one of the great rebbes.[59]

To attend a university, Heschel would first have to spend a year at a high school for Jews that was accredited by the Polish government. The Gymnasium in Vilna was founded in 1906 as a Jewish high school that taught courses in Russian and which had been transformed in 1918 into a Yiddish secular high school. Committed to his Jewish education, he was also eager to learn more from the scholarly worlds of philosophy, humanities, and the sciences. His mother understood that her son's passions rested in both worlds, remembering once seeing him kiss a history book after dropping it on the floor, the same way that a Jew would treat a sacred religious text.[60]

Heschel had learned about Vilna (which in the interwar period was named Wilno by the Polish authorities) from Jacob Perlow's younger brother, who had attended the school after his parents moved to the United States. He returned to Warsaw when Heschel was eighteen and reported to him about how exhilarating the experience had been. Heschel gathered more information on his own and earned money to support his travel by writing for the Yiddish association.[61]

Although she had supported his intellectual growth, his mother nonetheless worried when Heschel let her know about his desire to study in Vilna. Like many parents in the Hasidic community, her anxieties about assimilation were strong. She recruited her brother, Heschel's mentor, to dissuade her son from leaving. It didn't work. By the end of their conversation, Heschel's uncle reluctantly stated his support for his nephew's decision: "You can go, but only you," the rebbe said.[62] The family assumed that he would stay in the Hasidic fold and continue with his rabbinic studies.[63] At some level, they expected

that he would eventually return to Warsaw and use his secular knowledge to strengthen the Hasidic community in ways they could not imagine.

One night after the Sabbath ended, Heschel put on his cap, grabbed his bags, and boarded the train to Vilna. He bid his mother and sisters farewell. Before leaving, one of the men from his uncle's court, who had watched Abraham grow up, approached him. The old Hasid warned that Heschel should not allow his holy flesh to be "polluted from the world."[64]

At seventeen years of age, Heschel arrived at the Gymnasium. Vilna was also home to multiple types of Jewish communities. The city, which was the birthplace of the Bund in 1897, consisted of secular Jewish intellectuals, labor Zionists, and Yiddish literary writers, all of whom considered the Vilna Real Gymnasium to be an incubator of Jewish thought. It had been a hub for the Haskalah.[65] Vilna, known as the Jerusalem of Lithuania, was only a shell of what it had been decades earlier, but it remained an exciting arena for Jewish intellectual life. Control of the city had changed hands several times during the war and Russian Revolution, finally ending under Polish sovereignty in 1922. As in Warsaw, Jews constituted almost 40 percent of the population. If the Hasid symbolized Judaism in Warsaw, the cosmopolitan Yiddish scholar—tilting toward a radical bent— was the face of Vilna.[66] There were over seventy-six thousand Jews and one hundred synagogues. There was also the distinguished Jewish Scientific Institute (YIVO), established in 1925, which was considered to be one of the most important institutions of Yiddish culture in the entire world.[67]

By the time he arrived in Vilna, about 270 miles from his hometown, Heschel's physical appearance had changed. Like a growing number of religiously observant Jews in urban areas (who were calling themselves Orthodox to distinguish themselves from Reform Judaism), he had trimmed his facial hair, which had been meager to begin with. He started to dress in

standard European suits. He rented a barren room, furnished only with a bed, from an elderly Jewish man who lived in one of the most impoverished communities. Heschel continued to abide by traditional law. He kept kosher and adhered strictly to most of the rituals. He celebrated the Sabbath, prayed before and after every meal, and observed each Jewish holiday.[68]

Freed from the pressure of being a rabbinic son in the heart of Warsaw's Hasidic community, Heschel jumped into his studies, thriving in his classes in literature, German, history, psychology, and the sciences, all of which were taught in Yiddish (even the signs in the school for the bathroom and offices were in Yiddish). Several teachers at the Gymnasium had a profound influence on his thinking, including the playwright and novelist Moyshe Kulbak, who was a left-wing modernist, avant-garde writer considered one of the finest Yiddish poets, and an inspiring teacher.[69] "You will never be a great poet," Kulbak told him, "but you will become an excellent philosopher."[70]

During these early years of his development, Heschel came to appreciate the contributions of secular Jews to the quest of improving the world.[71] One of his friends was Nahum Faynshtayn, who would go on to establish a Communist newspaper. Faynshtayn was fascinated by the promise of radical economic ideas. Heschel joined a group of young writers, called Young Vilna, who were at the cutting edge of these leftward humanistic debates. They received intellectual support from Kulbak and the leaders of YIVO as well as from the journalist and activist Zalmen Reyzen, who helped establish them in 1929 and published their work in his newspaper, the *Vilner Tog*. Heschel passed his high school exams on 24 June 1927; two days later, on a Sunday, he celebrated his graduation.

Through his poetry, Heschel was starting to wrestle with the religious ideas that he studied in the yeshiva, his budding secular education, as well as the difficult circumstances he had encountered among those who were poor or lived in fear be-

cause of their Judaism. How to reconcile hardship and evil with his belief in God? Heschel wondered. He started a series of poems that explored the intimate and interdependent relationship between God and man: "Millions of eyes are clogged with a common tear / because of tangled fates—endless calamities. / God, pass me your weapons! / Let me slash through the gordian knots of that idolatrous embroidery of people's star-shaped fate! / No, I don't want to wear Your fists! I only beg, demand of You / that You tell bacillae 'Do not murder!' / Avert catastrophe and rampage, chase away bloodthirst in man and beast!"[72]

The seeds of Heschel's political outlook had been planted in Warsaw and Vilna. Increasingly fascinated with the nexus between the secular and the sacred, Heschel had observed the writers who had shed the physical and theological clothing of his community and were striving to achieve greater justice in society. Through literature, poetry, political writing, theater, and music, the Yiddish speaking communities that Heschel encountered were trying to change the world.

At twenty, Heschel received notice that he had been offered admission into the University of Berlin. He was excited to enter into this world-class educational institution and to move to a city known for being intellectually robust and sitting at the cutting edge of contemporary culture.

2

Berlin

STANDING AT A STOUT five foot, six inches tall, wearing thin, rimless glasses and a contemporary black suit, a clean-shaven Heschel walked off a train that arrived in Berlin in the fall of 1927. Having almost no money to his name, the stocky rabbi rented a bare-bones room in the apartment of a religious family who lived ten minutes from the University of Berlin. Despite his meager circumstances and often surviving on potatoes and bread, Heschel found that the city would open the doors to an exciting, cosmopolitan world. While Warsaw had its coffee-houses, theaters, and literary circles, not much could compare with the first-class educational and cultural institutions of Berlin. It was considered to be one of the most cosmopolitan cities in Europe.[1] "I admired the solidity of its architecture," he reminisced, "the overwhelming drive and power of a dynamic civilization. There were concerts, theaters, and lectures by famous scholars about the latest theories and inventions, and I was

pondering whether to go to the new Max Reinhardt play or to a lecture about the theory of relativity."[2]

Heschel's world was certainly a scholarly one, but it had been a self-contained form of inquiry focused on the same eternal questions and texts since the time of the Talmud. This kind of university living was different: it was about progress, science, and modernity. Weimar Germany in the 1920s was the epicenter of European culture and industry, with its cabarets, modernist art, and economic growth.

One of Heschel's toughest challenges upon resettling was to navigate a Jewish community so different from the one of his childhood.[3] The Jewish population, notably smaller than in his hometown, had generally embraced assimilation and shed their connection to tradition. They had been able to do so with greater ease than in Poland since there were fewer legal or political restrictions that prevented German Jews from participating in government, university, or cultural organizations. Jews were extraordinarily visible in the public life of the city.[4] A Nazi Party that claimed over seventy thousand Germans, drawing strength from German nationalism and false scientific arguments about racial hierarchy, still did not have much of a toehold in the city.[5]

For decades most of the city's top Jewish thinkers had maintained an uneasy relationship with Eastern Europeans, perceiving their brethren to be antithetical to the German ideal of Bildung, which meant achieving rationality and self-cultivation through education.[6] Many assimilated and prosperous German Jews had dismissed the newcomers as physically uncouth and uncivilized, an exotic other tied to a traditional, backward-looking past. The German Jews distanced themselves physically and intellectually from their Eastern European cousins.[7] German Jews feared that the influx of approximately thirteen thousand Eastern Europeans in the early twentieth century (20 percent of Berlin's Jewish population), whom they saw as less civilized, cultured, or modern, would threaten their standing

and successful assimilation into the mainstream culture. Indeed, their assimilation had depended on separating themselves from these communities. The Jews who came to the city from Eastern Europe scared them because they seemed to place their hard-earned identity at risk.[8]

Among the Germans, the Reform movement was prominent. "There is no cantor here, no words for prayer," Heschel observed.[9] Born in the nineteenth century, Reform Jews in Germany, as well as in other parts of Europe and in the United States, had sought to revitalize their religion by allowing practices to evolve with modern times. The goal was to preserve the relevance of tradition to emancipated Jews who were enjoying the fruits of integrating into the culture around them while still living in the shadow of violent anti-Semitism.[10] Reform Jews abandoned key liturgical practices (eliminating the mechitzah, the partition which physically separated genders during prayer) and reshaped the tenor of the weekly services to make them more appealing.[11] The elevated stature of Reform Judaism in Weimar Germany was evident in the New Synagogue on Oranienburger Strasse, one of the most beautiful structures in the city, seating over three thousand congregants. The Moorish Revival style was emblematic of the synagogues that had been built by the German Jewish community, a display of success and solidarity.

While finding his place in these non-Orthodox, secularized Jewish environs, Heschel grappled with the intellectual tensions and connections between his religious education and the disciplinary questions that animated Europe's premier universities. Founded in 1809, the University of Berlin was considered to be one of the finest institutions of higher learning. Heschel loved his teachers and instantly shined in the classroom.[12] He chose philosophy as his major with minors in art history and Semitic languages. Heinrich Maier, who chaired his dissertation, was a specialist in Kant who taught courses on

phenomenology and psychology. Max Dessoir, a Jewish scholar whose father had been a well-known Shakespearean actor, was an inspirational philosopher, as well as an amateur magician, who argued that different kinds of thought could be present in one individual, a theme that resonated with Heschel at this moment in his life. The Protestant theologian Ernst Sellin offered pathbreaking classes about the Bible that deployed historical and archeological analysis to understand the biblical narratives. Heschel's eyes were opened as he learned how Sellin used archeological findings from ancient Israel as a basis to reinterpret stories. In many of these courses, the relationship between the secular and the sacred was a topic of constant discussion. Heschel focused on the discipline of phenomenology, the exploration of the structures of consciousness and experience. This involved understanding how things appeared and the way they appeared from the first-person perspective. "In all phenomena of spiritual life, we encounter two types of qualities: the quality of actual being, and that of significance or meaning," Heschel wrote. "When, for example, a man stands in a garden and points his finger at a certain flower, two things are revealed to us: the movement of the finger (an occurrence within space and time) and its significance (the intention of the mover, which is evident from the movement). In these two ways the phenomenon (movement of the finger) is interpreted, and any correct evaluation must pay heed to both."[13]

Just a few blocks away was the Hochschule für die Wissenschaft des Judentums (Academy for the Science of Judaism), a neo-Orthodox institute established in 1872, where Heschel supplemented his university work. The Hochschule was situated on Tucholskystrasse, close to Adass Yisroel, the main synagogue of Orthodox Judaism. It offered beautiful lecture rooms and a magnificent heated library, all free of charge. This Hochschule was unusual in that it blended traditional Jewish textual study with contemporary German scholarship, straddling the line

between Orthodox rabbinic pedagogy and secular, scientific knowledge. The approximately 150 full-time students (including 27 women) debated the Bible as a historical text and analyzed Judaism as an evolving, rather than static, tradition. The teachers, some of whom came from outside the Orthodox faith, used historical methods to examine the Bible, treating the book as more than just God-given word.[14] Rabbi Leo Baeck, one of the major voices in Reform Judaism who had authored *The Essence of Judaism* (1905), taught students to understand religion through Kant. Julius Guttmann showed his class that philosophy could point to a science of Judaism. The reputation of the institution was so good that some Christian clergy enrolled to take courses. Like other Orthodox institutions in the city, scholars of diverse religious backgrounds were recruited to enrich the dialogue. Most of the German students wanted more than the secular education universities could provide. Eastern European students like Heschel were valued since they enriched the culture of the classroom by bringing a deep background in Judaism. The Weimar period was also notable for its admission of young Jewish women as students and scholars.[15] The novelist Franz Kafka called the Hochschule a "refuge of peace in wild and woolly Berlin and in the wild and woolly regions of my mind."[16]

Even as he experimented with other strains of Jewish learning, Heschel dived deeper into his understanding of Orthodoxy. In addition to his studies at the Hochschule, Heschel attended the Rabbiner-Seminar für das Orthodoxe Judentum, where he advanced his rabbinic training. The seminary was another innovative pedagogical group that had been formed by a scholar of mathematics and language who believed that traditional Jewish learning did not have to be antithetical to modern intellectual currents.

As a budding intellectual, Heschel thrived in the informal conversations that took place outside of the classrooms, part of

the reason that he loved to reside in an area that was filled with institutions of higher learning and education. Heschel was pleased to be invited into a renowned study group that took place at the home of David Koigen, a Ukrainian-born sociologist and philosopher. Koigen was greatly admired in Berlin. He was an independent scholar who had fled Kiev in 1921. Upon Koigen's arrival to Berlin, the philosopher Martin Buber promoted his scholarship throughout the city so that his friend could make a living by speaking and writing. The relationship was important to Heschel because Koigen, who grew up in a Hasidic family, was radical in his politics. He believed that Hasidic Judaism could serve as a powerful force for progressive change and spiritual renewal. He focused his research on developing a phenomenological understanding of religion, and believed in the holiness of every person and the essentialness of nonrationalistic thinking to a healthy soul.[17] Koigen, who was friends and a coeditor with Fishl Schneerson (they published the Yiddish literary journal *Kadima*), took Heschel under his wing and introduced him to prominent social scientists and humanists in Berlin. In seminar, Heschel pushed back against the philosophical arguments made by Koigen and other colleagues about the symbolism of God replacing the reality of God. This idea, to Heschel, was false. Heschel insisted, often in heated exchanges, that they had to begin their inquiry from the starting point of accepting the existence of a divine being; God was at the center of understanding all human ethical and religious activity. Unlike a mathematical formula or scientific theory, God was not something to be proven.[18] There was no room for the attitude of doubt; the starting point for the pious man was wonder about the world around him while holding an absolute belief in the existence of God.[19]

Heschel, a Hasid, was able to circulate through these vibrant intellectual networks with considerable ease since there was a growing thirst among secular Jewish scholars to discover

authentic forms of identity that varied from what cosmopolitanism or assimilation had to offer. Even if they differed on points of faith and theology, it was clear that Heschel's Hasidism served as a well for intellectual debate and discussion, one that could be repurposed to wrestle with contemporary questions of modernity. University scholars welcomed students who brought with them the fervor of spiritual practice but did so with a high level of cultural sophistication that was stripped of the grittier aspects of impoverished Warsaw.[20] By the interwar years there was more mixing of Hasidism and German Jews. World War I had also put Jewish German soldiers into direct contact with the residents of Jewish communities on the Eastern Front.[21] So too did the influx of immigrants who arrived into Berlin after the war that made the Hasidic population a more tangible presence in urban areas.[22]

By the 1920s, Hasidic culture had gained intellectual sway among Berlin's brightest thinkers. Despite the perception of the Hasid as living a life of cultural isolation and reaction against modern and cosmopolitan life, some intellectual Jews who had lost touch with their own Jewish backgrounds now looked to these communities as they struggled with a sense of existential emptiness—and sometimes horror—about Western European life.[23] They explored a romanticized vision of Hasidic life that helped with their own dissatisfaction with life in Berlin.[24] One of the most influential of them, the prolific philosopher Martin Buber, explained: "My spirit was in steady and multiple movement, determined by manifold influences, taking ever new shape but without a center. . . . Here I lived—in versatile fullness of spirit, but without Judaism and humanity."[25] Yearning for spiritual authenticity, an idealized Eastern European Hasid emerged within their writing as an aspirational model for how to practice the kind of "lived" Judaism that was missing from their generation.[26] The mysticism and exuberant prayer that they believed had existed with the founders, less rigid than the Ha-

sidic Jews whom they encountered in their own lifetime, embodied the spirit that some German Jewish intellectuals sought.[27] They admired the Hasid, whose intense piety appeared more genuine than the modernist impulses of twentieth-century Western culture.[28] Hasidic Jews were distinct even from the Orthodox of Germany, who adhered to a level of formality and halakhic rules that did not inspire the literary crowd. Imagining a Jewish neighborhood filled with joyous Hasidic men dancing and singing—speaking Yiddish—their written work transformed the image of the streets on which Heschel was raised from being a place of dirtiness, backwardness, and danger into a source of raw spiritual energy.[29] When he was twenty-six, Buber, who had come to forget much of the Hebrew he learned as a child, had his awakening when reading a short book about Rabbi Israel Baal-Shem that left him feeling "overpowered in an instant, I experienced the Hasidic soul."[30] Buber's writing about Hasidic texts and mysticism gained a cult-like following among younger Jews in the elite educational circles of Berlin.

Heschel and Buber became friends despite their theological disagreements. Buber thought of God, and the Prophets, as symbols to impart moral lessons. Heschel never abandoned his belief that God was real. They would continue their conversations over the years through letters. Their interaction, fraught as it was, deeply influenced Heschel as he worked out the relationship between individuals and the world around them.

The warm welcome Heschel received from the learned community did not dampen the profound discomfort that he felt about the thinness of their theological convictions.[31] As Heschel recalled, "I came with great hunger to the University of Berlin to study philosophy. I looked for a system of thought, for the depth of spirit, for the meaning of existence. Erudite and profound scholars gave courses in logic, epistemology, esthetics, ethics and metaphysics. They opened the gates of the history of philosophy. I was exposed to the austere discipline of

unremitting inquiry and self-criticism. I communed with the thinkers of the past who knew how to meet intellectual adversity with fortitude, and learned to dedicate myself to the examination of basic premises at the risk of failure." However, Heschel explained, "I became increasingly aware of the gulf that separated my views from those held at the university. I had come with a sense of anxiety: How can I rationally find a way where ultimate meaning lies, a way of living where one would never miss a reference to supreme significance? Why am I here at all, and what is my purpose? I did not even know how to phrase my concern. But to my teachers that was a question unworthy of philosophical analysis. . . . The problem to my professors was how to be good. In my ears the question rang: How to be holy."[32]

Bitter and mystified, Heschel spent many long nights walking the beautiful streets feeling out of sorts. He arrived in Berlin eager to learn from the best scholars yet had come to discover that a profound spiritual barrier separated them: "To them, religion was a feeling. To me, religion included the insights of the Torah which is a vision of man from the point of view of God. They spoke of God from the point of view of man. To them, God was an idea, a postulate of reason. They granted Him the status of being a logical possibility. But to assume that He had existence would have been a crime against epistemology."[33]

Heschel worked through his angst with poetry. The entrepreneurial Heschel reached out to prominent editors all over the continent, as well as in New York City, seeking a home for his writing. He received an enthusiastic response from a monthly Yiddish journal founded by the Socialist Labor Party based in New York called *Die Zukunft* ("the future"). The editor, Abraham Liessin, was a revolutionary Yiddish poet who had fled to New York in 1897 fearing arrest for his socialist activity. He had started editing the journal in 1913. By the 1920s, Liessin con-

cluded that Socialists lacked any kind of spiritual core. Looking to Jews who could write based on their knowledge of religious tradition, he jumped at the opportunity to work with Heschel. Much of the writing that Liessin published by Heschel focused on social injustice, concerns that grew directly out of the lessons he learned as a child from the stories of the Baal Shem Tov. His poems examined the relationship of God to man in a world of intense hardship. In one poem, Heschel angrily warned God about the suffering he witnessed: "You must tell every virus: 'Thou shalt not kill' . . ." In another piece, he wrote, "The pauper's sins are more beautiful / Than the good deeds of the rich."[34] His work gained the attention of Hayim Nahman Bialik, a pioneer in modern Hebrew poetry living in Palestine. One of Heschel's papers, "Visions in the Bible," received a distinguished award.[35]

Heschel's creative endeavors invigorated his scholarly pursuits. He completed his university courses on 24 January 1931 and started his dissertation. He decided to examine the consciousness of the Hebrew Prophets, depicting them as fearless figures who fought for justice when the priests, as well as the kings and judges, tolerated human suffering. They opened themselves up to God and could understand his compassion as well as anger. The Prophets denounced the wrongdoing of fellowmen and warned of the impending judgment of God. Heschel kept publishing his more artistic work as well, producing a string of powerful poetry and cofounding a journal, the *Berlin Pages of Poetry and Art*, with a Yiddish poet from Warsaw named A. N. Stencl, a pioneer of the modernist style.[36]

His intellectual maturation occurred against the backdrop of intensifying physical, legal, and economic anti-Semitism. Right as Heschel dove into his doctoral research, the Weimar Republic disintegrated as the Nazi Party rose to power. What had been a vibrant city dedicated to cultural experimentation turned into a site of utter horror. Ever since the world econ-

omy started spinning into a downward spiral in the late 1920s, Germany had been on the decline. With high rates of unemployment in cities like Berlin, more Germans were listening to the voices of right-wing political leaders who blamed Jews and other "outsiders" for their economic hardship. In the 1932 elections the Nazi Party won more than 37 percent of the final vote, making Adolf Hitler a major political leader. After several months of parliamentary wrangling, Hitler took power.

One night when Heschel was attending the opera, Hitler entered the hall. The young scholar trembled in terror when he observed everyone rise from their seats to honor this frightening figure. Heschel walked out as soon as he could.[37] These ominous political developments pushed Heschel to think more carefully about weaving together the theological principles he was learning in his rabbinical studies, the rational humanism in his university education, and the terrifying events that were taking place throughout his new home country. Heschel felt disenchanted with German Christians, who were doing little to protest or stand in the way of the Nazis. But he wasn't ready yet to leave Germany. Like many Jews in Berlin, Heschel could glean the dangers but not imagine the totality of evil that would sweep the country.

Heschel completed his oral examinations in February 1932 and had a collection of poems, *The Ineffable Name of God: Man*, released by a publisher in Warsaw. The poems about suffering and divinity were crafted in a somber tone, shaped by Hitler's rise to power. In "Repentance" he wrote, "God, You greatest mute! / You answer screams with riddles / You're no defender of the criminal / You never say to hatred—'Out! Stop!' . . . / We— God and man and dogs, let's repent together or each one for the other. / And forgive us our sins as we forgive You Yours." The poems also revealed that at this early age Heschel was acutely sensitive to the condition of those around him who suffered. "Street-walkers are my bastard sisters," Heschel wrote in

"Forgiveness," and "sinister criminals—souls perhaps trans-migrated from me."[38]

The climate for Jewish intellectuals only worsened. His future became more uncertain when the publisher Schocken, a house owned and run by a German Jew named Salman Schocken (founded in 1931), rejected his manuscript based on a critical report by Buber.[39] This left Heschel without anywhere to go. He saw the danger in other ways as well. In April 1933 the Nazis forced Jewish-owned stores to place yellow stars on their doors, a sign for consumers to stay away. This was part of a national boycott launched by the Nazis on Jewish businesses and professionals. On 10 May, university students, coordinated by the Nazi regime, gathered to burn over twenty-five thousand books that were deemed to be un-German. Almost forty thousand people congregated in the central square to hear Joseph Goebbels declare, "No to decadence and moral corruption! Yes to decency and morality in family and state." The work of some of the most famous Jewish authors of the time were among the first to be thrown in the fires. "Now, as the smoke of our burned books rises into the sky," one journalist wrote in a firsthand account, "we German writers of Jewish descent must acknowledge above all that we have been defeated. Let us, who were fighting on the front line, under the banner of the European mind, let us fulfill the noblest duty of the defeated warrior: Let us concede our defeat."[40] Putting his angry thoughts about this night on paper, Heschel published a poem in the Yiddish newspaper *Haynt*, under the pseudonym Itsik, called "On This Day of Hate." He wrote, "Race-pure Germans, happy holiday to you. On this, your blasphemous, holy day, hatred is your sanctity. . . . In the mob's heart there's noise and robbery. Every desire gets stolen ten thousand times." Heschel ended the poem with a stanza that was filled with rage: "On every windowpane, the hand spits a burning Star of David / The facades of Jewish houses gleam / Like holy curtains over outraged Torah-arks / The Inef-

fable Name—a brilliant darkness / The K I K E on every window-pane in flames."[41]

Heschel was racing against time. He wanted to establish himself as a scholar even as the world around him was disintegrating into anti-Semitic hell. In December 1934, Heschel found a desperately needed break when the Polish Academy of Sciences agreed to publish his book as long as he contributed enough money for a subvention—a financial contribution raised by the author to support the production of a book. The good news came just a few months after he finished his degree at Hochschule and was ordained as a rebbe for the second time. Since it would take time for the book to be published, Heschel asked for an extension from his dean, who agreed to push back the deadline for graduation. The dean closed the letter with an exclamation point, "Heil Hitler!" Realizing that his time was limited, Heschel moved in with some friends in Berlin so that he could save the rent money as he built up his publishing coffers. Impressed with Heschel's work, the distinguished publisher Erich Reiss commissioned Heschel to write a short biography about the renowned medieval Jewish theologian Maimonides, in celebration of the eight hundredth anniversary of his birthday. Though Heschel didn't want to take on the project, he agreed to do so since he was desperate for money; he finished the book in a year, scrambling to complete the work so that he could make certain that his dissertation saw the light of day.

In Maimonides, Heschel found a role model, which was ironic given the fundamental differences in how they understood God. Maimonides saw God as transcendent; Heschel perceived God to have human emotions and to be in need of man. Heschel was intrigued by Maimonides's clarity about what he was meant to contribute to his community and especially interested in the evolution of his thoughts about God after his brother David's death. "The love of thinking was the fundamental motif of his life," Heschel wrote. "He related to think-

ing as to something personified. Every act of thinking was the reception of a revelation for him."[42] His depiction of a scholar who sought to make his consciousness of God accessible to as many people as possible, a democratization of the spiritual knowledge, held immense appeal to Heschel, a Jew anxiously trying to survive life under the Nazi regime.[43] The final product, written in German, earned him terrific reviews in a number of major journals. The book sold well, and within a year it was translated into French.[44]

With this accomplishment under his belt, Heschel secured a job in Frankfurt at an institution that focused on Jewish education for adults. He received his doctoral degree on 11 December 1935, and the Polish Academy published Heschel's dissertation in March 1936. Buber invited Heschel to be his successor as the director of the Mittelstelle für Jüdische Erwachsenen Bildung in Frankfurt, a prestigious adult education center and one of the most exciting institutions in the country. It had been founded by Franz Rosenzweig to reengage Jews with their tradition. Thousands of people attended the courses. Europe's greatest Jewish intellectual powerhouses taught there: Rosenzweig, Buber, Baeck, Gershom Scholem, Erich Fromm, and others. The building was bubbling with lectures, cultural performances, in-house courses, and training for teachers. Buber had reopened the doors in 1933, four years after it had closed upon Rosenzweig's death, reconceptualizing the mission from being the education of Jews to coexist within German culture toward the education of Jews who were now finding themselves isolated and under attack from the Nazis.[45]

On 1 March 1937, at the age of thirty, the soft-spoken Heschel moved full-time to Frankfurt. He rented a room from an Orthodox family in the suburb of Eschersheim, Jacob and Amalie Simon and their two daughters, just a short walk from the largest Orthodox synagogue. Much of his time was spent leading seminars and giving lectures. Shortly after Heschel's ar-

rival, Buber invited him to dinner at his home. Over the course of the evening the two men, as they often would, ended up vigorously debating the Prophets. Though Buber commented that Heschel was stubborn, they thoroughly enjoyed the exchange.[46] Otherwise, Heschel, who was very serious at this point in his life, spent most of his time in solitude and didn't socialize much. On numerous evenings, he devoted many hours to writing letters to his mother and sisters in Warsaw.[47] In his spare time, Jacob Simon tutored him in English, which he had learned through his work in business, and Heschel improved his linguistic skills by reading the *Times* of London.[48]

The work he loved. Heschel was on a mission to teach Jews, even the most secular and radical figures, about why biblical text mattered. In this period he published a book about the life of the Jewish philosopher Isaac Abravanel, who lived through the fifteenth-century expulsions of his people from Spain and Portugal—a theme he knew would have meaning to Jews who were facing the Nazis.[49] "When the ancient faith came under this heavy attack, disappointment broke the backbone of the faithful," Heschel wrote. "Their disillusionment approached despair. In that hour of crisis, Abravanel wielded his authority, his scholarship, and his faith."[50] He penned articles for a number of Jewish publications—from book reviews to essays with meditations about the holidays.[51] Heschel sent letters to intellectual luminaries in the United States. He wrote to Louis Finkelstein, a major up-and-coming scholar at the JTS. Accepting an invitation from Rudolf Schlosser, the prominent head of an anti-Nazi Quaker community in Frankfurt, Heschel spoke to the group about the role of religious leaders in the struggle against Nazi persecution.[52] Heschel praised them as an antidote to the passivity that most Christian Germans exhibited even though they knew what the Nazi Party was doing but feared taking any steps.[53]

"It is not easy to work or to think with a whole heart,"

Heschel wrote Buber. "Maybe God has pity for the world."[54] Indeed, it became increasingly challenging for him to concentrate on his intellectual work. He avidly read the newspapers to follow the major events in the brewing war in Europe. On 12 March 1938, Germany invaded Austria, leaving his many relatives in Vienna under Nazi control. When Heschel traveled back to Warsaw to visit his family in April for Passover, he was stunned to see the broken state of the city. He wrote Buber that Jews were facing an "epidemic of despair."[55] After having grown up surrounded by poverty and economic hardship in cities rife with anti-Semitic sentiment, Heschel now watched government forces brutally and systematically crack down on the freedom of fellow Jews.

On 28 October 1938, Heschel's life unraveled. The Gestapo raided Jewish homes to deport eighteen thousand Polish Jews who were living in the country. With two suitcases filled with books and unpublished papers, taking the collections rather than his clothing and other possessions, Heschel was placed in a detention camp called Zbaszyn, which was situated at the Polish border. Through family and their contacts in Warsaw, Heschel was able to obtain his own release. Heschel accepted an invitation to join the Warsaw Institute of Jewish Study, where he reconnected with his family, moving back in with his mother and sisters. But that situation was untenable. On 9 November, the same night as *Kristallnacht*, a violent pogrom by Nazi Germans against Jewish institutions, Heschel wrote Buber that he needed to leave Europe.[56] With German authorities standing by silently, hundreds of synagogues had been destroyed or vandalized; thousands of businesses ransacked. Jews were physically assaulted, and almost one hundred were killed. There were also mass arrests. From that point forward, it became impossible to ignore the dire threats he and others faced. "Here everybody is in agony because of bitter premonitions," he told his friend. "It would be of great importance for me to get away."[57]

His salvation came unexpectedly from the training ground for Reform Jewish rabbis in the United States. Julian Morgenstern, an Illinois native who had become the acting president of the Hebrew Union College (HUC) in 1921, the seminary in Cincinnati, Ohio, that ordained Reform rabbis, invited Heschel to serve as a research fellow. Morgenstern, who officially became president the following year, had devoted his tenure toward developing a more coherent vision of what their members stood for and reconnecting students with Jewish tradition.[58] He advocated recruiting more Eastern European Jewish students and scholars into the institution who could open up a largely German Jewish population to ritualistic spirituality. Also devoted to social justice, Morgenstern in 1938 actively lobbied the State Department to allow HUC to recruit European Jewish intellectuals to be part of a College in Exile.[59] In a city where the Jewish community had proven to be dedicated to philanthropy and social justice, the board of governors at HUC had voted to let Morgenstern start recruiting German Jewish scholars to the school, providing them with room and board, access to the library, and a small living stipend.[60]

Heschel had come to Morgenstern's attention through Buber, who had written a letter strongly endorsing his work. Another exile from Berlin, Ismar Elbogen, a scholar of Jewish liturgy who had been a professor of Heschel at the Hochschule and who had arrived at HUC as a research professor, likewise recommended his former student. Although Heschel came from a Hasidic background and Morgenstern headed a Reform seminary, this kind of interdenominational fluidity was common during the interwar years. "Orthodoxy, Conservatism and Reform are coming together," one Indiana rabbi observed in 1935, "not because they are recognizing themselves in agreement but because they face a common enemy, assimilation."[61]

The opportunity to emigrate to America came not a moment too soon. On 6 April 1939, Heschel received a letter of-

fering him a position as a research fellow at HUC with an annual salary of five hundred dollars as well as room and board.[62] Heschel wrote back to accept the invitation a few weeks later: "I appreciate your generous kindness in communicating to me on my appointment as Research Fellow." It was, Heschel noted, "very kind of you to think of me and to help me in this sorrowful time." But Heschel added that he had already met with great difficulties trying to obtain a visa and would need assistance in this respect.[63] Numerous people wrote to the American Consulate on his behalf, including the Quaker Rudolf Schlosser, whose group he spoke to in Frankfurt.[64]

The path to America was circuitous, as it was by then for any Jews fortunate enough to escape. In July, still unsuccessful in obtaining his official documents, Heschel temporarily moved to London by capitalizing on family connections. His brother, Jacob, had resettled there six months earlier. After having been rescued from the terror of totalitarianism, Heschel established the Institute for Jewish Learning under the auspices of the Theodor Herzl Society, a Zionist organization, where he taught adult refugees.[65] "In recent years," Heschel said at the opening ceremonies, "we have come to know the ignominy of human beings. We have experienced their metamorphosis into brutal barbarians," including those who "occupied an important position in Western culture and education." The reason, Heschel said, was that the "educational ideal" didn't address a person's inner life and atomized individuals from society. Jewish education, in his mind, should foster Jewish memory: "The vital sources of Jewish education are not the books but the people, the bearers of memory. The essence of education is not in the letters, but in those who engage with the Spirit and bear witness to it. The duty of Judaism is to educate the Jews to be bearers of that which has been passed down. Being educated means to be bearers of the Spirit. Without a living tradition, as Jews we would go under. This is why the break with the tradi-

tion is so dangerous to our survival."[66] In an article he published in the society's newsletter in its first year, called "On Return," Heschel pointed to education as the salvation for Jewish suffering: "We have been challenged by the darkest powers, and no indignity could be more shameful than crawling away. What is our answer? The answer to expulsion is return—to the Jewish community, to the Jewish spirit, to the Jewish land." Connecting these ideas to Nazi Germany, he continued: "Ghosts spread over the ruins of values. Power and hatred took up residence there, and soon they conquered an entire Reich. In this Reich there was no place for Jews. Why? Because independent of our will and our knowing, the meaning and duty of Jewish existence is to be a witness to the Spirit and to maintain the path to goodness."[67]

Six weeks after he left Warsaw, tragedy struck Heschel's family when the Nazis invaded Poland. His sister Esther was killed in the bombing. His mother and Gittel had to flee from their apartment. He couldn't contain his sorrow as he reached out to friends and colleagues for support during his time of mourning. He wrote his mother and surviving sisters constantly. "Each day that we receive a letter from you," his sister wrote, "is a holiday for us."[68] The loss was unimaginable.

It would take almost a year of Morgenstern's efforts before the American consulate in London granted him a visa. When Heschel finally received the official notice, he wrote Morgenstern to "express once again my deep gratitude for the confidence you have honoured me in inviting me to come" and said that he would arrange to leave as soon as possible.[69] Heschel immediately declared his intention to become an American citizen. Heschel sent a letter to Buber, who had resettled in Jerusalem, to tell him that he was leaving the "sea of suffering" in Poland.[70]

On 9 March 1940, he boarded the 16,243-ton Cunard White Star Liner *Lancastria*, a luxury ship that the British had

converted into a vehicle for rescuing and transporting refugees, in Liverpool. The ship was hit by a wave so strong that it broke through a number of portholes and flooded some quarters.[71] Along with 480 passengers, 360 of whom were refugees as well as an English portrait painter, Simon Elwes, and several musicians, Heschel ended his twelve-day journey in New York. On 21 March his cousin Mordechai Shlomo Friedman, one of the first Hasidic rabbis in the United States, whose congregation was on the Lower East Side, welcomed him. "Dear Mr. President," Heschel wrote Morgenstern, "I have just arrived in New York!"[72] The excitement that he temporarily expressed about reaching the United States could not erase the underlying sadness and trauma that had defined his final years in Europe. Less than three months after he landed, the *Lancastria* was sunk in a Nazi air attack resulting in the loss of over four thousand lives.

3

Cincinnati

On 21 March 1940, Heschel arrived at the port of New York. On the day that his ship reached the docks, Americans were reading about a world that was unraveling. The front page of the *New York Times* reported a retaliatory German air attack had taken place on a convoy of British ships off the Scottish coast. Oliver Stanley, Britain's secretary of state for war, decried critics of the Allied forces, comparing them to people who came down from supper to safely watch others fight while urging them to hit harder. The combat in Europe was "not for the entertainment of other people but for their own lives," he said.[1] President Franklin Delano Roosevelt, who had been inching the nation closer to war even as Americans still lived in relative isolation, had been ordered to continue staying in bed after having already been away from his desk for several weeks with a high fever. The worst of the Great Depression—a devastating eco-

nomic crisis that left 25 percent of the nation's workforce unemployed—was closer to ending, but it had been a long decade.

Even still, the air felt different in America. On the Lower East Side, Heschel discovered a Jewish community that was living free from the immediate fears that he and his family in Warsaw encountered. When he embraced his sister Sarah, at whose apartment at 132 Henry Street he temporarily stayed, Heschel knew that she and her husband, and now he, were all relatively safe. This was a big difference from the dire conditions in Europe, where he had barely escaped with his life.

True to form, Heschel wasted no time. He traveled to America not only for his personal safety but to expand his intellectual and religious horizons. It would be in the new country where he would dig further into his old traditions, exploring the hybrid of the sacred and secular that animated his thinking.

Heschel's first stop was the JTS, the spiritual and canonical center of "Traditional Judaism." The mission, as the future president Cyrus Adler explained, was to walk the line between "those who had set the idol of modernity upon their alters . . . and those who held to the mode of the Ghetto in its worst period."[2] The leadership of JTS transformed the institution into a hotbed of Judaic scholarship. Many of the best faculty had emigrated from Eastern Europe and were Orthodox in their religious outlook. It was a comfortable institution for an observant Jew like Heschel. Initially, the seminary did not have any connection to a specific denomination. The faculty, and JTS, came to be identified with the Conservative movement—the denomination which sought a middle path between Orthodoxy and Reform—only after the board agreed to house the Rabbinical Assembly (originally formed in 1901 and renamed in 1919) and the United Synagogue, created in 1913, which turned into the federation of Conservative congregations.

While Heschel would have preferred to settle in New York,

the financial challenges JTS faced in the late 1930s prevented them from housing as many refugees as the HUC.[3] The newly arrived rabbi asked Morgenstern if he could spend a few weeks in Manhattan to visit with his family and become better acquainted with the scholarly resources that were available for research; Morgenstern agreed to his request.[4] Heschel used this interregnum to attend the annual convention of the American Oriental Society and meet with scholars at JTS, including a dinner at the apartment of the recently appointed chancellor, Louis Finkelstein.[5] Finkelstein, whose father, Simon, had been an Orthodox rabbi who emigrated from Eastern Europe to Cincinnati, felt inspired to "see in my own home a lineal descendant of the famous Maggid of Mezeritch eight generations back and (on his mother's side) from the equally famous 'Compassionate One,' Rabbi Levi Yitzhak. He was related by blood-kinship or marriage to almost every important Hasidic 'dynasty' in Europe."[6] Besides their similar European roots and commitment to strengthening Jewish practice in the United States, Finkelstein and Heschel both taught theology and were ordained rabbis with doctorates from elite universities (Finkelstein from Columbia).

On 9 April in the late evening Heschel dutifully boarded an overnight train at Penn Station in New York that pulled into Winton Place in suburban Cincinnati at 4:45 p.m. At the age of thirty-three, the unassuming immigrant from Poland arrived at his new home in America's heartland anxious to see the HUC and meet the man who had saved his life. He exited the train looking more like the person who came of age in Berlin than the Hasid from Warsaw—clean-shaven, short hair, black rimless glasses, and a plain black suit.

While settling into his new home, Heschel worried too that Americans, as much as their condition was better than that of his brethren in Eastern Europe, still faced dangerous levels of anti-Semitism. Heschel quickly learned how anti-Semitism continued to be woven into the nation's cultural fabric. During the

1920s, a surge of white supremacist organizations targeted African Americans and Jews. The Anti-Defamation League, an organization established in 1913 to combat attacks on Jews, reported that twelve hundred anti-Semitic organizations formed between 1933 and 1940.[7] The automobile giant Henry Ford published blistering anti-Semitic screeds in his newspaper, the *Dearborn Independent*, that garnered international attention. Many professional and social organizations did not admit Jews. Harvard and Yale instituted quota systems to limit the number who could be admitted. The Great Depression in the 1930s bred stronger public support for demagogues like the radio show host Father Charles Coughlin, who in 1937 and 1938 delivered fiery broadcasts blaming a conspiracy of Jews for the problems the nation faced. There were a growing number of incidents of anti-Semitic violence and vandalism; polls showed more Americans subscribing to negative views of the religion. "Today, as never before in their history," one observer noted in 1941, "American Jews are apprehensive over their security. A great anxiety weighs on them."[8]

Despite ongoing hostility, American Jews had built an impressive infrastructure. Since the mid-nineteenth century, Jews immigrated to Cincinnati and other major cities in sizable numbers. The first wave of Jewish immigrants arrived between the 1820s and 1880s primarily from Central Europe. They established communities that became financially secure. Between the 1880s and the mid-1920s, over two million additional Jews from Eastern Europe flooded into the United States.[9] Like the Central Europeans before them, they sought improved economic opportunity, freedom from government regulation, and escape from the violence of pogroms.[10] In New York, Philadelphia, Chicago, and Columbus robust communities formed, tied together by dense networks of synagogues, Yiddish and Hebrew newspapers and magazines, retail merchants, kosher butchers, and civic organizations.[11]

After Congress enacted legislation in 1921 and 1924 that imposed quotas restricting the entrance of Eastern Europeans, Jews wove themselves into the fabric of the country's life. Jewish Americans, for instance, were a national presence through their role in popular culture. Entertainers like Groucho Marx and Irving Berlin starred on the national stage. Bankers and business leaders such as Jacob Schiff and Julius Rosenwald emerged as powerhouses of industry. The Jewish community established a vast cadre of philanthropic organizations like B'nai B'rith (1843) and political groups like the American Jewish Committee (1906) and American Jewish Congress (AJC, 1918).[12] Most notable about American Jews by the late 1930s, who constituted about 3.7 percent of the population, was the rising number who moved into middle-class areas. With social and cultural handicaps stacked against them—from the exclusion they encountered in professions, social clubs, and universities to the redlining by bankers and realtors—they were able to achieve some degree of upward mobility and cultural integration. Over half a million Jewish men and women would serve in the military during the war effort. With prosperity and assimilation came predictable concerns among rabbis that their community was moving dangerously far away from tradition—a problem that most ethnic groups encountered in this period.[13] As one writer noted, "Today in America, Jewry, like a chameleon, has taken on the color of its new surroundings. Its soul remains divided between the memory of its Eastern heritage—of traditions nursed through centuries of ghetto life—and the interests of the community, which has received it. Its thought has been cast increasingly in the American vernacular."[14]

American Jews had splintered into three major denominations. Reform Judaism possessed an infrastructure of synagogues and civic associations from Dixie upward through the Midwest. The movement housed its rabbinical seminary in Cincinnati, the HUC, and nurtured strong, dynamic leaders through the

Central Conference of American Rabbis. Continuing to alter core ritual practices, Reform Jews in America abandoned the bar mitzvah ceremony and only read selections from the weekly Torah portion, even jettisoning the second day of a number of major holidays.[15] The movement had expanded in the nineteenth century but contracted in the early twentieth century as new immigrants turned elsewhere. Orthodox Judaism secured a much smaller foothold, though gaining strength with the influx of Eastern Europeans.[16] Based on a small Lower East Side yeshiva established in 1886, Yeshiva College was founded in 1928 offering a mixed curriculum of Talmud along with a smattering of secular education as well as a rabbinic seminary for the Orthodox. The Union of Orthodox Jewish Congregations of America was founded in 1898. Other Americans looked to the middle way of Conservative Judaism, which sought to balance traditional ritual with secular life in ways that were stricter than Reform. Though the faculty strived to be independent, JTS became clearly identified by much of the religious public as a base for the movement and a training ground for Conservative rabbis. The Rabbinical Assembly organized the Conservative rabbinate; the United Synagogue its synagogues. Each denomination of Judaism was concentrated on the Eastern Seaboard while expanding populations of all three could be found in most states.

Cincinnati, which the historian Henry Howe described as a "sort of paradise for the Hebrews," became one of the most vibrant Jewish communities outside the Northeast.[17] The immigrants who settled there starting in the 1830s, deeply influenced by German culture, transformed it into a home for the Reform movement. Rabbi Isaac Mayer Wise established the HUC in 1875 as a seminary to train rabbis. From its inception HUC enraged Orthodox leaders. The seminary mistakenly served non-kosher food, including crab and shrimp, at the celebration for the inaugural class of rabbinic graduates in 1883

(known as the Trefa—"unkosher"—banquet). These menu items, a result of poor oversight, came to symbolize an acceptance of total assimilation.[18] In 1885, Reform Jews formalized their doctrine with the Pittsburgh Platform, a document that officially articulated their philosophy of reinterpreting Judaism to meet the intellectual realities of the secular culture. Reform Jews, the platform said, accepted "as binding only the moral laws, and maintain only such ceremonies as elevate and sanctify our lives, but reject all such as are not adapted to the views and habits of modern civilization."[19] Under Rabbi Kaufmann Kohler, who became president in 1903, HUC added to its focus on rabbinic training an initiative to be one of the world's finest Judaic research institutions. Upon taking over in 1921, Julian Morgenstern continued Kohler's initiatives. The seminary benefited from the prosperity of Cincinnati's Jewish community in law, banking, and retail. The adoption of the Columbus Platform in 1937 restored a certain number of laws to observance but didn't change the fundamental nature of the movement.[20]

Reform Judaism was the most influential voice in town, but the other strands of Judaism were present as well. Mid-nineteenth-century immigrants had established a stable Orthodox community. By 1940, there were ten Orthodox synagogues. They received support from the Manischewitz family, manufacturers of baked matzah, and the Oscherwitz family, who packaged kosher meat. The Conservative synagogue, Adath Israel, under the leadership of Rabbi Louis Feinberg, created a model for the kind of traditional congregation that the Rabbinical Assembly promised to achieve. The services were in Hebrew, men and women sat on separate sides of the sanctuary without a formal barrier, and many of the congregants kept kosher homes (not with the same level of strictness as Orthodox families) and observed the laws of the Sabbath.[21]

Heschel settled into his two-room dormitory suite. Living conditions for the sixty students and fellows who were attend-

ing HUC were relatively good since the residential building had been renovated in the 1920s.[22] As part of their recruitment package, HUC provided Heschel with free room and board, access to the dining hall, and the use of the Bernheim Library. On 29 May 1940, Heschel obtained his certificate of arrival at the U.S. District Court to officially start the naturalization process.

As it was for many Eastern European immigrants, mastering English was extraordinarily important to Heschel. Though he had published in four languages (Yiddish, Hebrew, German, and Polish), being able to communicate through the native tongue of his new country would be a "triumph of signal importance," as one acquaintance explained. He strove to learn ten to twelve words a day by reading *Roget's Thesaurus*.[23] Morgenstern assigned a rabbinic student, Herbert Drooze, to assist him (in exchange, Heschel tutored Drooze in Hebrew). When Heschel asked him for great examples of modern English literature, Drooze brought speeches by Abraham Lincoln, *Moby-Dick* by Herman Melville, as well as the works of Thomas Wolfe and William James. Heschel was enchanted by what he read: "This is the English language!" One morning Heschel approached Drooze trembling with excitement. "Herbie, a wonderful thing happened to me last night." Drooze asked what, and Heschel replied, "I dreamed in English!" "A new language had taken residence in his unconscious," Drooze realized.[24]

The size and diversity of American Judaism impressed Heschel. The encounter with Reform Judaism was unsettling. HUC had saved his life, for which he would always be deeply grateful, but it did not promote a style of Judaism that appealed to him. He grew increasingly frustrated with the spiritual and ritualistic character of his colleagues. The political passivity that he saw from elected officials and Jewish organizations as they confronted the greatest human rights catastrophe of modern history—the Nazi slaughter of millions of Jews—profoundly saddened him.

In many respects, Cincinnati was a disappointment. The lifestyle among rabbinical students bothered him. Living in a city that was popularly known as Porkopolis because of the production of the (very) non-kosher meat, saddened him. Reform Jews were willing, in his mind, to abandon most of what he believed to be the essence of their tradition. Whereas in Warsaw Reform Judaism competed with the robust world of Hasidism, in the Midwest the inheritors of the Jewish Enlightenment were winning over hearts and minds. Unlike in Warsaw or Berlin, where he had observed Reform Judaism from the outside, now he lived right in the middle of their world. Following several decades of declining membership, Reform Judaism was experiencing a resurgence in the 1940s as more fellow Eastern European Jews joined their congregations.[25]

At HUC, rabbinical students showed little commitment to basic rituals that Heschel considered vital. On the Sabbath, they used electricity and worked despite the biblical injunction to rest. In the classroom, students could barely speak Hebrew and were unfamiliar with classic texts. Heschel could not consume most of the food in the dining hall because the meat was not kosher and mixed with dairy products.[26] He lived on a diet of tuna fish and hard-boiled eggs.[27] After meals, most of the students and faculty would quickly depart, leaving Heschel alone to recite the blessings.

Many of the students treated him like an oddity because of his practices; a few openly mocked him. The response to Heschel reflected prevalent tensions that existed between the Germanic character of Reform Judaism, many of whom were extremely conscious about distinguishing themselves from their Eastern European Hasidic brothers and sisters, whom they saw as being of a lower class and less cultured (as had been the case in Germany).[28]

Nor did Heschel like the fact that a majority of faculty and students were opposed to Zionism, which he and many Eastern

Europeans supported. Some Reform leaders, like Rabbi Stephen Wise, embraced the cause of creating a homeland for Jews in Palestine. But most in the movement, whose followers hung American flags in their synagogues and sang "America the Beautiful" in services, believed that Zionism constituted an acceptance of the inevitable marginalization of Judaism.[29]

Heschel's experience in Cincinnati was not anomalous. In contrast to Eastern Europe, where Jews were officially defined by their religion, constitutional freedoms meant that decisions about observance were left up to the individual.[30] And there were many Jews throughout the country who chose to allow cherished rituals to go by the wayside. During the 1920s and 1930s, membership in synagogues shrank. Fewer Jews kept kosher or celebrated the Sabbath. One study of Jewish life in New York City in 1929 revealed that three-fourths of Jewish schoolchildren did not know Hebrew and were barely literate in rituals.[31] Between 1928 and 1930 only about one-eighth of Reform Jews lit Sabbath candles on Friday night and recited the blessings over the wine (Kiddush); just a third celebrated Passover. A minuscule number of Jews learned Talmud.[32]

The frustration that Heschel felt at HUC also centered on the treatment of scholarship. Many of the faculty at the seminary did not acknowledge the quality of his work.[33] For a man of the book who defined so much of his identity around his intellectual prowess, a budding scholar who had been privileged to circulate among the most renowned minds in Berlin, the hostility that Heschel felt at HUC was hugely unfamiliar. He was dismissed by colleagues as a foreigner with irrelevant ideas, someone who did not have a permanent place in the city. "I was an immigrant, a refugee," he recalled. "No one listened to me."[34]

Part of the problem was that American Jewish scholars were increasingly hostile toward the study of theology. They brushed aside the topic as irrelevant and supernatural. Operating in an era when the social sciences had been triumphant, in-

stitutions of Jewish learning were structuring their curriculum around Halakha, or Jewish law, emphasizing how ideas emerged out of specific historical and sociological contexts, as well as legalistic rabbinic commentaries. This stood in sharp contrast to Christian seminaries, where theology never lost its hold.[35]

His thirst for intellectual community prevented Heschel from withdrawing. Instead, he searched for any meaningful connections that were possible.[36] Heschel formed an unexpected bond with one of his colleagues, also an ardent pacifist and social justice activist named Abraham Cronbach. This professor, the son of German immigrants, was one of the most controversial figures at the seminary. Cronbach held onto a radical understanding of Judaism that emphasized the constant pursuit of social justice and breaking down border walls with other religions ("We should bring Jesus into the Synagogue").[37] He introduced Heschel to many of the fellow social activists in the city.[38] On several occasions Heschel joined Cronbach during his weekly Sunday trips to small Ohio towns where he visited prisons, homes for unmarried mothers, and old-age institutions.[39] Heschel was also fortunate to mentor some talented HUC students. Eugene Borowitz and Samuel Dresner were known by their peers as the "Kavanah Boys" and the "Piety Boys." Both were brilliant intellects who appreciated Heschel's pedagogical style and spiritual fervor.[40] Another student, Joseph Gumbiner, was deeply impressed by the way Heschel exuded the spirit of the Hasidic tradition. "We had never been exposed to anything like this," Gumbiner said. "At first the students listened in silent amazement."[41] Heschel also befriended the headwaiter, a Christian African American named Larry D. Harris, who told Heschel stories about the dire conditions of his community.[42] In a memorable experience, he attended the church on a Sunday morning where Harris was a deacon.[43]

Heschel displayed a strong egalitarian streak. When Drooze introduced him to American beer at a local restaurant, which

he loved, the rabbi enjoyed witty back-and-forth banter with the waitress. Upon leaving the establishment, Heschel placed his hands on Drooze's shoulders and said, "America is a wonderful country." When Drooze asked why, Heschel responded: "America is a wonderful country because that waitress *really* believes that she is just as good as I am." Unlike in Europe, where a university professor was seen as elite, here he and the waitress were equals. "The American self-respect and easygoing comradery had touched Dr. Heschel profoundly," Drooze recalled.[44]

Heschel was also able to find some solace by venturing outside of HUC. Almost every Sabbath afternoon, he walked four miles to the Cincinnati Bureau of Jewish Education at 658 Rockdale Avenue.[45] The bureau, which the United Jewish Social Agencies opened in 1927, convened adult education programs based on Orthodox practice.[46] Heschel was energized by the Sabbath afternoon Talmud study, where participants dove into deep textual analysis, speaking in Hebrew. To the shock of his HUC colleagues, Heschel volunteered on other days to teach young children in the bureau's Hebrew School. So enthralled was Heschel that often he kept going with his young students until there was not enough light available for them to read. Then, as one of his mentees recalled, "Heschel began to sing a *nigun*, and those American-born youngsters who had never before heard such melodies . . . joined eagerly. Mind and soul together were being nourished. Study became worship. The lives of the students were never the same after that year."[47]

An especially rewarding encounter took place at a dinner party organized by Jacob Rader Marcus. It was here that Heschel met Sylvia Straus. Sylvia was friends with Marcus's wife, Antoinette, a classical musician. Born in Philadelphia in 1913, the younger sister to three brothers, and raised in Cleveland by unobservant Russian Jewish immigrant parents, Straus was a talented and beautiful classical pianist who had studied in Cleve-

land under the tutelage of Severin Eisenberger, a distinguished Polish-born musician. After dinner, Sylvia performed a piece for the guests. Heschel was moved by the intimate performance and enchanted by her beauty. She found the aspiring scholar to be handsome and was intrigued by his religious background. They went on a few dates and exchanged letters. The romance was interrupted though when she moved back to Cleveland and then relocated to New York to study under a different mentor, Arthur Rubinstein.

On the shores of the Hudson River in New York City Heschel found the place he wanted to truly make his home. Summers being a special time for Heschel, starting at the end of his first semester at HUC he spent the hot months of July and August on the Upper West Side, where he could enjoy the world-class intellectual life and Jewish institutions the city had to offer. He rented a small room at 362 Riverside Drive, within walking distance of the JTS. He instantly fell in love with the city, from the vibrant scholarly conversations at JTS to the YIVO Institute on 123rd Street, where he dove into manuscripts, seminars, and lectures about Yiddish culture.[48] The institute had temporarily moved to New York at the outset of the war and found a permanent space uptown in 1942 when it became clear that returning to Vilna would be impossible; the Nazis had captured the city one year earlier. Heschel was invited to join the board of directors by the research director, Max Weinreich, one of the founders of the institute when it had been in Vilna. Weinreich was a Yiddish linguist who felt a deep cultural attachment to Eastern European Jewry and had a strong appreciation for the German academy, having received his doctoral degree in 1923 at Marburg University.

Whether he was in Cincinnati or New York, Heschel spent most of his nights consumed with fears about the deteriorating situation in Europe. In the late hours, he would sit in his bedroom all alone writing letters to his mother and sisters, de-

spondent about their inability to obtain visas.[49] "I miss your wisdom and friendship," Heschel confessed to Martin Buber. "But it is impossible to write. To experience the atrocious in the distance makes me mute."[50]

The world was rapidly descending into a devastating global conflagration. A few months after Heschel's first summer in New York, the Japanese attack on Pearl Harbor on 7 December 1941 gave Roosevelt the support he needed to take the United States into the world conflict, first with a declaration of war against Japan and then Germany. The escalation of war was rapid. Three million American men were inducted into the Selective Service in 1942. The Germans, who occupied almost all of Western Europe, were fighting in Russia, North Africa, and the Balkans, suffering some strategic defeats such as in the Battle of Stalingrad. Throughout that perilous year, Jewish leaders learned of Hitler's "Final Solution" to exterminate the population in death camps like Auschwitz and Treblinka.[51]

Just as he had felt with regard to German Christians in Berlin, Heschel grew increasingly despondent about the indifference that he sensed among American politicians, including President Roosevelt, toward the dangers Jews confronted. Roosevelt, who received overwhelming support from Jewish voters, had refused to allow refugees to enter the country. In June 1939 the administration had turned back 937 passengers on board the *MS St. Louis*, most of whom were Jewish, who were trying to escape Germany; 254 of the passengers would be killed by the Nazis. Others who survived went to concentration camps. Born out of his frustration, Heschel sympathized with a network of Jewish dissidents who protested Roosevelt's timidity. Jewish leaders like Rabbi Stephen Wise, they also complained, protected FDR from criticism even as the evidence of atrocities mounted.[52] Heschel felt that most mainstream Jewish organizations were not doing enough to mobilize pressure on elected officials.

His frustration did not quell his belief in the possibility of piety in the modern world. In his writing, Heschel pushed back against those who claimed that it was impossible for God to communicate with humans after the age of the Hebrew Prophets. Instead, Heschel argued that any individual could directly encounter God by living a pious life. "The pious man is still with us," he wrote in "An Analysis of Piety" (1942), his first significant scholarly work in English.

"He has not vanished from the earth, and indeed more frequently than is generally realized, situations in normal life are to be encountered which are full of the evidence of pious devotion. The presence of piety among us is thus an incontestable fact, so why should prejudice deter us from investigating this phenomenon and, at least, endeavoring to understand it?" Heschel added that piety "stands staunchly as the champion of something more important than interest and desires, than passion or career. While not denying the beauty and grandeur of the world, the pious man realizes that life takes place under wide horizons, horizons that range beyond the span of an individual life or even the life of a nation, of a generation or even of an era."[53]

On 21 July 1942, Heschel joined the twenty thousand people who packed into Madison Square Garden to protest Nazism. The rally, convened shortly before the holiday of Tisha B'Av (an annual fast day to mourn the destruction of the Temples), was co-organized by the AJC, the Jewish Labor Committee, and B'nai B'rith. Heschel listened with the rest of the crowd to a number of luminaries, including Rabbi Wise and William Green, the president of the American Federation of Labor, as they spoke out in support of the Jewish refugees. The New York City mayor Fiorello La Guardia declared, "I am through protesting. . . . We are not going to win this war by making speeches, slogans, epigrams, or headlines. This war is going to be won with the lives and the blood of the freemen

fighting the Nazis." Governor of New York Herbert Lehman warned that halfway measures would not work in the fight to save democracy: "There must be no appeasement or compromise in this fight for freedom. Either we destroy the Nazi, the Fascist, and the Japanese warlords, or they destroy us." The crowd was excited to listen to a written statement from FDR: "The American people not only sympathize with all victims of Nazi crimes but will hold the perpetrators of these crimes to strict accountability in a day of reckoning which will surely come." Toward the end of the rally, the crowd chanted the mourner's prayer, the Mourner's Kaddish, in memory of the slain Jews. It concluded with a declaration from the AJC: "We join in mourning for the destruction of the innocent and helpless victims of Nazi terror, and at the same time highly resolve that we shall not permit the world to forget these crimes so that the perpetrators may be brought to answer for them before the bar of civilization."[54]

It was not enough. The mass rally ended up being a letdown to Heschel since nothing concrete happened after it was done. When he returned for the beginning of the semester, Heschel was shaken by the fact that so few people seemed concerned about what was happening. He remembered that upon coming back to the HUC, he "recited Psalms, fasted, and cried myself out. I was a stranger in this country. My word had no power."[55] He conveyed the sense of urgency that he felt about the state of humanity. In February 1943, he published a piece in the HUC *Bulletin*, "The Meaning of This War," in which he characterized the tragedy in Europe as an outgrowth of humans having lost their connection to spirituality and ethics in the total embrace of scientific rationalism. "Who is responsible?" Heschel asked of the war. Seeking to understand who was responsible for such a broken world, Heschel answered his own question by imploring fellow Jews: "Let Fascism not serve as an alibi for our conscience. We have failed to fight for right,

for justice, for goodness; as a result, we must fight against wrong, against injustice, against evil. We have failed to offer sacrifices on the altar of peace; now we must offer sacrifices on the altar of war." The piece marked an important moment in the evolution of Heschel's thinking in which he started to hone in on the actions of humankind to understand why God might seem absent from the world.[56] The polity had to be rooted in a divine order if it was to remain just. With an eye toward Europe, Heschel argued, "The outbreak of this war was no surprise. It came as a long-expected sequel to a spiritual disaster. Instilled with the gospel that truth is mere advantage and reverence weakness, people succumbed to the bigger advantage of a lie—'the Jew is our misfortune';—and to the power of arrogance—'Tomorrow the whole world shall be ours.' The roar of bombers over Rotterdam, Warsaw, was but the echo of thoughts bred for years by individual brains, and later applauded by entire nations." Heschel wrote, "We labored to perfect engines and let our inner life go to wreck. We ridiculed superstition until we lost our ability to believe." The problem was not the absence of God but that "God will return to us when we shall be willing to let Him in—into our banks and factories, into our Congress and clubs, into our homes and theaters."[57]

In the spring of 1943, on the first day of Passover, German troops began liquidating the Warsaw Ghetto. Jews followed the news with bated breath.[58] Heschel spent the early morning hours in the HUC dormitory sleepless and terrified about the fate of his relatives. He listened to reports from the military front on a shortwave radio that Herbert Drooze had loaned him. Heschel was so consumed by the latest information that he would switch on the radio before sundown on Friday and leave it running throughout the Sabbath (so that he did not have to turn the device on or off during the holiday); he kept it on for so long that some of the tubes burned out.[59] To friends and colleagues, he rarely spoke about the situation or his fears.[60]

Moyshe Kulbak and Hillel Zeitlin, his friends from Europe, perished.[61]

But much worse was when he learned that his mother had died of a heart attack when German police raided her apartment. He organized a shiva service in the dormitory to mourn her passing. Soon after, he received word that his sister Gittel had been sent to Treblinka, where she would be killed.

Heschel was totally devastated by the death of close family members and friends at the hands of the Nazis. Living alone as a single man far from home with few intimate personal connections, he struggled to overcome his deep sadness, feeling a mix of guilt and despair. His worst nightmares had literally come true as the violent forces he fled stole much of his family away.

During these horrendous times, Cincinnati's Orthodox community provided Heschel with the greatest psychological comfort. In particular, he derived satisfaction from his relationship with the chief rabbi, Eliezer Silver, who had taken over the main Orthodox synagogue in 1931, Congregation Kehillah B'nai Israel.[62] Rabbi Silver, who was short, heavy, and spoke with a thick Yiddish accent, was an extraordinarily charismatic leader. After working for a spell in the garment industry, he had moved through a number of rabbinic jobs in Pennsylvania and Massachusetts before finally settling in Cincinnati in 1931. He was elected as the president of the Union of Orthodox Rabbis and cofounded the American chapter of Agudas Yisroel in 1939.[63] The rabbi won several battles with the city's Reform leaders, including a campaign to establish a kosher kitchen in the Jewish Hospital. To enhance his power, he formed an Orthodox City Council, a Vaad Ha'ir, that operated as a governing alliance of affiliated synagogues.[64]

Heschel saw in Silver a kindred spirit who was frustrated with the political passivity of Jewish organizations. Rabbi Silver's ambition for Orthodox Judaism was coupled with a strong belief in the imperative of taking direct action to save obser-

vant European Jews.[65] He believed it to be a mitzvah to rescue them. As a Lithuanian-born Jew who had emigrated from Russia in 1907, Silver was deeply sympathetic toward the refugees fleeing Nazi Germany. He founded the Vaad Hatzalah (an international rescue committee) in 1939, an organization dedicated to saving Jewish rabbis and yeshiva students. Silver worked with Senator Robert Taft, an Ohio Republican, to increase the number of emergency visas that the State Department granted and to build support for opening Palestine to Jewish refugees.[66] Silver believed in the creation of a Jewish state despite his ties to Agudas Yisroel.

On 6 October 1943, Heschel joined Silver at the "rabbis' march" in Washington, DC. The idea for the protest originated with Peter Bergson, a radical activist from Palestine who worked with the Irgun (the Jewish underground) and had come to the United States, changing his name from Hillel Kook, to fight for national Jewish liberation and the safety of Jewish refugees. He was one who felt that the U.S. government was not doing enough.[67] Bergson, who was not religious, anticipated that the image of Orthodox rabbis marching through the streets of Washington could have a big impact on elected officials. He relied on Rabbi Silver's organization to recruit marchers. Three days before Yom Kippur approximately four hundred Orthodox rabbis disembarked from a train at Union Station. Upon arriving at Capitol Hill, they were greeted by Vice President Henry Wallace. The rabbis read out loud a petition demanding that the United States respond more aggressively to the extermination of Jews that was taking place and that they recognize Palestine as a legitimate settlement for Jewish refugees. Wallace, otherwise liberal in his politics, refused to make any commitments given the administration's ongoing resistance since they refused to let the passengers on the *MS St. Louis* ashore.

The rabbis then moved on to meet with individual legislators, including the Speaker of the House and the Senate Ma-

jority Leader. "These rabbis were not clean-shaven or well-dressed," according to one account. "They were avowedly Eastern European. They represented not 'American types' from the posh synagogues. On the contrary, they might just as well have been the rabbis whom Hitler was then putting in death-camps along with their congregants."[68] The next stop for this rabbinic brigade was the Lincoln Memorial, where they gathered to pray. With the statue of the president who saved the Union behind them, the rabbis once again read the petition calling for the salvation of Eastern European Jews. As each passerby tried to catch a glimpse of this unusual procession, the rabbis kept moving toward their final stop, the White House, as they alternated between chanting the Mourner's Kaddish and singing traditional Hebrew prayers to the tune of "The Star-Spangled Banner." Standing at the entranceway, the rabbis were informed that Roosevelt was too busy to meet. The president's advisor Samuel Rosenman and Rabbi Wise had urged FDR not to see them since Bergson did not represent the mainstream Jewish community.[69] Roosevelt's decision was disappointing, albeit predictable.

The rabbis' march gave Heschel his first real taste of grass-roots activism in the pursuit of justice. In DC, he saw firsthand the power of protesters who were not tethered to the establishment, free to shake up the status quo, and criticize people in power, whether they were Jewish leaders or elected officials. The rallies and marches were a stark contrast to Rabbi Wise, who, just a few days after the march, delivered a sermon in his New York synagogue on the Day of Atonement that centered on the beauty of everyday life rather than on the genocide being committed against Jews overseas.[70]

Even as he marched, Heschel never lost sight of the necessity of producing his theological and philosophical writing. His intellectual pursuits were directly connected to these experiences even if he did not always articulate the relevance of this

relationship. His early taste of activism in New York and Washington, and, more important, the acute horrors of World War II only heightened his desire to explore his theological interests.[71] The ravages of war, in his mind, were a product of the spiritual crisis of humankind—among Jews and Gentiles—in the age of modernity, science, and cosmopolitanism. His work was enough to persuade colleagues at HUC to convert his job into a full-time faculty position in 1943.

Heschel struggled to fulfill his professional obligations at HUC despite his immense sadness. His father had died young; his mother and two sisters had been killed by the Germans. Yet another tragedy occurred when the Nazis murdered his sister Devorah Miriam in May 1944 in Auschwitz. The young rabbi sat shiva for the fourth family member to be killed in the Shoah— a term used by American Jews during the war, which translated into "the Catastrophe"—within the span of five years. Heschel became deeply depressed, so much so that his assistant worried he might be suicidal.[72] "Our world seems not unlike a pit of snakes," he wrote in *Liberal Judaism* (in a revised version of the piece he had published in the HUC *Bulletin*). "We did not sink into the pit in 1939, or even in 1933. We had descended into it generations ago, and the snakes have sent their venom into the bloodstream of humanity, gradually paralyzing us, numbing nerve after nerve, dulling our minds, darkening our vision. Good and evil, that were once as real as day and night, have become a blurred mist."[73] Heschel and Sarah, his sister in New York, were the lone survivors in his immediate family.

On 12 April 1945, Heschel and the rest of the nation went into mourning when news broke that Roosevelt had died. A few weeks later, Adolf Hitler killed himself after being surrounded by Allied troops in his bunker. The eighth of May was Victory Day as the Allies formally accepted Germany's surrender. At nine o'clock in the morning eastern standard time, President Harry Truman announced the news. In London, over a

million people took to the streets to celebrate. The rallies would continue for the rest of the month all over Europe and North America. The death of Hitler, as well as the official end of the war in Europe, was only bittersweet for Heschel. Not only did the war with Japan continue, ending on 15 August with surrender after the United States dropped devastating atomic bombs on Hiroshima and Nagasaki, but every event was overshadowed by new revelations about how much destruction Jews had suffered. Six million had been vanquished. Entire towns and urban neighborhoods were eviscerated. "The stirring events that took place during the last weeks are tragically contrasted with the silence of death that hovers over Poland," Heschel wrote Morgenstern.[74]

The only relief for Heschel came with good professional news from the East Coast. In addition to his officially becoming a U.S. citizen, JTS offered him a full-time faculty appointment. Based on the advice of the JTS faculty member Rabbi Mordecai Kaplan—who had enjoyed a conversation in Cincinnati with Heschel in 1943 during which they discussed a new prayer book that he was editing and who had been taken by his reading "An Analysis of Piety"—Finkelstein concluded that the Hasidic refugee from Warsaw could be part of his ambitious plan to turn the seminary into an institution that could help the Western world recover from the crisis of war.[75] The chancellor saw in Heschel someone who could enhance the public reputation of the faculty and be a spiritual mentor to rabbinical students. On 29 May, Heschel wrote Finkelstein to formally accept the position. "In accepting this great task and high distinction I am fully aware of the responsibility it implies," he noted.[76]

Heschel's colleagues in Cincinnati were upset when they learned of his decision to take the job at JTS. Few were surprised. "It is with deep personal regret that I inform you that your letter of resignation as a member of the Faculty of the Hebrew Union College was submitted by me yesterday to the

meeting of the Board of Governors of the College," a gracious Morgenstern wrote Heschel, "and was in turn accepted by them as you requested." The man who had personally saved Heschel's life added, "A deep appreciation of the motives of honor and integrity which prompted you to reach this decision was expressed by the Board of Governors."[77]

Heschel left Cincinnati a different person from the man who arrived five years earlier. Four of his closest family members had been killed or died as a result of the war. Entire communities in Europe had been decimated by the Nazis. He had seen how in the face of such terror, political leaders in an enlightened democracy as well as mainstream Jewish organizations could be extremely slow, or totally unwilling, to respond.

While Heschel still felt relatively isolated, he was not. He was among several dozen European-born and -trained Jewish scholars and writers who had arrived on American shores before or during World War II and now found themselves after the mass genocide grappling with the existential question of how to revitalize a ravaged Judaism within the United States and across the globe. Sensitive to the brittle nature of democracy and the battered condition of their own people, refugees like Heschel turned their attention to worldly questions about spirituality, morality, God, and community.

The Holocaust posed a profound challenge to their deeply held beliefs.[78] Germany, which was seen as a beacon of scientific inquiry and modern cosmopolitan culture, turned into a center of moral depravity and brutality. Heschel spent the rest of his life trying to make sense of this, wrestling with the question of whether and how Judaism—and all religion—could offer the key toward preventing this kind of mass injustice from rearing its head again.[79]

4

New York City

THERE WASN'T ANYWHERE in the world in 1945 that could boast of a Jewish culture as vibrant as that in New York. Though the war had resulted in devastating losses and the wartime mobilization on the home front had been immense, prewar communal life resumed with remarkable ease since all of the fighting had taken place overseas. Within Jewish communities, even after the death of six million, Heschel encountered a spirited atmosphere. Every denomination—Orthodox, Conservative, Reform—claimed synagogues, educational centers, cultural events, publishing outlets, and intellectual talent unrivaled anywhere in the world. Most of the Jewish population, which peaked at a little over two million by 1950, lived in the Bronx and Brooklyn.[1] There were about one thousand synagogues scattered throughout different neighborhoods. Only 16 percent of the Jewish community resided in Manhattan, but their presence was ubiquitous, with many of them commuting into the

city for work. "To the kid from Chicago," noted the social critic David Bazelon, who arrived in 1943 at the age of twenty, "New York was an astoundingly bright new world, filled with Jews of marvellous variety: like a supermarket kind of candy store, with versions of heritage. . . ."[2] Jews were a prominent force in a number of industries, including in the realm of culture. "The chief contribution of the Jews to the City of New York," according to the sociologist Daniel Bell, born in the garment district and educated at the City College of New York, "has been their role as 'consumers of culture.' The large symphony orchestras, theaters, trade-book publishing, the avant-garde magazines, the market for drawings and paintings—all have, as their principal audience and consumer, the Jewish middle class."[3] Besides the immigrant hamlets of the Lower East Side, more affluent Jews in Manhattan were moving into wealthier areas uptown such as the Upper West Side, which was often being called the "gilded ghetto" because it was home to over ten synagogues and an array of kosher restaurants and butchers.[4]

By the time Heschel arrived at the Upper West Side, the JTS overshadowed both the HUC and Yeshiva University. The institution continued to strive, as Solomon Schechter said, to be a place for "the mystic and the rationalist, the traditional and the critical."[5] Under the direction of Schechter (president in 1902–15), JTS had recruited a cohort of top scholars to its roster. Cyrus Adler (chancellor in 1908–40) and Louis Finkelstein (chancellor in 1940–72) made great progress during the 1930s and early 1940s in strengthening the faculty.[6] In addition, the new location at 3080 Broadway placed JTS near Columbia University, and the Union Theological Seminary gave the institution the feel of a robust campus. So too did the opening of student dormitories, a kosher dining hall, social spaces, and a first-rate library. JTS became well respected for its rabbinical school curriculum and graduate program for Conservative clergy.

Chancellor Finkelstein envisioned JTS as being on a mis-

sion to save the future of Jewry after its decimation in the war. On 31 August 1945, the chancellor wrote the faculty, "The Jewish world has after all suffered during the past five years the gravest catastrophe in all its history. We find ourselves responsible for the training of rabbis and teachers whose influence will be felt in every part of the world because American Jewry is the only really influential Jewish community in the diaspora surviving the war."[7] A central part of Finkelstein's agenda was his drive to improve how Christian Americans perceived his religion by working with rabbis to reshape conventional narratives about Judaism.[8] "The era of isolationism is at an end, whether it applies to the isolation of nations, of peoples, or of culture spheres," he announced. Finkelstein continued: "Moreover, we came to realize that the political, the economic, the cultural and even the moral and spiritual realms are interdependent." His press release continued: "There can be no religious piety without social justice; no lasting economic prosperity without the sense for the spiritual; no political stability without compliance with moral principles."[9] The lesson of the war, in his mind, was that democracy started at home. Jews would have to be at the forefront of the fight for human and civil rights if they were to prevent another massacre of the sort that occurred in Europe from happening again.

Finkelstein served as a leader when the boundaries between Orthodox and Conservative remained porous. Much of the faculty at JTS continued to perceive of the connection with the Rabbinical Assembly as a practical partnership rather than a defining mission. "If someone calls us traditional, orthodox, or conservative," Finkelstein said, "it is he who makes a division of Judaism, not us."[10] Cyrus Adler agreed. As he wrote to the philanthropist Jacob Schiff, JTS was "a religious institution with a definite aim in view to preserve the Jewish tradition and make it livable in modern surroundings. You once called this reasonable orthodoxy. Some people call it conservative Judaism.

I prefer the name of traditional Judaism or historical Judaism."[11] Like his predecessors, Finkelstein aspired to find a viable set of practices resting somewhere between rigid Orthodoxy and Reform Judaism, embracing modernity while respecting tradition.

If JTS could promote positive understandings of "Traditional Judaism," then cultural assimilation and adherence to Jewish tradition would no longer be in as much conflict. The chancellor thought a great deal about how to implement his strategy. It required smart outreach. He had established the Institute for Religious and Social Studies in 1938 to connect great Jewish thinkers to influential religious leaders from other faiths. He launched a national radio series, *The Eternal Light*, that aired on the National Broadcasting Company and in 1952 became a television show. Finkelstein sensed that the translation of Judaism to broader publics would have to take place on popular platforms. Television was appealing, as it reached almost 65 percent of American homes by 1955. Books and articles were likewise important. He recruited faculty members whose writing had the potential to reach beyond narrow scholarly circles.

Finkelstein admired Heschel's work on Maimonides as well as his unapologetic spiritual approach to Judaism, something he felt was sorely lacking among faculty and students. As improbable as it seemed, this rabbinic scholar from Warsaw fit nicely into his vision of promoting Judaism to the broadest possible public. Heschel spent much of the next decade producing a series of books and articles that sought to rekindle an appreciation for piety in the secular era of science and modernity. Within the span of about fifteen years, Heschel turned himself into a public intellectual who was known for his writing about the reciprocal relationship between God and man. Heschel's publications outlined how Judaism allowed pious individuals to open themselves to God. Heschel developed his argument that God was a God of pathos, who expressed humanlike emotions of love and hate. His work continually explored

the ways in which living a pious life could allow a person to move beyond their ego and to see the wonders of the world as well as the injustice that existed around them. By the early 1960s, though his work was controversial among Judaic scholars because it was not considered rigorous enough and was too loose with texts, Heschel stood as one of the most prominent Jewish theologians in the country, featured in the national press.

As his professional career took off in the 1940s and 1950s, Heschel's personal life flourished. He rekindled his romance with Sylvia Straus. The couple, who adored each other's company, married in an Orthodox ceremony in Los Angeles, where her parents had moved, on 10 December 1946. Heschel was thirty-nine and his wife six years younger. Soon after, they began their life together at an apartment at 425 Riverside Drive.[12] Being in the city allowed Heschel to spend time with family members, including his sister and first cousin Aaron, who resided in Brooklyn.[13]

The driving issue behind much of his writing had to do with one defining problem: How could society prevent the kind of brutality which ravaged European Jews? "The horrors of the Second World War," he said in his inaugural lecture at JTS, "have filled the hearts of all upright men with reproach and shame. Never has there been so much guilt and distress on this earth."[14] The fact that the relationship between God and Man had weakened, Heschel came to believe, was at the root of the spiritual crisis that revealed itself with World War II and the advent of atomic weapons. It was not that God had abandoned humankind but that humankind had closed themselves off from God. Societal indifference had allowed the evil of Hitler and Nazi Germany to lurch forward. Heschel's theology pointed to the existence of devout humans who could achieve self-transcendence through prayer, belief, righteous deeds, and religious practice. Like the Hebrew Prophets, these were the persons who could express the voice of God, which he called "the ineffable."[15]

Heschel was one of several religious philosophers wrestling with their theological convictions in the shadow of the traumatic geopolitical events that unfolded with the Holocaust, World War II, and the atomic bomb. The end of the war did not ease concerns about the possibility of further disaster. At the onset of the Cold War against the Soviet Union, President Harry Truman announced in 1947 that the United States would seek to contain the spread of communism all over the globe and that it would vastly expand the national security apparatus. When Communists wrested control of the Chinese government in 1949—the same year the Soviets exploded their first atomic bomb—international tensions rapidly escalated.

Many of the scholars exploring these questions lived in New York during what the historian Jon Butler has called a period of "individual and institutional religious creativity unsurpassed in any other twentieth-century American locale, urban or rural." Manhattan, a city which for many Americans had become a symbol of secular modernity, sacrilege for some, was also a hotbed for religious thinkers who were grappling with the existential crises of the era.[16] Paul Tillich, a Lutheran theologian who defended Jews at the outset of the Nazi regime and eventually fled his home country of Germany to join the Union Theological Seminary, had become an influential Protestant theologian and philosopher who ruminated over the implications of this unsettling new world.[17] As he worked to save refugees from Europe after arriving to the United States in 1933, Tillich spent his time writing about faith and doubt as well as Christianity and existentialism. The impact of the war, he claimed, was to produce a "sacred void." Tillich had been brought to the States by Reinhold Niebuhr, one of the nation's most important Protestant theologians and an esteemed figure within New York intellectual circles. Niebuhr outlined a vision of Christian realism that questioned liberal confidence in reason and moral suasion. His work emphasized the reality of sin. In his

book *Moral Man and Immoral Society: A Study in Ethics and Policy* (1932) he warned that persons were more likely to sin when acting as a collective rather than as individuals. He was extremely vocal in the late 1930s and early 1940s about the Nazi atrocities being committed against the Jews. In *The Children of Light and the Children of Darkness* (1944), Niebuhr wrote, "Man's capacity for justice makes democracy possible, but man's inclination to injustice makes democracy necessary." During the war, though he used to be pacifist, Niebuhr implored fellow countrymen to join the battle against fascism since there was no middle ground in a battle against evil. *Time* magazine featured him on the cover in March 1948.

Less known to the public but widely esteemed in the city's religious circles, Rabbi Joseph Dov Soloveitchik grappled with these questions as he tried to reinvigorate Orthodox Judaism so that it could survive in modern times. Like Heschel, Soloveitchik descended from a family of prominent rabbis. He was born in Pruzhan, Poland, in 1903 and trained in the finest yeshivas, while also being educated at secular institutions, receiving his doctoral degree in philosophy at the University of Berlin in 1931 (he and Heschel both thanked the neo-Kantian philosopher Max Dessoir in their final doctoral work).[18] He emigrated to the United States one year later and worked at a number of jobs until ending up as the head of Yeshiva University in 1941. Considered to be a riveting speaker whose lectures seamlessly flowed between biblical texts and cutting-edge psychology, Soloveitchik was strictly traditional in his observance. His writing and public statements emphasized the clear authority of rabbis and opposed changes to Jewish law. Strictly abiding to Halakha was at the core of his philosophy. Nor did he support theological discussions between Jews and Christians, although he encouraged ecumenical conversations about practical issues. Because he believed that Jewish practice was what defined his religion, the theological differences with Chris-

tianity were insurmountable and there could be no basis of dialogue.[19] At the same time, Soloveitchik broke with many of his colleagues—pioneering what would come to be known as the Modern Orthodox movement—by striving to demonstrate the ways that Jews who lived a life that revolved around Halakha could make the modern world stronger. "When halakhic man approaches reality," he wrote, "he comes with his Torah, given to him from Sinai, in hand. He orients himself to the world by means of fixed statutes and firm principles. An entire corpus of precepts and laws guides him along the path leading to existence."[20] Soloveitchik responded to the predicaments of humankind by showing how observance could liberate Jewish individuals to achieve more meaningful lives. Soloveitchik rejected the outlook of Haredi Jews, who lived in almost complete isolation from those around them. Jews, he felt, had an obligation to use their laws as a foundation upon which to improve the world around them, including the pursuit of social justice.[21]

For Heschel, the effort to make sense of the tragic period began with an examination of his own community of origin, Eastern European Ashkenazi Jews. In 1949, he published *The Earth Is the Lord's: The Inner World of the Jew in Eastern Europe*, an expanded version of a well-received lecture he had delivered at YIVO in 1945 (at the conclusion of which the crowd stood up unprompted to chant the Mourner's Kaddish). "I feel justified in saying that it was the golden period in Jewish history, in the history of the Jewish soul," he told readers. This piece presented the culture of Ashkenazi Jews in contrast to what he saw as the rigid, formal, hierarchical world of the Sephardi. "The culture of Spanish Sephardic Jews was shaped by an elite," Heschel explained, "it was derived from above and was hardly touched by the archaic simplicity, imaginative naivete, and unaffected naturalness of the humble mass."[22]

Heschel's romantic memory of Eastern Europe's Ashkenazic culture, a world that he left behind in search of the cos-

mopolitan city, introduced readers to a place where religion was a democratizing force. Religion empowered every male in the community by allowing them to learn ancient texts and to participate equally in prayer regardless of economic status. "In almost every Jewish home in Eastern Europe, even in the humblest and the poorest, stood a bookcase full of volumes," Heschel wrote. "Poor Jews, whose children knew only the taste of 'potatoes on Sunday, potatoes on Monday, potatoes on Tuesday,' sat there like 'intellectual magnates.'" Torah was more powerful, in his estimation, than physical hardship: "The stomachs were empty, the homes were barren, but the minds were crammed with the riches of Torah."[23] Ashkenazi Jews were bound together by the common idiom of Yiddish and their "revolutionary" approach to prayer. The Hasidic Jews were mystical and steeped in the traditions of the Kabbalah. "Under the spell of the Hasidim, the rich and ponderous speculations of the Sephardic mystics were stripped of their tense and stern features without any loss of profundity or earnestness. The lofty and elaborate doctrines of the Kabbalah were melted into thoughts understandable by the heart." Although the book did not directly address the Nazis, the Holocaust hovered over the narrative. Heschel lamented the fact that "persecutions, pogroms, and murders shattered the ground from under the feet of the people."[24]

The book was written in the poetic style that would characterize most of his work—a style meant to evoke emotion and feeling in his readers, to shake them out of their spiritual slumber, since he believed that they had been hardened in a climate dominated by rationalistic, scientific thought. As the philosopher David Hartman argued, "Heschel was willing to sacrifice the intellectual rigor of formal theology for the intensity of religious narrative, and he was less concerned with conceptual consistency than with making God a living reality for modern Jews embarrassed by religious language and culture."[25]

The Earth Is the Lord's generated its share of criticism. Some

negative reviews noted that he romanticized Warsaw. Heschel, for instance, didn't acknowledge the overweening power of the rebbe or the stifling conservatism that had taken hold by the time he left for Vilna. Nor could one understand from his stories why the author had voluntarily departed from his community of origin for a secular education. Poverty, illiteracy, and hardship were overshadowed by the image of a world filled with budding scholars whose study of Torah overwhelmed all else.[26] Stylistically, there was an absence of scholarly footnotes.

Yet much of the response was positive. The work resonated at a moment when the national media were publishing sympathetic portraits of Eastern European Jews following the tragic fate of Warsaw and other cities.[27] As a result of World War II, the fate of Jewry was coming to be seen as an integral element to the human rights question. Finkelstein thanked the publisher, Henry Schuman, for producing a "brilliant work" that captured the "spiritual life of East European Jewry" with a "complete understanding and thorough appreciation."[28] Morgenstern sent Heschel a note to express the "joy I experienced in reading it. It imparts the flavor of Eastern European Jewish life as no other book of which I know succeeds in doing." As someone who helped save refugees from this region of the world, Morgenstern stated with authority that "it is a living monument to an aspect of Jewish culture, which, alas, has now come to an end."[29] Maurice Friedman, a former socialist and labor organizer, who was studying for his doctoral degree at the University of Chicago, wrote his friend, "Most of the criticisms of which you told me were quite beside the point. Since you were writing a popular and not a scholarly work, you did not need to document and dispute, and the background which you did select was quite apt for your purpose. Nor were you obliged to do any more than you did in recognizing the weak points in the east European Jews. You were trying to capture the vision which they embodied in their lives, and this you did quite suc-

cessfully and without sentimentality."[30] And Niebuhr wrote, "I marvel how a man who does not have the English tongue as a birthright can write so beautifully in English. This in addition to the profundity of the thought."[31]

North American Jews looked to displaced émigré intellectuals in the United States to convey through their vivid prose the character of the Eastern European culture that many of them had fled. Trained in the finest universities, equally as conversant with modern social science as they were with Torah, these writers were unapologetic about their heritage, as some earlier thinkers had been, eager to share the tradition that they loved and now yearned to preserve. Heschel and his cohort had been there in person through their early adulthood and were thus capable of writing about Jewish life from memory, not just books.[32] In his review for the *New York Herald Tribune*, Marvin Lowenthal praised *The Earth Is the Lord's* as a "prose rhapsody on the theme of Ashkenazic Jewry." As long as readers understood that his portrait of Eastern Europe was not "literally true" as a historical account, they would "rise from the book a wiser man, and spiritually refreshed."[33] In *Conservative Judaism*, Herman Kieval concluded that the book was especially pertinent since so "many of us fail to see any values in that murdered culture which can serve the needs of our own situation." For all the review's exaggerations, Kieval felt that Heschel conveyed to contemporary readers why the Hasidic culture offered "a spiritual goal for democratic education, a way to find the beauty of holiness in everyday life, a faith which sustained a persecuted people through every crisis and terror."[34] The book constituted a eulogy for a way of life.

The Earth Is the Lord's entered into an important conversation that American Jews were starting to have about the Holocaust in the late 1940s. Within their families and communal institutions, American Jews privately wrestled with the aftermath of World War II even as they enjoyed the bounties of

economic growth and leaned into the suburban boom. The anguish about the slaughter of six million people manifested itself in many ways. Synagogues, summer camps, filmmakers, fiction writers, as well as civic organizations were finding ways to commemorate the tragedy inflicted upon their people.[35] Soon after the war ended, Henry Shoskes, a Jewish writer from Bialystok who had settled in New York in 1940, published *No Traveler Returns: The Story of Hitler's Greatest Crime*, which looked at the fate suffered by the Jews from the Warsaw Ghetto. In January 1947, YIVO sponsored a traveling exhibit called "Jews in Europe, 1939–1946" that featured photographs and physical objects documenting the "extent and ramifications of the Nazi crimes against the Jewish people." In 1950, as part of its "Studies in Prejudice" series, the AJC published Paul Massing's *Rehearsal for Destruction* (Massing, a professor at Columbia, was not Jewish), which uncovered the origins of anti-Semitism in Imperial Germany.[36] Equally important were Jewish intellectuals who honed in on the problem of man's relationship to God in an effort to wrestle with the evil so evident in the modern world. Though the Holocaust was not always their explicit topic (the term was not really used until the mid-1960s), it was never far below the surface. "For us," Heschel wrote, "contemporaries and survivors of history's most terrible horrors, it is impossible to meditate about the compassion of God without asking: 'Where is God?' "[37] His quest for spirituality was always connected to the nightmares from the war. As he told a group of Orthodox day school educators in 1949, "When the annual congress of the Nazi Party convened in Nuremberg in 1937, journalists from all over the world, such as the *Times of London*, described with enthusiasm the demonstrations of the various Nazi organizations. They could not find enough adjectives to praise the physical beauty, the order, the discipline, and the athletic perfection of the tens of thousands of young Nazis who marched ceremoniously and festively before the leader of the 'move-

ment.'" Heschel continued: "These writers who were so excited by the exterior splendor lacked the ability to see the snakes in the form of humans—the poison that coursed through their veins, which not long after would bring death to millions of people."[38]

For a majority of American Jews, the establishment of the state of Israel in 1948 was one big answer to these existential questions. Many American Jews had not been part of the Zionist movement but after World War II came to support the state.[39] In fact, polls showed a broad shift among most Americans on this issue; in 1945, 72 percent opposed U.S. involvement on the Palestinian question whereas by 1946, 76 percent of those polled favored the right of Jews to have a homeland in the territory.[40] Israel generated renewed optimism throughout the Jewish world, a counterpoint to the horrors of World War II. According to the *American Jewish Yearbook*, it was "the most dramatic and perhaps most significant event in post-exilic Jewish history."[41] Overflow crowds packed into Madison Square Garden in New York City to celebrate the creation, with former first lady Eleanor Roosevelt, Republican Senator Robert Taft of Ohio, and former New York governor Herbert Lehman speaking. "Salute to Israel" the organizers called it.[42] Thousands of Jews joined parades in Cincinnati, holding banners that read, "The Spirit of 76 in Israel Today" and "Long Live Jewish Palestine." As women and children waved miniature paper flags, Rabbi Fishel Goldfeder of the Avondale Synagogue announced to the crowd, "This is the day for which we have so long hoped. Rejoice and be happy. This is the day which marks the rendezvous of Israel with destiny."[43] The reaction was similar elsewhere. "New York and other American cities yesterday wore a festive air as blue-and-white flags bearing the Star of David fluttered from rooftops in celebration of the birth of the Jewish State," one reporter observed.[44] Most of the prominent voices who opposed Zionism in the United States had faded from the

mainstream. To Heschel, Israel always constituted a central part of Jewish history and the decision of the United Nations to legitimate the state represented a monumental step forward after the reign of the Nazis.

But Heschel, who was a Zionist, focused on the Jews immediately surrounding him. And he wasn't alone. Despite the positive feelings about Israel, the new nation-state did not dominate American Jewish life after the initial celebrations passed. During the 1950s, for instance, merely forty-eight out of more than one thousand Jewish education teachers reported that they had taught Israel as a "subject of study."[45]

The main concern of American Jews remained the health of Judaism in their own country as they confronted assimilation and secularity. After World War II, the work of congregational rabbis and scholars took place against the backdrop of a booming economy and thriving suburban middle class. Collective bargaining agreements provided industrial workers with unprecedented economic security and upward mobility. Quota systems that had restricted Jews from entering into prestigious professions and cultural associations, as well as universities, started to fall. College-educated middle-class citizens were enjoying the benefits of being part of a growing middle class, owning large homes in the suburbs that were filled with televisions and washing machines, having at least one car in the garage, and securing access to endless convenient fast-food restaurants and department stores. In this milieu, Americans came to define themselves by how much they could enjoy the fruits of this bountiful economy. Jews whose education and middle-class jobs allowed them to move out of the cities and into this consumerist paradise were eager to participate. As they wove themselves into the fabric of the nation, it became less appealing to preserve tradition. Though intermarriage rates were low in the 1950s (under 5 percent), for many families in suburbia, Sabbath no longer meant going to synagogue but leisure time

for going out to eat at non-kosher restaurants, shop at local stores, and jump into cars for long family outings. Holidays such as Hanukkah were remade by absorbing customs from the larger culture. "Hanukkah, in short," one sociologist concluded, "becomes for some the Jewish Christmas."[46]

Despite these challenges, Finkelstein insisted that American Jews thirsted for stronger connections to their roots. "I remember how stricken we were when 47 Jews were killed in a pogrom in the Ukraine," he told a reporter for *Time* magazine. "We had days of mourning and fasting. But six million! That dreadful calamity—and the whole spiritual and material crisis of our time—are bringing American Jews back to the faith of their fathers."[47] Since there was no straight path forward to achieve what Finkelstein called for, a robust debate unfolded about how to make their thousand-year-old tradition more relevant to contemporary Jews living in a secular environment.

Heschel's emphasis on spirituality differed from the central thrust of mainstream rabbinic scholarship, which revolved around Jewish law, Halakha. The cutting-edge scholarship being produced at JTS aimed to unpack the formal structures of behavior that could create the basis for preserving the Jewish tradition. The writing of many of the greatest minds tackling these issues centered on promoting an understanding of, and adherence to, Halakha that was of divine origin rather than nurturing some sort of religious consciousness. Grappling with rabbinic commentaries was the key, according to this outlook, to building a strong Jewish foundation that could survive in the modern world. The "positive-historical" approach, as it was known among the experts, aimed to situate rabbinic thought within specific social and historical contexts. One of the legendary practitioners from this school of thought was the JTS Talmudist Louis Ginzberg, a Lithuanian born émigré who joined the JTS faculty in 1903, four years after arriving to America.

The fault lines between Heschel and his colleagues were

evident to one of the renowned scholars at the institution, Saul Lieberman, whose emphasis was on understanding Jewish law. Lieberman, who lived in the same apartment building as the Heschels, was born near Pinsk, Belorussia, in 1898 and trained at an Orthodox yeshiva. He went on to pursue his education at the University of Kiev as well as in France before obtaining several positions in Jerusalem, where he taught Talmudic and rabbinic literature. Finkelstein recruited Lieberman to join JTS in 1940, the same year as Heschel. Lieberman, who continued to live and practice as a strict Orthodox Jew, became one of the most renowned and prolific Talmudic scholars in the world. Like many Litvaks, he dismissed mysticism and expressed little interest in theology.[48] Lieberman was always working and had an extraordinary memory, so good, it was said, that he didn't read the newspapers so as not to fill his head with information not pertinent to his writing. His writing provided commentary on different tractates of the Talmud. One of his best-known works was his epic, multivolume edition of the Tosefta, early rabbinic oral laws in the Tanaitic period, a tumultuous time during which rabbis wrestled with the destruction of the Second Temple. Lieberman's scholarly stature and closeness to Finkelstein allowed him to set the tenor of pedagogy at JTS. He was considered to be the rabbi of the weekly services and the most influential figure on the faculty.

For the homiletics professor Mordecai Kaplan, the answer to invigorating American Judaism revolved around the synagogue. Kaplan was the son of an Orthodox rabbi who arrived in the United States from Lithuania in 1889. Holding a degree from Columbia University, Kaplan was ordained in 1902 as one of the first graduates from JTS. He started his career in New York's Orthodox synagogue, Congregation Kehilath Jeshurun. But Kaplan became frustrated with the dogmatism he encountered among congregants and colleagues. In 1909, he accepted a position as dean of the Teachers Institute

of JTS. He simultaneously helped establish the Jewish Center in 1918 on the Upper West Side, an institution where religious practice mixed with social activities. Four years later, he moved on to create the Society for the Advancement of Judaism, a synagogue grounded in his distinct vision of Judaism. Twenty-five years older than Heschel, Kaplan had been arguing for decades that Judaism needed to be reconstructed so that its values and practices made sense within the modern era of science and democracy, without replicating the style of Reform Judaism that departed too far from the organic culture of Jews. Kaplan thought the emphasis of the Reform movement on a belief in God didn't help individuals see why Judaism still mattered. The Orthodox adhered to strictures that were incompatible with modern moral sensibilities, ethics, and needs. Conservatism was too often incoherent. "The problem of Judaism is inherently the problem of how it is to meet modern life," he noted in his diary.[49] He felt that American Jews faced immense challenges in the modern economy if they sought to preserve their traditions. "There is no time for Judaism, and there are no energies left for it," he wrote. His first book, *Judaism as a Civilization* (1934), laid out his arguments.[50] Drawing on theories from the social sciences, Kaplan claimed that religious symbols, knowledge, philosophy, arts, practice, and literature were essential to preserving the collective consciousness of an evolving Jewish civilization.

Paying attention to nurturing Jewish culture through a seven-day-a-week, multipurpose synagogue-center was more important in his mind than strict adherence by individuals to theological doctrine or spirituality. Kaplan, who appreciated Heschel's embrace of the mystical side of Judaism (he wrote a poem in 1942 adapted from "Analysis of Piety"), described God as a "cosmic process" and an idea derived from the social unity of Jewish civilization.[51] He pursued a pragmatic, antiauthoritarian, and scientific logic to explain the essential importance

of religion. God was not a being, according to Kaplan, that stood outside of and above the universe. World War II left Kaplan feeling urgency about the project of reconstructing Judaism. "I am entirely unequal to giving anything like adequate expression to the feelings that well up in my heart at the thought that the war in Europe is at an end. If only it were like waking up from a terrible nightmare!" Kaplan wrote in his diary in August 1945. "But unfortunately the unspeakable atrocities committed by the insane murderers are too real to disappear with the break of the dawn, and the living victims of the war are too much part of our own lives to be forgotten."[52]

Kaplan's emphasis on Jewish folkways rather than on the biblical commandments broke with the conventional thinking of many colleagues at JTS and were thus controversial. Ginzberg, Kaplan said, saw him "as a menace . . . [when confronted with his ideas]. He grows hysterical, he screams at the top of his voice, he foams at the mouth and shakes his fist as he cries . . . you are destroying Judaism."[53] "The Jewish people are not here to maintain Torah," Kaplan argued defiantly. "Torah exists for the sake of the Jewish people." Kaplan went so far as to say that key rituals such as keeping kosher should be practiced only when they "[did] not involve an unreasonable amount of time, effort, and expense." "There is no God and Kaplan is his prophet," one Orthodox critic quipped.[54] Yet Kaplan's vision of the synagogue as an institution that could bind Jewish communities gained a strong foothold among young rabbinic students who were spreading out and putting down roots in the suburbs. "If the *bet am* is to function as a means of generating Jewish atmosphere, it should aim to utilize existing needs for Jewish association, and to direct Jewish creative ability upon Jewish interests, projects and objectives," he wrote. "The following are some of these needs: Jewish elementary school facilities, boys' and girls' clubs; recreation facilities such as gymnasia, showers, bowling alleys, pool tables and game rooms; adult study and art

groups; communal activities; religious services and festival pageants and plays; informal meetings of friends and associates." The point of all this, he explained, was that to "live Judaism as a civilization" meant to not only pray together but also "to work and to play as a Jew, that is, to carry on, as a Jew, activities which answer to fundamental human wants."[55] His teaching resonated with local congregations who were increasingly demanding that their rabbis adapt customs, such as allowing for more prayers to be chanted in English rather than in Hebrew and devoting greater financial resources to facilities that could be used for life-cycle celebrations.[56]

Heschel found Kaplan's approach to be insufficient and flawed. Both men were challenging the prevailing scholarship at JTS but doing so from very different directions. The problem for Heschel was modern life, not traditional Judaism. God was very real, Heschel argued, not an idea or an abstract concept that symbolized something else. The challenge was for modern humans to remake their consciousness so as to be able to hear God.[57] Heschel privileged a nonpragmatic, mystical, and supernatural interpretation of God that was filled with mystery. Whereas Kaplan and his followers sought to cultivate social cohesion and communal self-expression, Heschel trained his eyes on the obligations of the individual and the biblical commandments. Rituals without a proper orientation grounded in this understanding of the Divine, Heschel insisted, would lose their attraction. So too would the most beautiful of buildings. Each biblical commandment had to be approached with true "Kavanah," the rabbinic concept of having the right intention. Rabbis had to teach individual congregants how to achieve this goal. The failure to take Kavanah seriously, Heschel warned, was one of the main problems facing modern Judaism.

Like Kaplan, Heschel tried to fulfill Finkelstein's mission by explaining the import of Jewish traditions, connecting them to questions about the basic fabric of America. Laced into his

account of the sacred elements of the Jewish cycle was a sharp critique of consumerism and material desire that complemented the message of other writers, like the journalist Vance Packard, who were in their own ways lamenting the commercial obsessions in the postwar period.

Published by Farrar, Straus and Young in 1951, one of New York's premier houses, Heschel's *The Sabbath* turned to the sanctity of time in this secular, consumer world. The space that Jews created from commerce and material want was not physical; it was a block of time demarcated by the Sabbath. At a time when many Jews were focused on the importance of territory with the creation of Israel, Heschel's book moved in a different direction with a contrasting emphasis on temporality. Heschel reminded his readers that in Genesis the first thing declared to be holy was the seventh day, as opposed to a place or physical object. "Holiness in space, in nature, was known in other religions. New in the teaching of Judaism was that the idea of holiness was gradually shifted from space to time, from the realm of nature to the realm of history, from things to events. . . . The emphasis on time is a predominant feature of prophetic thinking," Heschel wrote.[58] He explained that the seventh day of the Jewish week, which started at sundown on Friday night and ended at sundown the following evening, provided a period of introspection to direct people's energy toward something greater than the material demands of the secular world. Jews were to avoid work, commerce, and even the use of electricity. Indeed, one was supposed to spend twenty-four hours away from the most iconic of American goods—the automobile. A strong anti-consumerist ethos ran through the text. "He who wants to enter the holiness of the day must first lay down the profanity of clattering commerce, of being yoked to toil. He must go away from the screech of dissonant days, from the nervousness and fury of acquisitiveness and the betrayal in embezzling his own life. . . . Six days a week we wrestle with the world, wring-

ing profit from the earth; on the Sabbath we especially care for the seed of eternity planted in the soul. . . . Six days a week we seek to dominate the world, on the seventh day we try to dominate the self."[59] Since the Hebrew Bible characterized the seventh day as one that God made holy, Heschel wrote, "what we plead against is man's unconditional surrender to space, his enslavement to things." The publisher decorated the pages with handsome wood engravings by the New York–based Polish artist Ilya Schor, who also came from a Hasidic family in Poland and devoted his artwork to making Judaica that commemorated the spirit of the Eastern European shtetl.

Heschel garnered strong reviews even as more of his JTS colleagues started to grumble about the intellectual heft of his writing. Professor Nahum Glatzer of Brandeis University compared Heschel to a few of the world's greatest Jewish scholars, including Leo Baeck and Franz Rosenzweig.[60] *The Sabbath*, another reviewer noted, was "destined to become a classic."[61] "I have just finished reading Dr. Heschel's *The Sabbath: Its Meaning for the Modern Man* and am still under its wonderful sabbatic spell," wrote the reviewer in *Our Voice* in West Palm Beach. "He has written a piece of holiness and beauty."[62] In the *Brooklyn Jewish Center Review*, Israel Levinthal, the founding rabbi of the renowned Brooklyn Jewish Center, a visiting spot for prominent Americans like Albert Einstein, marveled at "one of the most beautiful interpretations of the Sabbath to be found in Jewish literature, especially in modern times and in the English language."[63] *The Jewish Parents* called it a "powerful argument for spiritual living in our day—of which the Sabbath is the climax."[64] In a personal note to Heschel, Samuel Schulman, a Russian-born Jew who was the rabbi-emeritus of the prestigious Reform Temple Emanuel in New York, praised *The Sabbath*: "As I read your little book I was happy because I recalled the spirit of the Sabbath as it sanctified life in the humble home of my parents. Thus I had the feeling of nostalgia which must

be shared even by you."[65] Marvin Fox, a philosopher at Ohio State University, wrote to say that "you have succeeded in restoring the Sabbath to its full glory. Every Jew who values Jewish institutions is indebted to you for your excellent work."[66] The teenager Jacob Neusner, a future Judaic scholar who grew up in a Reform home in Connecticut, was deeply impacted by the book, which was given to him by his father. "I was very moved by it," he recalled. "I had never read anyone who wrote about anything Jewish that had any human meaning to it."[67] Kaplan shared his impression, the "inspirational quality of your writing applied to the theme with which you deal should make this book a very important factor in acquainting both Jews and Christians with the beauty and the sanctity of the Sabbath."[68]

Heschel was enjoying the experience of becoming immersed in New York's prestigious communities of the mind. While he waxed nostalgic about this lost world in Eastern Europe, he was sufficiently self-aware to realize that ever since Berlin, he identified with the contemporary intelligentsia. This was clear when he sent Maurice Friedman, who was visiting the seminary in 1950, to spend time with the Hasidic community in Williamsburg. Friedman returned to JTS absolutely enthralled by the joyous prayer he witnessed, asking Heschel why he and Sylvia didn't relocate there. Heschel responded, "When I left my home in Poland, I became a modern Western man. I cannot reverse this."[69]

Heschel next set out to tackle the existential dilemmas that faced humankind following all of the catastrophic experiences that had occurred in the twentieth century. Modernity, markets, and science had not produced a peaceful world. "Horrified by the discovery of man's power to bring about the annihilation of organic life on this planet, we are today beginning to comprehend that the sense for the sacred is as vital to us as the light of the sun; that the enjoyment of beauty, possessions and safety in civilized society depends upon man's sense for the sa-

credness of life, upon his reverence for this spark of light in the darkness of selfishness; that once we permit this spark to be quenched, the darkness falls upon us like thunder."[70] Given the events that he himself had witnessed, Heschel understood why so many people were desperate to know the answer to the question, "Where is God?" But even though his readers had lived through "history's most terrible horrors," with the earth more "soaked with blood" than ever before, Heschel insisted that it was a "major folly" to shift "the responsibility for man's plight from man to God, in accusing the Invisible though iniquity is ours. Rather than admit our own guilt, we seek, like Adam, to shift the blame upon someone else."[71]

The key for Heschel was that individuals needed to achieve a religiously oriented consciousness. In his next work, published a few months after *The Sabbath*, entitled *Man Is Not Alone*, Heschel examined the complex problem of man's relationship with God.[72] Man was not alone but he had to be able to open himself to the presence of God. Deeply influenced by the Hasidic and Kabbalah traditions, Heschel expressed his belief that humans bore immense responsibility to live a life that would enable God to hear them and for them to hear God. Doing so was more urgent than ever before given that "we live in an age when most of us have ceased to be shocked by the increasing breakdown in moral inhibitions. The decay of conscience fills the air with a pungent smell. Good and evil, which were once as distinguishable as day and night, have become a blurred mist. But that mist is man-made. God is not silent. He has been silenced."[73]

"As civilization advances," Heschel warned, "the sense of wonder almost necessarily declines. . . . Mankind will not perish for want of information; but only for want of appreciation."[74] Maintaining a deep respect for the physical and social sciences, Heschel simultaneously insisted that individuals needed to be able to achieve a fundamentally different mindset. The key, he said, was that being pious helped nurture a sense of wonder

about the universe. Heschel wrote, "Standing eye to eye with being as being, we realize that we are able to look at the world with two faculties—with reason and with wonder." It was "wonder rather than doubt" which was the "root of all knowledge."[75] Wonder, he argued, was an orientation to the world that allowed an individual to be perpetually surprised by everything which surrounded them. The problem was that in the secular era of science, pragmatism, and rationalism, most individuals didn't know how to naturally think this way. Frequent worship was one way to develop a sense of wonder about the most ordinary of things so that life did not become stifled by routine. The pious person living in a state of wonder was capable of achieving a higher sense of "radical amazement," which was more complete and more total, even leaving them in awe of wonder.[76] When walking with his students and colleagues in Riverside Park, this was the reason he liked to say, "Don't forget the trees, don't forget the river."[77]

Once an individual entered into a state of "radical amazement," then they could transcend their ego.[78] Piety, in his telling, was antithetical to selfishness. For the pious person, God's needs superseded an individual's needs. "Man reaches a new vertical dimension, the dimension of the holy, when he grows beyond his self-interests, when that which is of interest to others becomes vital to him, and it is only in this dimension, in the understanding of its perennial validity, that the concern for other human beings and the devotion to ideals may reach the degree of self-denial."[79] By becoming aware of the "ineffable," an individual could prepare themselves for an encounter with God. "We are penetrated by His [God's] insight. We cannot think any more as if He were there and we here. He is both there and here. He is not *a being*, but *being in and beyond all things*."[80]

The God in *Man Is Not Alone* exhibited humanlike qualities. Far from the transcendent God portrayed by Maimonides and the Greek philosophers, Heschel presented a God that pos-

sessed human emotions about the state of humankind: rage, love, and compassion.[81] In his work, God's anger stemmed from a moral judgment about the sins of humankind, feelings that would eventually be followed by love and compassion. God, Heschel wrote, was "the father of all men, not only a judge; He is a lover engaged to His people, not only a king. God stands in a passionate relationship to man."[82] The Hebrew Prophets, who had been the subject of his doctoral dissertation, were moved by the "divine pathos" of God that they felt deep in their souls. The reciprocal relationship that the Prophets had achieved with God was the source of their acute moral sentiment.

By feeling God's pathos, an individual gained the capacity to express divine love as well as divine anger about the state of humanity: "The sense of the ineffable introduces the soul to the divine aspect of the universe, to a reality higher than the universe."[83] The person who achieved this state of consciousness would be better positioned to create a just society. Once we become "alive to our living in the great fellowship of all beings, we cease to regard things as opportunities to exploit."[84]

With an eye toward his colleagues, Heschel wanted to show through this book that Jewish law and faith were deeply intertwined. Heschel did not dismiss the importance of Halakha at all, but he believed that humans' having a sense of divine pathos was necessary to allow for a commitment to law to take effect. "After the Holocaust," he liked to say privately, "Jewish scholarship should be devoted to Yiddishkeit."[85] "As faith cannot exist without creed, piety cannot subsist without a pattern of deeds; as intelligence cannot be separated from training, religion cannot be divorced from conduct. Judaism is lived in deeds not only in thoughts," Heschel wrote.[86] The proper orientation of individuals toward the universe was essential for Judaism to achieve its potential to improve the world.

In a review that caught the attention of New York's literary community, Reinhold Niebuhr predicted in the *New York Her-*

ald that Heschel "will become a commanding and authoritative voice not only in the Jewish community but in the religious life of America." He didn't stop there. "This volume is so impressive because it is the work of a poet and mystic who has mastered the philosophical and scientific disciplines," Niebuhr went on to say, "and who with consummate skill reveals the dimension of reality apprehended by religious faith, as distinguished from all the coherences and sequences and causalities which science charts and philosophy arranges into a total rational scheme."[87] The publisher issued a press release highlighting the review and referenced a personal note from Niebuhr calling the work a masterpiece.[88] In a private letter, Finkelstein, who read the book over the Jewish High Holidays, commended Heschel for producing a piece that "helps improve one's soul. . . . The manner in which you have been able to present very difficult and abstract theological problems in lucid, easily-read, poetical prose is quite remarkable. . . . I have no doubt that the publication of this book will have a most beneficent influence on the thinking and action of many people in this day of widespread religious and philosophical confusion."[89] The publication also found interest in a burgeoning literature in the United States (many of which had the word "man" in the title) of philosophic, political, and fictional work in the 1950s that sought to understand the threat humankind faced in the aftermath of totalitarianism, world war, and severe economic depression.[90]

One person taken by Heschel's work was Alexander Altmann, the chief rabbi of Manchester and an influential scholar of the history of philosophy with a doctorate from the University of Berlin. He believed that Heschel's writing represented an exceptional contribution to the canon of Jewish studies. Altmann had fled from Nazi Germany in 1938 after having served as a rabbi in Berlin. He had known Heschel since their time together at the Institute of Jewish Studies in London. In a private letter, Altmann described Heschel's "Analysis of Piety" as a

"masterpiece of giving expression to the inexpressible, an objective account and poetry at the same time. . . . It had all the quality of a true Heschel product."[91] Upon receiving *Man Is Not Alone*, Altmann wrote his friend to "offer you my cordial felicitations on your successes and achievements in the literary field and, what is more, on your courage in teaching a philosophy of life which in many ways runs counter to the prevailing mood of your environment. I am glad to find that American Jewry does appreciate you." Altmann admiringly called Heschel's work a major achievement (though he liked *Earth Is the Lord's* better because it was "more earthbound and more expressive of your own self").[92]

Though the work may have been lyrical in the minds of some scholars and short on references, Heschel's writing was a far weightier treatise on religion than almost anything the average American Jew encountered. A promotional letter that the publisher sent out to congregational rabbis across the country, signed by three prominent rabbis, including the Orthodox Leo Jung of New York, proclaimed that the book should be required reading for congregants, sisterhoods, and men's clubs since it could "lead them to an understanding of our calling as rabbis of Israel." The book, they said, filled a void that had been created by the "tragic dearth of literature breathing with the spirit of Judaism."[93] *The Eternal Light* featured an episode on the work, the fourth of its "great book series."

Beneath the crass materialism that writers lamented, there was a thirst for religion in Cold War America. Heschel found space in a publishing market where religion was becoming a hot commodity. Prestigious houses as well as reputable religious publishers like Henry Schuman were signing authors at a rapid clip. Christian intellectuals were motivated to go public by the belief that the nation faced a true moral crisis after the triumph of communism.[94] Some religious figures with a more explicit political agenda sought to provide theological cover to

anti–New Deal conservatives.[95] There was even a blockbuster Hollywood film, the second most successful movie of the decade, Cecil B. DeMille's *The Ten Commandments*, starring Charlton Heston, that managed to rake in ticket sales with the life story of Moses. Others simply yearned for the ethical and moral foundation that they believed religion provided. The Jewish community had an appetite for theology which stemmed from an existential quest to make sense of the Nazis. "The modern Jew has been prone to forget that the world is unredeemed," Heschel wrote, "and that God is in exile. The present generation is beginning to realize how monstrous an illusion it was to substitute faith in man for faith in God."[96]

This series of books that came to define Heschel's thinking was released at the moment when synagogues were multiplying in every region of the country. Paralleling the rapid growth of church membership in the early Cold War, the American Jewish community intensified its own institution-building, but with the added impetus of a people desperately trying to revitalize a religion that had been devastated by mass genocide. Rabbis, philanthropists, and other religious leaders felt a sense of gravity about strengthening the organizational foundation of their community. In a 1951 cover story in *Time* magazine that featured Finkelstein, the reporter noted, "The old, half-deserted synagogues are filling up again, new congregations are forming, new synagogues are being built. Young married couples are sending their children to religious schools to learn the fundamentals of their faith—then forming study groups so that they will know what their children are talking about. The word that such young Americans use, over & over again, when they are asked what they are looking for, is 'heritage.' "[97] The Conservative movement was doing well, expanding from approximately 35 communities in 1945 to more than 800 by 1971. Jewish summer camps like Camp Ramah were established in multiple locations; dense networks of philanthropies formed. The num-

ber of children attending Jewish schools increased from 239,398 to 553,600 between 1948 and 1958.[98] There would be almost 4,200 synagogues in the United States by 1958.

Heschel's work was attractive to pulpit rabbis who were seeking to offer their congregants as much Jewish culture as possible. The United Synagogue of America, working with all of the major Conservative organizations, incorporated *The Sabbath* into a two-year national campaign in 1951 and 1952 as a centerpiece of the "Sabbath Observance Project." Although the Sabbath had suffered in "our technological age," the United Synagogue explained, "the Sabbath, properly observed, offers us the opportunity to cast off the chains of routine and hyper-tensions, to preserve our psychological, physical and spiritual equilibrium." Rabbis, cantors, and their educational directors received kits to organize weekends that were devoted to teaching congregants about the tradition, including excerpts from Heschel's *Sabbath* to circulate with discussion points.[99] The American Jewish Press distributed a serialized version of *The Sabbath* to twenty-eight newspapers.[100] The United Synagogue purchased twenty-five hundred copies of the book, which they distributed to local communities at a discounted rate ($1 instead of $2.75). They also organized a widely publicized ceremony at JTS to honor Heschel. The publisher Roger Straus Jr. presented copies to the leaders of the New York Public Library, the Hebrew University in Jerusalem, and the Library of the Seminary.[101] In *Sabbath* Heschel produced a cerebral product to satiate the hunger for Jewish culture in suburban communities that were so far removed from the rich ethnic life of the neighborhoods of Warsaw or even New York City. A congregant in a synagogue in New Jersey would read Heschel's latest work about how individuals could encounter God via the same ethnic curiosity that brought them to sisterhood shops to purchase dreidels, mezuzahs, Sabbath candles, and challah covers.[102] "In the last five years American Judaism had to reckon seriously with

a new phenomenon—the writings of Abraham Joshua Heschel," wrote Maurice Friedman in *Congress Weekly*, an influential Jewish publication.[103]

At the same time, Heschel's work gave an emphasis different from the Conservative movement's focus on adherence to Jewish law and building institutions in the fight against assimilation. A majority of young rabbis was arguing that the best way to preserve tradition was to keep the Sabbath, eat kosher, celebrate the major holidays, and go to synagogue regularly. Graduates of JTS attempted to find new methods to promote the Sabbath and holiday services so that middle-class Jews continued to feel attached to the liturgy while partaking in the world around them. Influenced by Kaplan, they were placing their energy into building and filling synagogue centers that provided social and educational services to make Judaism more attractive to the secular family.[104] However, they paid insufficient attention, Heschel feared, to faith.

Even as rabbis offered up Heschel's *Sabbath* to inspire congregants, he did not back down from his critique of their work. "Has the synagogue become the graveyard where prayer is buried?" he asked provocatively of Conservative rabbis who gathered at the Breakers Hotel in Atlantic City for their annual convention in June 1953. Inside the "Aristocrat of Kosher Hotels," Heschel warned that "there are some people who believe that the only way to revitalize the synagogue is to minimize the importance of prayer and to convert the synagogue into a center," a not-so-subtle attack on Kaplan, who sat in the audience listening. "Services are conducted with dignity and precision," he said. "The rendition of the liturgy is smooth. Everything is present: decorum, voice, ceremony." But, he complained, "one thing is missing: *Life*. . . . Our motto is monotony. What was will be, and there is nothing new in the synagogue. The fire has gone out of our worship. It is cold, stiff, and dead." Heschel blasted rabbis for failing to teach their congregants how to pray

as they instead directed their energy toward acting as pundits: "Sermons, indistinguishable in spirit from editorials in *The New York Times,* urging us to have faith in the *New Deal, the Big Three* or *the United Nations,* or attempting to instruct us in the latest theories of psychoanalysis, will hardly inspire us to go on to the *musaf* [the last part of the service]." Heschel urged rabbis to think differently about the mission of their vocation: "Preach in order to pray. Preach in order to inspire others to pray." Heschel's words were so condemnatory that he immediately understood he might have gone too far, telling a JTS colleague, Yakov Rozenberg, as they walked along the boardwalk that it was wrong of him to depict rabbis as "page boys" who only stood in front of their congregations and announced the pages in the service.[105] His biting remarks made it into the press. "Religious Places Held Void of Spirit" read the headline of Irving Spiegel's story in the *New York Times.*[106] One year after his pointed speech, Heschel, with the support of a prestigious Guggenheim Foundation fellowship, further roiled the rabbinic waters by taking direct aim at the suburban synagogue in *Man's Quest for God.*[107]

With publications like *Man's Quest for God,* it was not surprising that Heschel encountered some friction. A number of JTS scholars derided him as a mystic, an indirect slam to put down his work as vague, light, and shallow. At a moment when his colleagues took a historicist approach to textual study that was influenced by modern academic disciplines, many dismissed his writing as second-rate. A number of philosophers did not give his work much respect, though he was earning the admiration of Niebuhr.[108] According to Maurice Friedman, "Critics who have no sympathy with what Heschel has to say and deny that he has made any contribution to philosophy patronizingly praise his works as beautiful prose poems and as 'satisfying and moving' works of art."[109] Heschel's skepticism about social science, along with his deep embrace of mysticism and Kabbalah,

was too much for JTS faculty who were eager to merge modern analytical methodology with Judaic scholarship. He insisted on writing and teaching about a living God as most of his colleagues were trying to demonstrate the congruity between their analysis and contemporary thought.[110] Critics complained that Heschel was prone to irrationality and subjectivity. They didn't like the way he treated textual analysis. Even praise about his moving prose, one admirer noted, was a backhanded way of denying weightier philosophical contributions.[111] A few critics went so far as to note that his work received more favorable attention from non-Jewish writers than from top-tier JTS scholars. In other words, he was a rabbi for the Christians, a comment that was intended to be an insult. Despite Heschel's help in fulfilling Finkelstein's hopes about reaching the general public, the chancellor became less responsive to his research and pedagogical needs, aggravating the sense of distance between Heschel and his home institution.

Some rabbinical students complained about Heschel's pedagogical style, feeling that he was dismissive and uninterested in teaching. His expectations about what constituted an adequate background clashed with what second-generation seminary students brought with them from public and Hebrew school educations. This was not entirely unique to Heschel, as many seminary faculty continued to see a gap between themselves as scholars and the students in their classroom seeking vocational training as Conservative rabbis.[112] Students would sit in Heschel's cramped office, the air filled with smoke from his Dutch Masters Panetela cigars and a musty smell from the books stacked from floor to ceiling, trying to discern the meaning of the esoteric lessons he imparted to them through oblique metaphors and Hasidic tales. "When I needed a professor (as in reading and commenting on my papers) you wanted to be a *rebbe*. And when I needed a *rebbe* (on the edge of pouring out my heart), you kept to the role of professor," one admiring stu-

dent confided to him.[113] Despite their many intense conversations in the hallways of JTS about issues such as Hasidism and modernity, Kaplan became more critical as their personal relationship deteriorated. "I may be reading some prejudice of mine into his attitude toward those who disagree with him [Heschel], but I cannot help feeling that it is one that is insinuatingly patronizing and sanctimonious. As if to say: 'Now listen to me, my friend, you really should be pitied for being such as benighted fool,'" Kaplan, who was also known for being unpleasant with students and colleagues, jotted down in his personal diary. "But as a scion of famous Hasidic dynasties, I am endowed with the divine grace that enables me not only to see through you, but to be of help to you, if you only wouldn't be so pigheaded and listen to what I am telling you."[114]

The tensions between Lieberman and Heschel, as well as other faculty such as Kaplan, took on mythological status within the halls of the seminary.[115] Students gravitated toward these stories during their studies as personalized ways to think about and to debate the conflicting philosophies of Judaism to which they were exposed. A little gossip was also a way to relieve the stress from their studies.

In an institution filled with big minds and healthy egos, the differing interpretations of Halakha, theology, and pedagogy quickly turned personal.[116] Heschel felt that the animosity directed toward him was the reason the administration delayed his promotion to full professor until 1959 and stuck him in a small office, Room 603, in the less prestigious Teachers Institute Building.[117] The conflicts inside the hallowed halls of JTS weighed heavily on Heschel since he was someone who prided himself on his natural ability to connect with different kinds of people. He never liked direct confrontation, which was somewhat ironic given how he would spend the final decade of his life. When Heschel found himself in an argument, he usually contacted the person by the end of the night so as to resolve the

issue before going to sleep. He avoided fights and refrained from responding to attacks. Heschel didn't even correct people who called him Herschel so as not to upset them.[118]

Heschel's efforts to produce a road map to individual piety culminated with the publication of *God in Search of Man*. Unlike *Man Is Not Alone*, this work was filled with footnotes, quotations, and tighter textual references.[119] Written in conversation with philosophers spanning from Plato to Descartes to Buber to John Dewey, Heschel put forward his distinctive take on the philosophy of religion. Divided into three sections that revolved around the encounter he was writing about (God, Revelation, and Response), the book started by expressing sympathy with Americans who felt that religion was alien. "It is customary to blame secular science and anti-religious philosophy for the eclipse of religion in modern society," Heschel confessed to his readers, but "it would be more honest to blame religion for its own defeats. Religion declined not because it was refuted, but because it became irrelevant, dull, oppressive and insipid."[120] By beginning the work with this abrupt confessional, he candidly acknowledged the angst that existed among Jews and non-Jews about the relevance of religion. When Albert Einstein was revealing the laws of physics and scientists were creating vaccines to prevent deadly diseases, why should any Jew in America believe in a supernatural being? He argued that religion and science asked different kinds of questions. "The end of science is to explore the facts and processes of nature," he wrote, "the end of religion is to understand nature in relation to the will of God. The intention of scientific thinking is to answer man's questions and to satisfy his need for knowledge. The ultimate intention of religious thinking is to answer a question which is not man's, and to satisfy God's need for man."[121]

Religious leaders and institutions were not making it easy, they were in fact the problem, Heschel said in response to his own question. He returned to his emphasis on faith, spiritual-

ity, and intention in addition to the law. "When faith is completely replaced by creed, worship by discipline, love by habit; when the crisis of today is ignored because of the splendor of the past; when faith becomes an heirloom rather than a living fountain; when religion speaks only in the name of authority rather than with the voice of compassion—its message becomes meaningless."[122]

More than any other book until that point in his career, *God in Search of Man* specifically tied Heschel's philosophy of religion to the Jewish tradition. He showed how his particular understanding of religious consciousness came directly out of Jewish theology. "Religion consists of *God's question and man's answer*."[123] Judaism revolved around a covenant between God and the individual; the Hebrew Bible was a record of their encounters. The key moment of revelation occurred at Mount Sinai with reciprocity, *matan torah*—the giving of the Torah to the Jewish people—and *kabbalat torah*—their acceptance of the tablets.[124] Both parts of the encounter for the "chosen people" were essential for the revelation to occur. With this point, *God in Search of Man* reiterated Heschel's thesis that God needed man in order to achieve a just world. In contrast to the many interpretations that revolved around man finding God, Heschel reversed the narrative by explaining that God was always looking for man. The key was for man to open himself to this relationship so that God could be able to find him. "*The grand premise* of religion is that *man is able to surpass himself*; that man who is part of this world may enter into a relationship with Him who is greater than the world; that man may lift up his mind and be attached to the absolute; that man who is conditioned by a multiplicity of factors is capable of living with demands that are unconditioned," Heschel wrote.[125] As he argued in *Man Is Not Alone*, Heschel reiterated that God needed man. "God is not indifferent to man's quest of Him," Heschel wrote. "He is in need of man, in need of man's share in redemption.

God who created the world is not at home in the world, in its dark alleys of misery, callousness and defiance."[126] Judaism required of a devout person that they be able to appreciate the holy dimension of the most apparently inconsequential elements of their lives: "This is one of the goals of the Jewish way of living: to experience commonplace deeds as spiritual adventures, to feel the hidden love and wisdom in all things."[127]

By practicing the Mitzvot, the 613 commandments of God, and praying in the right way, Jews could open themselves up to this encounter. Practicing the commandments allowed them to cultivate the kind of spiritual consciousness that was necessary to hear God. The weight that he placed on the importance and power of the Mitzvot reflected the deep influence that the Hasidic tradition had on his thinking. During his youth, he had learned from rebbes who expressed great devotion and passion about the secret power of these commandments.[128] The self was the obstacle in this greater awareness. "Shamed, shocked at the misery of an overloaded ego," he wrote, "we seek to break out of the circle of the ego."[129] Indifference to the "sublime wonder of living is the root of sin."[130]

Heschel devoted part of the book to address the tensions that existed between Jewish law and nonlegalistic thinking. "To reduce Judaism to law, to halacha," Heschel argued, "is to dim its light, to pervert its essence and to kill its spirit." In his effort to address the debate that he had been involved in with his colleagues since arriving at JTS in 1940, Heschel insisted that Halakha and Aggadah (nonlegalistic thinking) depended on each other: "The law does not create in us the motivation to love and to fear God. . . . The code of conduct is like the score to a musician. Rules, principles, forms may be taught: insight, feeling, the sense of rhythm must come from within."[131]

All of these arguments came together in his effort to suggest how individuals and societies could deal with the problem of evil. "The world is in flames, consumed by evil," Heschel

pondered, certainly thinking about the carnage of the Holocaust and atomic bomb. "Is it possible that there is no one who cares?" The "essential predicament of man," he explained, "has assumed a peculiar urgency in our time, living as we do in a civilization where factories were established in order to exterminate millions of men, women and children; where soap was made of human flesh. What have we done to make such crimes possible? What are we doing to make such crimes impossible?" With memories of his own family, he acknowledged that there was a "high cost of living to be paid by a Jew" in current times. "In trying to understand Jewish existence, a Jewish philosopher must look for agreement with the men of Sinai as well as with the people of Auschwitz," he lamented.[132] His answers to these dilemmas came back to the spiritual crisis he believed was gripping humankind and the promise that Judaism offered. The belief in God and the daily ritualistic practices that Judaism required, done in the right spirit, compelled every individual to appreciate the wonders of the world that surrounded them: "Judaism is an attempt to place all of life under the glory of ultimate significance, to relate all scattered actions to the One. Through the constant rhythm of prayers, disciplines, reminders, joys, man is taught not to forfeit his grandeur." By sanctifying time, Judaism offered a way to root out moral indifference and to provide for the most effective response to evil: "Man's task is to make the world worthy of redemption."[133] The influence of Hasidism in this and his growing corpus of work was clear. As Samuel Dresner later wrote, "There are, for example, clear echoes of Hasidic concepts and concerns in Heschel's excursions upon the Sabbath as a bride, upon 'divine pathos,' the 'ineffable,' 'radical amazement,' the illusion of God's absence, the 'holy dimension' of all reality, the 'primacy of inwardness,' . . . the centrality of prayer. . . . Some of the section headings in *Man Is Not Alone* might, in fact, be transposed to a book on Hasidic philosophy."[134]

In the *New York Times*, the Reverend A. Powell Davies, a priestly champion of liberal causes from Washington, DC, wrote that Heschel's book "does for Judaism what Protestant theologians have been attempting to do for Christianity. . . . His book is not for Jews alone but for those also who, while not adopting his special emphasis, can respond to the range of his mind and the depth of his insight."[135] For all the talk about godless communism and the role of faith in America, Davies believed that there was an unfortunate scarcity of serious writing for the general public about the substance of religion. "Thus, with brilliant insight and matchless expression," proclaimed Rabbi Emanuel Rackman, "he presents to us a complete text for our understanding of God and Israel, their Law and their love."[136] Rabbi Jack Riemer called Heschel an "immense influence on the development of American Jewish thought . . . the guide and the teacher to a generation in search—the spiritual spokesman for those who seek to find the meaning of their lives as Jews." Riemer loved that the book asked "us to turn from debates over creed to concern for faith. It pleads that we make our observance a genuine joy instead of a mechanical chore."[137] *Time* magazine's editors were so taken with the book that they profiled Heschel, who, according to the piece, "writes prose that sings and soars in the warm intuitive tradition of the great 18th century Hasidic leaders from whom he is descended."[138]

Heschel was a writing machine. His rate of productivity impressed everyone as he released an endless stream of work about Jewish theology. He could be extraordinarily tough on himself. When one rabbi asked why he wrote so many books, Heschel related the story of a Jew who was ordered by a Cossack to sing. "Jew! I have heard it said that Jews can sing. Sing me a song!" When the Cossack offered up that any song would do, the Jewish man started singing for his life. "I didn't like that song, Jew!" the Cossack yelled. "Sing me another!" And he did. The Cossack once again complained, proceeding to beat

him violently. The cycle kept repeating itself. Taking a breath, Heschel explained to the rabbi: "I am my own Cossack. Each time I read what I have written, I say to myself, 'I didn't like that one. It wasn't good enough. Write another.' And so I write and I write and I write."[139]

As his publishing career flourished, Heschel experienced great satisfaction from his family. He and Sylvia raised their daughter and only child, Susannah, born on 15 May 1952. The three formed a tight unit. Heschel was loving with their daughter, purposely reciting nursery rhymes with mistakes just so his daughter could correct him or playing hide-and-seek throughout each nook of the apartment.[140] Though her father was not very interested in popular culture, Susannah recalled, he loved their strolls in Riverside Park and playing games like Simon Says. With his daughter, he was full of passion, warmth, and joy. When there was a problem, he would shrug his shoulders and say, it's "Narishkayt," which meant it was nothing.[141] Sylvia and her husband spent immense amounts of time with their daughter, taking her to dinners and cultural events as well as on vacation.[142] Susannah enjoyed reading her books. Her parents ended each evening with a game of Chinese checkers, sometimes with Sylvia playing a piece on the handsome piano in the living room, chatting and drinking tea before retiring to bed.[143]

The Sabbath was the most joyous day of the week. Sylvia and Susannah would start preparing early on Friday morning by purchasing food for dinner. Heschel would return home from his office in the afternoon, and they would turn off all the electricity before sunset. "Friday evenings in my home were the climax of the week, as they are for every religious Jewish family." Susannah wrote about her father's love for the holiday. "My mother and I kindled the lights for the Sabbath, and all of a sudden I felt transformed, emotionally and even physically. After lighting the candles in the dining room, we would walk into the living room, which had windows overlooking the Hud-

son River, facing west, and we would marvel at the sunset that soon arrived."[144] Occasionally, Heschel invited guests to join them for dinner, prayer, and conversation. One frequent visitor, the closest of friends, was Wolfe Kelman, the director of JTS. Born in Vienna in 1923, Kelman was the descendant of a Hasidic rabbinic dynasty who had immigrated from Poland, though his family settled in Toronto, Canada. Kelman, whose father died when he was thirteen, served in the Royal Canadian Air Force during World War II before entering JTS as a rabbinic student, where he was ordained in 1950. Kelman didn't like much of his experience with the notable exception of his work with Heschel, who felt to him like a kindred spirit. After deciding to remain at the seminary in a professional capacity rather than pursuing a pulpit or becoming a teacher, Kelman dedicated himself to building a rabbinate that possessed a strong professional and spiritual infrastructure. Like his friend Heschel, Kelman was always searching for ways to preserve the essence of the Hasidic heritage even while working and living in the institutions of Conservative Judaism. Friends and colleagues considered him to be a rabbi's rabbi.

On Saturday mornings, Heschel attended the service at the JTS, which still used a very traditional prayer book; the men's and women's sections were separated by an aisle. On the walk home, he and his colleagues would discuss the sermon, which was usually delivered by a rabbinical student. "The walk took only fifteen minutes, but my father had a habit of taking a few steps, then stopping to talk over a point before moving on, so that the walk often lasted half an hour," Susannah remembered. The Sabbath afternoon consisted of a nap and, during warm weather, a walk through the park. He spent afternoons reading, but, because it was the Sabbath, he read only Hebrew texts rather than philosophy or politics; since writing was prohibited he marked pages he wanted to reread by inserting napkins or attaching paperclips to them.[145] Elie Wiesel, the distinguished

writer who had survived the Nazi concentration camps, frequently visited at four o'clock. As Wiesel remembered in his memoir, "We spent hours together, sometimes strolling up and down Riverside Drive discussing God, prayers, Polish Hasidism compared to Hungarian Hasidism, Lithuanian Yiddish folklore, and Polish literature. He loved to reminisce about Frankfurt, where in the thirties he succeeded Martin Buber at the Institute of Jewish Studies."[146]

If Heschel did not return to JTS for the third meal in the student cafeteria, where he would hold court just like his uncle had done in Warsaw, he invited rabbinical students to his apartment instead. Sylvia served them some cheese, bread, fish, and crackers. Heschel would sit in his favorite blue chair in the light-filled living room. Susannah explained, "My father was attentive to each student, asking about his studies, hometown rabbis and goals for the future."[147] If anyone would bring up gossip or business, he would show a gentle smile and say, "Not on Shabbat!"[148] The conversations could be intense. Heschel liked to mix humor with anecdotes in a manner that could often be difficult to understand but that always conveyed some larger point. "You had to get the hints and the allusions and you really had to hold on tight. It was hard," recounted Levi Kelman, the son of Wolfe, "[as] people are not used to concentrating. You really had to concentrate in conversation with Heschel."[149] As the Sabbath afternoon came to a conclusion when the sun set, he handed each of them a siddur, and they chanted the evening service, the Ma'ariv, ending the Sabbath with the havdalah.[150]

Heschel's Hasidic roots often opened the eyes of twenty-two-year-old rabbinic students who had grown up in suburbia. During the Sabbath services, Heschel would pray by vigorously shuckling, singing with zeal and avoiding the chatter that had become a familiar part of Conservative services. Nobody matched Heschel during the holiday of Simchat Torah, when

Jews celebrated the conclusion of the annual Torah reading. The festivities always included Jews singing and dancing with the Torah scrolls. But most of the relatively tame young rabbinical students had never seen anything like Heschel dancing in exuberant fashion, swaying wildly with his eyes closed in a state of euphoria, without any apparent sense of restraint, putting his younger colleagues to shame.[151]

The Heschels spent their summers in Los Angeles, visiting Sylvia's parents and three brothers. They sublet a wing at the home of Victor and Ruth Goodhill. One of the great attractions of the home was a grand piano that Sylvia played and its comfortable setting (though he was terrified of the Goodhills' small poodle). Heschel spent most of his days writing at the research library at UCLA, bringing his papers with him in a brown grocery sack.[152]

The Heschels took their first trip to Israel in 1957 when he was invited to participate in an international conference. Heschel had been eager to visit since 1948; the conference was the first opportunity to afford such an expensive trip. On the way over, the family spent time in London as well as Paris. "Such experiences add perspective and scope even to a parochial mind," Heschel wrote Kelman.[153] Next, the family flew to Israel. Before their travels, Heschel grew a beard. He told Eugene Borowitz, "I thought to myself, how will it look for you to go to Jerusalem without a beard? So, I grew a beard."[154] Upon his arrival to the Holy Land, government officials and the media treated him like a celebrity. He was a guest of President Zalman Shazar, who had been a childhood friend. Traveling through the country, Heschel met with distinguished leaders, including Prime Minister David Ben-Gurion.[155] Being in Israel in the aftermath of the Holocaust made Heschel feel strongly that the existence of a Jewish state was a powerful refutation of anti-Semitism by the global community. "We stand at a climax of Jewish history,"

Heschel said to the World Council of Synagogues. "Like a branch plucked from the fire, this generation has gone through the experience of disaster and has also tasted the mystery of deliverance. Dark and dreadful would be our life today without the comfort and joy that radiate out of the land of Israel. Crippled is our people, many of its vital organs destroyed, some of its limbs chopped off, and yet we also witness the wonder of thriving communities in new lands, anxious to continue to live in the presence of God and in loyalty to His Torah."[156]

Notwithstanding his love of Israel, Heschel did not lose focus on the dialogue about the spiritual condition of world Jewry. The Diaspora and Israel were part of a larger continuum. The land meant less than the spiritual strength of the Jewish people. If Jews were not spiritually engaged, Israel would not mean very much beyond its territorial value. Upon his return to the United States, Heschel told the Rabbinical Assembly that his awe about walking through the streets of the Jewish state was tempered by his anguish that most Jews didn't live a pious existence: "The question is not how to make the State meaningful to the Jews of America but how to make the State worthy of 2000 years of waiting."[157] During a meeting at the Jewish Agency in New York on 6 January 1958, which revolved around the relationship of the state of Israel to the Diaspora, Heschel told two esteemed colleagues Salo Baron (Columbia) and Rabbi Robert Gordis (JTS) that American Jews were not yet ready to discuss the connection since "we do not know what the diaspora is." It was not true, Heschel argued, "that we live in Galut [the concept of being uprooted from the homeland]; we live in Olam Hazeh [the present age]." Heschel insisted that the major issue to discuss was the condition of Judaism in the United States: "What is the Jewish individual: what is his relation to Jew and Judaism, to the Jewish People, and his tradition and to God? What relevance has the Bible and Jewish tradition on the

individual in America?" Only by resolving these questions about the individual could they start to turn to the larger issue of the interconnection between Israel and the Diaspora.[158]

Nor did the politics surrounding Israel always sit easily with Heschel. He angered Zionist leaders in 1959 when he publicly opposed a resolution by the United Synagogues to join the World Zionist Organization—the political arm of the movement. The proposal was being pushed by Kaplan, who was now promoting a vision for an international Jewish people with its core in Israel. Heschel argued that the path for Jews to become connected to Israel and overcome the "embarrassment of being absent" was to participate in "an inner spiritual and cultural *aliya* on the soil of America."[159] Heschel also preferred that synagogues be free of politics. "The primary function of the synagogue is to inspire the soul and instruct the mind; its task is to cultivate faith in God, love of man and understanding of Torah; its goal is holiness; its methods are personal, intellectual, spiritual. The primary function of a political organization is to serve the self-interest of the group it represents; its goal may be holy, yet its methods are adroitness, opportunism, and expediency. We must shun any attempt to use political authority in order to achieve spiritual goals as well as resist involvement in activities that are determined by political tactics." While individuals could not live in "isolation, detachment" from these sorts of questions, he believed it would be "suicidal to reduce Judaism to collectivism or nationalism."[160] The proposal was defeated.

During these years of his professional maturation, Heschel formed only a handful of close friendships. In addition to Kelman, Heschel felt a strong bond to one of his star rabbinical students, Marshall Meyer, the energetic Brooklyn-born graduate of Dartmouth College who ended up becoming the head rabbi of the Bet El congregation in Buenos Aires, Argentina, in the late 1950s. Meyer took every one of Heschel's seminars and

worked as his secretary. The two grew close; Marshall thought of him as an uncle. They consulted over personal and professional problems, spending hundreds of hours together between his arrival at rabbinical school in 1952 and departure to Argentina in 1959. Once when Meyer was ill with the flu, Heschel brought him food at the dormitory. They took long walks in Riverside Park and visited the Metropolitan Museum of Art, where Heschel loved to see Rembrandt's paintings. On another occasion, when Heschel was worn down, Meyer introduced him to the music of the operatic singer Jussi Björling, the sound of whose voice soothed his mentor.[161] Meyer quickly developed a passion for building a global Conservative movement and applying the Jewish tradition to the pursuit of human rights.

After Niebuhr delivered a paper at a joint meeting of JTS and the Union Theological Seminary, he befriended Heschel. The relationship made sense intellectually. Both were fascinated with the Hebrew Prophets; Niebuhr, more than almost any other American intellectual, had helped popularize their tradition. Niebuhr respected Heschel's work. They liked to walk home from their offices together; their apartments were only a few blocks apart, the Heschels at 425 Riverside Drive and the Niebuhrs at 404.[162] The two theologians were a sight to see. Heschel, about five foot six, and Niebuhr, well over six feet, with his body leaning over as a result of a stroke, sauntered past the storefronts as they were deeply engaged in conversation about the philosophical and theological problems that informed their writing. "I have enjoyed these walks so much as I also appreciate your gracious friendship through the years. You are a blessing to your friends," Niebuhr wrote.[163] Niebuhr's wife would later observe that Heschel became her husband's closest friend, as there was a "happy empathy" between them that a third person wouldn't want to spoil.[164]

Heschel was one of the most memorable members of the Admissions Committee. As students hoping to gain entrance

into the rabbinical school were interviewed by the committee, Heschel asked the questions that often stuck in their memories. When one midwestern graduate from New York University, William Lebeau, had his interview, Heschel asked, "Mr. Lebeau, did you see God today?" Lebeau, who had grown up in a secular family and become interested in the rabbinate only after spending a few summers at Camp Ramah, thought long and hard about the question, struggling to provide a good answer. All he could come up with was having devoted the morning to his preparation for the interview and rushing over to be in the building on time. "I've seen God on a beautiful day in the park, in the flowers and trees and the smiling faces of children," Lebeau finally responded, thinking that he had a smart answer for the rabbi. "I asked if you saw God today," Heschel repeated in a follow-up, exuding dissatisfaction with the response. "No," Lebeau humbly acknowledged, "I was distracted by my meeting with the committee. I don't believe I saw God today." Heschel told Lebeau, who would be admitted, that "as a rabbi, you must learn to feel God's presence everywhere—even in the most mundane and trying of circumstances."[165]

Heschel was becoming a popular guest on the Jewish speaking circuit, a role he accepted given the need to compensate for his modest JTS salary. He received numerous invitations to be a scholar-in-residence at synagogues and universities. He could be difficult to understand, his words esoteric and mysterious, his Yiddish accent thick, but audiences loved the experience. When a former student of Heschel overheard one congregant singing praise about one of his talks, he asked her what it was that he said which was so powerful. The congregant responded, "I don't know what he said, but it sure made me feel good just sitting in his presence and listening to him."[166] His national stature by the late 1950s was evident in the way that the weekly synagogue bulletins advertised his talks. "He has been gener-

ally acclaimed as a brilliant lecturer and one of the greatest Jewish scholars of our days," noted the B'nai B'rith with regard to a gathering where he would appear at the Deer Park Lodge.[167] Whatever the rabbinical school scholars were saying, a growing number of laypeople, as well as their rabbis and cantors, were eager to have him in their presence. He was emerging as an iconographic figure in American Jewish life.[168] Whereas his Eastern European accent and demeanor would have scared off German Jews at the turn of the twentieth century, the fact that a majority of suburban Jewish families had come from a background similar to his made prosperous communities eager to learn from an authentic voice of spiritual wisdom that resonated with their past. Through Heschel, second- and third-generation Americans quenched their nostalgia for the religious world of their fathers and mothers. Heschel shared his ideas "before rapt synagogue audiences," the historian Howard Sachar recounted, "few of whom may have grasped his thinking, but most of whom were entranced by his bearded, 'prophetic' appearance, trademark beret, and somewhat theatrical delivery." Usually disappointed with the nature of the organized Jewish life he encountered, Heschel was nonetheless impressed with the laypersons he met along the way, sensing immense potential in the next generation. As Dresner recalled, "After returning from a lecture tour, Heschel once observed to me, considering the discouraging conditions of the Jewish community—the lifeless synagogue, the bar-mitzvah-oriented school, the home drained of Yiddishkeit—it was remarkable that so many American Jews, especially young people, were still open to Jewish ideas. Had he been raised in such an atmosphere, Heschel mused, he wondered if he would have remained an observant Jew! He admired the young Jew who had been given so little of Jewishness and still holds on, as if hoping for something to happen." For this reason, Heschel believed

that rabbis and other leaders needed to provide a "ladder of observance" to meet them where they were and then show how to gradually elevate their practice.[169]

Heschel's strong identification as a religiously observant Ashkenazi felt less threatening to many Jewish Americans than it might have in the 1930s since open hostility had vastly diminished in the political, economic, and cultural realms.[170] Though still a distinct minority, Orthodox Judaism (including Hasidic communities) was enjoying a resurgence that made Heschel's traditional beliefs seem less remote.[171] Heschel traveled the country as a teacher of the Jewish religion in a secular and scientific age when "modern man has, by and large, lost contact with the dimension of reality that gives rise to religion," as Fritz Rothschild noted in a collection of his friend's work that he edited.[172] Heschel spent two months as a visiting scholar at the University of Minnesota in 1959, where he let his salt-and-pepper hair and his goatee grow out in response to Kelman's observation that his friend didn't look "mystic enough."[173]

The spiritual crisis facing humankind in the nuclear age informed Heschel's position about almost every problem he tackled. During a class at JTS, he asked students if gelatin was kosher, which generated a spirited discussion. But when he subsequently asked, "Nuclear weapons: kosher or *treyf?* [non-kosher]" the room went silent.[174] Increasingly, he felt that such silence about the major issues of the day was inexcusable.

In April 1960, Heschel spoke at the Conference on Children and Youth in Washington under the auspices of President Dwight Eisenhower. Kelman and Marc Tanenbaum, the director of interreligious affairs for the American Jewish Committee, had passed his name along to Eisenhower officials who organized the event. They saw him as a natural spokesman given his extensive writing on the Prophets.[175] Tanenbaum had a keen appreciation for Heschel, with whom he had studied and served as an assistant while a rabbinic student at JTS in the late 1940s.

Tanenbaum's parents were Orthodox Jewish Ukrainians who had fled from Europe; he was raised in a religiously observant home, haunted by memories of anti-Semitism. Though he didn't like the rigidities of the Orthodox community in his undergraduate studies at Yeshiva University, Tanenbaum was committed to his tradition and valued what Heschel was trying to do with his work on spirituality. For Tanenbaum, Judaism had an important role to play in the political battles over key social issues that faced the nation. Serving as the executive director of the Synagogue Council in the 1950s, an umbrella association of rabbis from different Jewish denominations, Tanenbaum had become very well-networked in politics, including through his strong relationship with the civil rights activist Reverend Martin Luther King Jr.

In his address at Eisenhower's conference, Heschel lived up to the promise. He argued that the problem facing young Americans was really "the spirit of our age" and the "emptiness in the heart, the decreased sensitivity to the imponderable quality of the spirit. . . ." People had become so concerned with power that society had "dangerously stunted his concern for beauty and grandeur." Young people, Heschel said, were suffering as a result. "We have denied our young people the knowledge of the dark side of life" by pampering them. "They do not feel morally challenged, they do not feel called upon," he said. The "glorification of fun as the chief purpose of existence" had turned their attention away from the deeper meaning of life. If one sought to understand the roots of juvenile delinquency, for instance, it was necessary to see how kids were no longer taught to have a sense of wonder. "The basic issue," Heschel concluded, "is how young people can be brought up with a proper sense of responsibility in an affluent society," which could come only from having a feeling of "reverence for the sublime aspect of human existence." The country needed not only better schools but also better parents, parents who

were "worthy of being revered as an example of devotion and responsibility." He called for a "radical reorientation" of thinking to teach through example the centrality of "moral and spiritual exaltation." It was vital, Heschel said, that society start to understand that "our greatest threat is not the atomic bomb. Our greatest threat is the suffering of man." The address received widespread attention, even in unusual venues. He published the remarks in *Law and Order*, a trade magazine for police, whose editors told readers that Heschel's ideas were worth considering in order "to recognize the souls of all policemen."[176]

The condition of elderly Americans, who were often poor and without the resources they needed, had become another topic of national debate. Eisenhower extended Heschel another invitation in 1961 to participate in a White House Conference on Aging. Heschel's talk to over seven hundred persons in attendance at the Mayflower Hotel went well. His fellow participants were impressed. In the session "The Older Person, Family Life, and the Service They Need," Heschel appeared alongside Senator Barry Goldwater of Arizona, the right-wing Republican who would run for the presidency in 1964. Goldwater blasted the "liberal or radical philosophy" of individuals turning to government welfare. In sharp contrast to the senator, Heschel disagreed. Turning to the delegates, Heschel said, "I see the sick and the despised, the defeated and the bitter, the rejected and the lonely. I see them clustered together and alone." He added, "A vast amount of human misery, as well as enormous cultural and spiritual damage are due to these twin phenomena of civilization: the contempt for the old and the traumatic fear of getting old. . . . [T]he cult of youth is idolatry. Abraham is the grand old man, but the legend of Faust is pagan."[177] Thinking about priorities, Heschel argued that "a nation should be ready to sell, if necessary, the treasures from its art collections and the sacred objects from its houses of worship in order to help one sick man. Is there anything as holy, as

urgent, as noble as the effort of a whole nation to provide medical care for the old?" His remarks received strong praise from Secretary of Health, Education, and Welfare Arthur Flemming, who cited Heschel's ideas in his closing address.[178]

His growing engagement in the struggles of the secular world pushed him to understand better the rabbinic traditions that had shaped him. Heschel aspired, as he told the host of the CBS radio show *Way to Go*, to save the "inner man from oblivion."[179] The first volume of *Torah min HaShamayim* (Heavenly Torah) was published in 1962 (the second volume would come out in 1965). In *Torah min HaShamayim* Heschel produced a masterpiece, written in rabbinic Hebrew, about rabbinic literature revolving around theology and nonlegalistic moral and spiritual interpretations (Aggadah) that were traditionally overlooked for work that centered on a strict reading of Jewish law (Halakha). "In Halakhah you find power and might," Heschel wrote, "while in Aggadah there is grace and love. Halakhah has a voice of power—it breaks the cedars—while Aggadah is the still, small voice. Halakhah is like a rush of mighty waters; Aggadah, the spirit of God hovering over the waters." The work, which he dedicated to his mother and three sisters who perished in the Holocaust, joined an important canon of synthetic books about rabbinic thought by Abraham Geiger, Solomon Schechter, George Foot Moore, and Louis Finkelstein. He sought to write a work that was inspirational by showing the plurality of approaches in the Jewish tradition.[180]

In *Torah min HaShamayim*, Heschel wanted to use the rabbis to unpack different ways in which Jews thought about fundamental questions about God, revelation, and more. In order to contrast the mystical and rational approaches to rabbinic interpretation, Heschel explored the differences in the ways of understanding God and revelation between the rationalism of Rabbi Ishmael and the mystical and apocalyptic work of Rabbi Akiva.[181] Heschel presented these interpretations as being part

of an ongoing dialectic.[182] Taking the reader into the minds of the rabbinic sages, he demonstrated how they didn't always find agreed-upon resolutions to theological puzzles.

Rooted in his studies of Jewish mysticism and the notion that pious humans were able to unify God through good deeds, Heschel argued that humans sent God into exile by committing evil, thus leaving God incapable of healing the world. Despite being praised by the founder of the international Masorti movement, Rabbi Louis Jacobs, Heschel was bothered that other colleagues still refused to compliment him.[183] On one of their late-night walks on Riverside Drive, Kelman tried to comfort his friend. "How do you expect them to like you?" Kelman asked, if he was taking issue with their entire approach to studying the Prophets and Talmud. "You expect them to thank you for it?" Kelman asked half jokingly. Heschel listened to what his friend had to say.[184]

And then came *The Prophets*, published in 1962, Heschel's most influential and enduring work. For it was with this revised version of his doctoral dissertation that Heschel most clearly connected the questions that had animated his writing since Berlin with the political questions that were on the front pages of the newspapers. Expanded into two volumes, *The Prophets* spoke to readers at a fraught moment when the possibility of military conflict between the United States and the Soviets seemed very real.[185] It resonated with idealistic activists who were dedicating their lives to social justice. Whereas some Americans joined programs like the Peace Corps, others took to the streets. By this time civil rights activists had created a mass grassroots movement—anchored in African American leaders in the South, many of whom were preachers—polarizing public opinion about race relations and equal rights.

With the Holocaust always looming over his thoughts, Heschel dedicated the work "to the martyrs of 1940–1945." He set out to analyze their consciousness in God, a sharp contrast

to the secular consciousness of the world in which Heschel lived that troubled him so much.[186] In Heschel's account, the Prophets felt and expressed God's outrage about the corruption of the state of Israel. The Prophets embodied the relationship between God and man that was at the heart of a functioning moral universe. Heschel highlighted the deep engagement of the Prophets to make the point that indifference to social injustice was unacceptable. "Above all," Heschel wrote, "the prophets remind us of the moral state of a people: Few are guilty, but all are responsible."

The first volume recounted the stories of Amos, Hosea, Isaiah, Micah, Jeremiah, Habakkuk, and the Second Isaiah. The second volume turned to prophesy as a general phenomenon in the Jewish biblical tradition. According to Heschel, the Hebrew Prophets, who lived the life of a "lonely man," differed from the rest of humanity in that they were able to experience God's pathos from within and communicate his desires, fears, love, and passions to the rest of the Israelites: "We and the prophet have no language in common. To us the moral state of society, for all its stains and spots, seems fair and trim; to the prophet it is dreadful. . . . Our standards are modest; our sense of injustice tolerable, timid; our moral indignation impermanent; yet human violence is interminable, unbearable, permanent. To us Life is often serene, in the prophet's eye the world reels in confusion."[187] The Prophets were not crazy nor were they delusional, in Heschel's account. Rather, the Hebrew Prophet was a "person overwhelmed by sympathy for God and sympathy for man. Standing before the people he pleaded for God; standing before God he pleaded for his people."[188] They were moved by divine pathos. "God is the focal point of his thought," Heschel wrote of the Prophets, "and the world is seen as reflected in God." God cared about and was affected by the actions of humankind: "He does not simply command and expect obedience; He is also moved and affected by what hap-

pens in the world and acts accordingly. Events and human actions arouse in Him joy or sorrow, pleasure or wrath." Heschel explained the Prophets as having an intimate relationship with God. They were moved by this relationship, understanding God's feelings. They reacted by being religious warriors for morality: "The prophets repudiated the work as well as the power of man as an object of supreme adoration. They denounced 'arrogant boasting' and 'haughty pride' (Isa. 10:12), the kings who ruled the nations in anger, the oppressors (Isa. 14:4–6), the destroyers of nations, who went forth to inflict waste, ruin and death (Jer. 4:7)." Though some observers believed that the Prophets employed hysterical language, Heschel interpreted their rhetoric as a sensible means to communicate God's anguish to the world. They saw the problems—corruption, poverty, human abuse, and misery—that escaped the attention of most people who had grown indifferent and callous. What society normalized, they protested. Their fierce sense of urgency reflected the feelings of God when he looked at his broken creation: "Prophecy is the voice that God has lent, to the silent agony, a voice to the plundered poor, to the profaned riches in the world. It is a form of living, a crossing point of God and man. God is raging in the prophet's words." To the Prophets, just as to civil rights activists like Martin Luther King Jr., the world was in a dire state. "This is what the prophets discovered. *History is a nightmare.* There are more scandals, more acts of corruption, than are dreamed of in philosophy. It would be blasphemous to believe that what we witness is the end of God's creation. It is an act of evil to accept the state of evil as either inevitable or final. Others may be satisfied with improvement; the prophets insist upon redemption."[189] The burden of being a Prophet was enormous. "In spite of public rejection," Heschel wrote, "in spite of inner misery, he felt unable to discard the divine burden, unable to discourage himself from the divine pathos. He knew why he had to yield; he knew

how to explain his inability to resist the terrible errand."[190] Just as Heschel's appreciation of Mitzvot in *God in Search of Man* stemmed from the Hasidic tradition within which he was raised, his appreciation of the Hebrew Prophets grew out of the Hasidic admiration of charismatic leadership (one of Heschel's students compared this to Buber's fascination with Eastern European Hasidism, of whose failings Heschel knew too much about).[191]

Most important to Heschel was the fact that the Hebrew Prophets refused to be neutral in the face of the evil they witnessed. Heschel argued that the greatest danger emanated from societal indifference: "There is an evil which most of us condone and are even guilty of: indifference to evil. We remain neutral, impartial, and not easily moved by the wrongs done unto other people." Through his study of the Hebrew Prophets, Heschel found that this kind of "indifference to evil is more insidious than evil itself; it is more universal, more contagious, more dangerous. A silent justification, it makes possible an evil erupting. As an exception becoming the rule and being in turn accepted."[192] This interpretation of the Prophets gave Heschel a way to understand the meaning of the universe: "Man-made history is not history's only dimension. . . . History is not a meaningless conglomeration of neutral facts, but a drama unfolding the relationship between God and man."[193]

Civil rights leaders, including King, Andrew Young, James Lawson, and Bayard Rustin, were gripped by Heschel's riveting portrait of the Prophets.[194] King, who was known for speaking with the same kind of fire and passion as the figures Heschel studied, had been trained via a deep engagement with the black social gospel.[195] Like many Jewish activists, King spoke about Moses and the Exodus, particularly in black–Jewish meetings where he hoped to emphasize points of connection.[196] A great number of other civil rights leaders were steeped in the prophetic tradition, viewing the United States more through the

lens of the Hebrew Prophets than through mainstream liberal-ism. They were deeply influenced by the Hebrew Prophets in the belief that institutions did not inevitably improve and that individuals had to play a role in triggering dramatic change even if their views rendered them to be outcasts.[197] King and his fellow activists were also drawn in by Heschel's condem-nation of indifference, which in his mind was one of the prime obstacles to civil rights—not the southern white racist but the moderate who did nothing, especially fellow clergy. Having these feelings, King shared the frustration that Heschel experi-enced in seeing German Christians who failed to mobilize against the Nazis.

In the *Los Angeles Times*, the reviewer Robert Kirsch, who called Heschel "one of the most important religious thinkers of our day," described the book as a "transcendent effort to re-store not only the significance of what they said but also what they were." By the end of *The Prophets*, according to Kirsch, "we are given a view of the prophetic experience which is as proximate as the mind of the philosopher can make it."[198]

As a result of *The Prophets*, Heschel entered into a new space, one in which his theology started to mesh with real-world activism. Watching the civil rights struggle unfold while writing about the Hebrew Prophets who devoted their lives to justice, he started to be drawn to the power of physical protest. He later said that working on *The Prophets* transformed his think-ing. "Early in my life, my great love was for learning, studying. And the place where I preferred to live was my study and books and writing and thinking. I've learned from the prophets that I have to be involved in the affairs of man, in the affairs of suf-fering man."[199] As a result of writing the book, he recalled that "from them I learned the niggardliness of our moral compre-hension, the incapacity to sense the depth of misery caused by our own failures. It became quite clear to me that while our eyes are witness to the callousness and cruelty of man, our heart tries

to obliterate the memories, to calm the nerves, and to silence our conscience. There is immense silent agony in the world, and the task of man is to be a voice for the plundered poor, to prevent the desecration of the soul and the violation of our dream of honesty."[200] Heschel had gained the attention of prominent civil rights leaders who were speaking with the same level of intensity as the Hebrew Prophets on matters of race and democracy. Then, his life changed dramatically.

5

Selma

Every morning Rabbi Heschel read the newspaper and each evening he watched the network news on a small black-and-white television set. Always an avid consumer of current events, he followed the unfolding civil rights movement with intense interest. Along with his wife and daughter, he watched Walter Cronkite's nightly CBS broadcast as the anchor reported on the struggles tearing apart the racially divided South, such as stories about the sit-ins that African American students conducted to protest segregated lunchtime counters at Woolworth. Heschel had made his first public statement on race relations in 1958 when he decried "our timidity and hesitance to take a stand on behalf of the Negroes" before a gathering of colleagues.[1] He saw painful similarities between the brutal condition of African Americans and the poverty that Jews experienced in Eastern Europe. He felt in the spirited prayer of the black church the polar opposite of the staid atmosphere in sub-

urban Jewish synagogues.[2] The courage that African Americans demonstrated in their fight for human rights inspired him. Heschel heard in the soaring rhetoric of Martin Luther King Jr. the same prophetic cries about social injustice that he studied.

The evolution of Heschel's understanding of the biblical commandments had also brought him to a place where he had a deep appreciation for individuals who were willing to step forward to achieve social justice. Whereas the Hasidic rebbes of his childhood were mostly interested in ritualistic commandments such as wrapping the Jewish phylacteries (tefillin) around one's arm and head for morning prayers or blowing the shofar (the ram's horn) during the High Holidays, Heschel emphasized the deeds that one human being could do for another, especially for those who were struggling. A person could find God and serve as God's voice on earth by being good to other people.[3]

Heschel's formal connection to the movement began in January 1963 when he addressed a major interfaith meeting of Protestant, Catholic, and Jewish groups on civil rights. By the time this gathering occurred, President John F. Kennedy was starting his third year in office, and the brewing tension over race relations was regularly on the front pages. Although the president was reluctant to propose legislation, fearful of angering the southern Democrats who ruled the roost on Capitol Hill, he was willing to use executive muscle to achieve progress. In 1962, for instance, Kennedy ordered National Guardsmen and federal troops to quell the white violence that unfolded when an African American named James Meredith enrolled at the University of Mississippi. The three-day interfaith conference at the Edgewater Beach Hotel in Chicago drew several thousand religious leaders. Three-fourths of them were African American pastors.[4] Reverend King, who was intent on showcasing the natural flow between theology and civil rights, advertised it as the "most significant and historic [convention]

ever held for attacking racial justice." The conference program started with a bold proclamation: "Religious groups in the United States hold that racial discrimination and prejudice are moral problems at their roots. Racial segregation is one of the most crucial problems facing our religious institutions and our democracy." King and the other organizers hoped to bring together "religiously committed people to speak with one voice on racial issues to their fellow citizens and the world." The themes of the sessions ranged from religious education on moral issues, to public policy and racial desegregation, to the dynamic of social exclusion. The declaration of conscience made at the conference deemed racism to be "our most serious domestic evil."[5]

The rabbis who recommended Heschel's name to the organizers promised that he would deliver a "prophetic inspirational" message.[6] And he did. In this singular moment, Heschel brought the full force of his people's tradition, life experiences, and personal meditations on the need to stand up to racial injustice as a human imperative. He culled from the biblical stories and Jewish laws he had been studying since his childhood in Warsaw to put forward a religiously infused narrative about the social conflict facing the nation. His talk about civil rights revolved around the story of Exodus, a familiar comparison for movement leaders who liked to connect the history of Jews escaping Egypt to the suffering of African Americans. At the "first conference on religion and race," Heschel half joked, "the main participants were Pharaoh and Moses," and the "outcome of that summit meeting has not come to an end. Pharaoh is not ready to capitulate. The exodus began, but is far from having been completed." Tying together Passover and the civil rights movement, Heschel told attendees that "it was easier for the children of Israel to cross the Red Sea than for a Negro to cross certain university campuses." He argued that the "spirit of religion" dictated that every person was God's "beloved child"

whereas the spirit of race was to "sunder, to slash, to dismember the flesh of humanity." He lamented that so few people understood how "insidious, how radical, how universal an evil racism is. Few of us realize that racism is man's gravest threat to man, the maximum of hatred for a minimum of reason, the maximum of cruelty for a minimum of thinking."

Religion and racism were diametrically opposed, according to Heschel. The two kinds of sentiment could not coexist in one person: "Prayer and prejudice cannot dwell in the same heart." Heschel went so far as to proclaim that "racism is worse than idolatry. Racism is Satanism, unmitigated evil." It was radical for a white American to depict racism as fundamentally evil: to "think of man in terms of white, black, or yellow is more than an error. It is an eye disease, it is a cancer of the soul." He implored the attendees: "Let us yield no inch to bigotry, let us make no compromise with callousness."[7] This stark message was diametrically opposed to—and a direct attack on—the legions of southern preachers who either were silent on this issue or who invoked scripture in defense of racial segregation and injustice.

Before a sympathetic crowd, Heschel criticized Americans who were not guilty of racist acts but who sat silently in the face of oppression.[8] Heschel refused to discuss racism as if it were just another social problem which needed to be rationally engineered through expertise and compromise. This was full-blown crisis. In his call to action, he anticipated the theme that King would explore a few months later while locked up in a Birmingham jail ruminating over the problems of moderation. With memories of the mass inaction that he witnessed when Jews were persecuted by the Nazis, Heschel warned: "By negligence and silence we have all become accessory before the God of Mercy to the injustice committed against the Negroes by men of our nation. Our derelictions are many. We have failed to demand, to insist, to challenge, to chastise." He be-

lieved that in trying to shake society free from its moral slumber, civil rights leaders were acting like the Hebrew Prophets: "All prophecy is one great exclamation: God is not indifferent to evil! He is always concerned. He is personally affected by what man does to man. He is a God of pathos." He was inspired by the fierce determination of the civil rights activists who until now he only read about: "Surrender to despair is surrender to evil. It is important to feel anxiety, it is sinful to wallow in despair."

In the loftiest of tones, Heschel described the struggle as the salvation of modern man. As he wrote about in *God in Search of Man*, civilization faced a spiritual crisis. When humans did not take seriously the spiritual condition of man, Heschel explained, social oppression became tolerable. With this address, Heschel shifted his emphasis from the threats facing universal humanity toward the particular challenges of African Americans: "The plight of the Negro must become our most important concern." Engagement in civil rights would not only rescue African Americans from their oppressors but also give its supporters a way out of their contemporary moral slumber, "a magnificent spiritual opportunity." In making this claim, he intended to appeal to white Americans by saying that at the centennial of the Emancipation Proclamation it was time for them to "strive for self-emancipation" by freeing themselves from bigotry: "We are all *Pharaohs or slaves of Pharaohs*. It is sad to be a slave of Pharaoh. *It is horrible to be a Pharaoh.*"

The audience erupted into a five-minute standing ovation; tears welled up in the eyes of African American attendees. Heschel's speech offered a welcome departure from what civil rights leaders had been hearing from mainstream white liberals. The rhetoric of Cold War liberals like Arthur Schlesinger Jr. emphasized pragmatism, incrementalism, and optimism. Secular liberals exhibited an unyielding confidence that human reason, freed from ideological dogmatism, was capable of solving

problems. Experts and levelheaded political leaders who eschewed the extremes, they kept promising, could craft policies to alleviate racism.[9] Most liberals shunned the moralistic politics of populism and were suspicious of anyone who spoke through a highly ideological prism (fearing a resurgence of McCarthyism).[10] The sociologist Daniel Bell had written, in positive terms, about the "end of ideology."[11] In the view of most prominent liberal intellectuals, institutions were capable of being repaired. King and other civil rights leaders, steeped in the teachings of the church, were drawn to the fiery biblical rhetoric they heard from Heschel. His messianic language about good and evil, divine and spiritual, blasphemy, prophecy, and redemption were frameworks that made sense to those fighting against, and surviving, violent racism. "The deep religious tone of Dr. Heschel's paper," noted the chairwoman of the National Social Action Committee of the National Women's League, "awed the group, many of whom had never heard him before."[12]

In contrast to other Jewish Americans involved in the struggle, Heschel emphasized the connection between theology, his religious tradition, and civil rights. He was not only a Jew who supported civil rights but also a theologian who, because of his Judaism, believed in racial equality. Heschel's speech, one reporter noted, was the opening salvo in proclaiming that civil rights leaders "need no longer work only through secular organizations. . . . They are approaching and being approached by their peers in the ministry and priesthood and have the possibility of spurring united religious action in this vital area."[13]

Through his rousing oratory, Heschel aligned himself with a civil rights movement that was on the cusp of transforming the country. The movement had amassed a sizable infrastructure since King emerged on the national scene via the Montgomery Bus Boycott (1955–1956). Civil rights activism spanned local chapters that had sprouted up throughout the South—

populated by ministers, working African Americans, intellectuals, and young students—to a national umbrella association in Washington, the Leadership Conference on Civil Rights, that coordinated the work of labor, liberal, and religious groups like the Southern Leadership Conference and United Auto Workers. After years of conflict between activists and white southerners that put the spotlight on racial injustice, movement leaders in early 1963 were pressuring Kennedy to propose legislation to outlaw segregation. At the same time, the white resistance only intensified. On the same day that Heschel spoke, the new governor of Alabama, George Wallace, vowed "segregation now, segregation tomorrow and segregation forever" as he was sworn into office.

When King addressed the conference the day after Heschel, he echoed similar themes. Calling on churches to remove the "yoke of segregation from its own body," King argued that faith-based organizations would "speed the day when an integrated society is a reality." Religion offered the key to social justice. "If the churches and synagogues take a forthright stand," he said, "there will be integration."[14]

During these frigid winter days, Heschel had the opportunity to spend time with King. They instantly formed a personal bond that would come to symbolize the power of the African-American-Jewish alliance. The friendship went beyond the imperative of the moment. Both men, each married to musicians, felt they had a great deal in common.[15] They shared a similar understanding of how their theological beliefs informed secular problems.[16] Heschel and King had been influenced by Niebuhr and Buber.[17] And therefore they viewed the world through the lens of their deep studies and religious practice. They also concurred on the similarities between the dangers facing African Americans in the South and what Jews suffered under Nazi Germany. Alabama, King once told a rally of Freedom Riders, "has sunk to a level of barbarity comparable to the

tragic days of Hitler's Germany."[18] King recognized that the "common struggle" of African Americans and Jews created unity "not only to rid ourselves of bondage but to make oppression of any people by others an impossibility."[19]

Heschel's message resonated with many American Jews who read about his comments in the newspapers. Jews in the United States understood how anti-Semitism and racism were cojoined, inflecting and undermining the country's credo of democracy and religious toleration. Since its founding, and certainly in its reincarnated form in the 1920s, the Ku Klux Klan warned of the twin dangers of what Jews were doing to America in the same breath that they denied the humanity of African Americans. To be sure, a majority of Jews still hesitated in partaking in the protests shaking southern towns and cities, either because they feared becoming linked to what they saw as radical causes in national politics or because they had come to enjoy the benefits derived from being accepted in the white communities of booming middle-class suburbs around New York, Philadelphia, Chicago, and Los Angeles.[20]

But by the early 1960s, the Jewish presence in the civil rights movement continued to expand. Jewish organizations such as the AJC were part of the Leadership Conference on Civil Rights, an umbrella association of civil rights advocates lobbying and mobilizing for legislation. A growing number of university students and young adults were deciding to join in the demonstrations. Unlike Heschel, these were full-time activists, devoting themselves to the daily work of movement building and literally risking their lives. The most prominent of all Jewish clergy was Rabbi Joachim Prinz, the president of the AJC, an organization founded by such giants as Rabbi Stephen Wise and Supreme Court Justice Louis Brandeis in 1918 to defend the rights of European Jews. AJC had become a leading advocate of liberal causes. Born in Bierdzany in the Prussian province of Silesia, Prinz had attended the University of

Berlin, received a doctorate in philosophy at the University of Giessen in 1923, and was ordained as a rabbi two years later at the Jewish Theological Seminary in Breslau. The charismatic young man had taken a pulpit in Berlin in 1926, where he proved to be a mesmerizing orator. During a visit to the United States in March of 1937, Prinz was shocked by the poverty and racism. Upon returning home, he published an article in the liberal journal *Der Morgen* disparaging what he had witnessed. "When people in New York City describe a neighborhood as being nice," he said, "they are not referring to its parks, trees or wide boulevards. They are talking about the fact that there are no blacks, Italians and Jews in that 'nice' part of the city." A few months later, the Gestapo expelled him and his two children and pregnant wife from the country. Despite his negative impressions of America, Prinz took the opportunity to emigrate there under the sponsorship of Wise. Prinz toured the States with the United Israel Appeal to speak about the dire condition facing German Jews. During his travels, Prinz befriended a number of African American ministers and learned more about the depth of racism, always contemplating the commonalities with anti-Semitism. In 1939, he was hired as the rabbi of Temple B'nai Abraham in Newark, New Jersey, one of the nation's oldest synagogues. As he helped the synagogue dig out of the financial hole from the Great Depression and proved himself to be a powerful presence on the pulpit, Prinz continued to speak out about hatred toward Jews and African Americans. Living in Newark, he witnessed the way racism worked in schools, employment, and housing. Following the war, he devoted himself to raising money to help refugees. Upon becoming the president of AJC in 1958, along with the American Jewish Committee, B'nai B'rith, and the Anti-Defamation League he became part of the Leadership Council on Civil Rights.[21] Prinz was not only supportive of the civil rights cause but also took on the role of serving as a frontline figure, working with leaders

like King (whom he first met in 1958 at the AJC convention) in his effort to build the movement.

Heschel would never become as involved in the movement as Prinz, but as a result of the Chicago speech he emerged as an important voice speaking to the relevance of the Jewish tradition to civil rights. Shortly after Heschel and King met, on 25 January *Time* magazine praised the rebbe from Warsaw as a leading thinker of the day. After the speech at the Chicago conference, Heschel's national profile grew rapidly. The *Time* editors' decision to feature him in their pages spoke to his newfound stature. The magazine published a lengthy review of *The Prophets*, identifying Heschel as "one of the world's most illustrious Jewish theologians." The article, which included a photograph of Heschel sitting beneath illustrations of the prophets Jeremiah, Habbakuk, and Isaiah, noted that he offered King's conference goers a "mordant critic of religious ineffectiveness in U.S. race questions."[22]

President Kennedy was also taking notice. In the spring of 1963, as he contemplated sending a civil rights proposal to Congress, the president invited Heschel to join a group of clergy in the Oval Office to discuss the measure. The moment was not lost on him. Though he had participated in Eisenhower's conferences on youth and aging, directly giving counsel to the president at the height of a racial crisis was an inspiring moment for someone raised amidst the poverty of Warsaw. A day before the meeting, the rabbi sent JFK a telegram: "I look forward to privilege of being present at meeting tomorrow, four p.m. Likelihood exists that Negro problem will be like the weather. Everyone talks about it but no one does anything about it. Please demand of religious leaders personal involvement not just solemn declaration." Underscoring the moral force of the issue, Heschel confessed: "We forfeit right to worship God as long as we continue to humiliate Negroes. Church, synagogue have failed. They must repent." He urged the pres-

ident to demand that the clergy in attendance contribute one month's salary to finance a program—like the Marshall Plan—to support housing and education for African Americans. The moment they were living through, he said, was a "state of moral emergency" and the "hour calls for moral grandeur and spiritual audacity."[23]

And these months felt like a state of emergency. In April, King and the Southern Christian Leadership Conference arrived at Birmingham, Alabama, to join local protests against racial segregation. On 12 April the police arrested King after he and almost a thousand protesters ignored an injunction banning them from marching into the business district. While sitting in his cell, King wrote "Letter from a Birmingham Jail," which was published in the *Birmingham News*. Reiterating a message similar to Heschel's speech in Chicago, his statement condemned the pragmatism and incrementalism of white moderates, describing them as a greater threat than racist extremists. "For years now I have heard the word 'Wait!' . . . It rings in the ear of every Negro with piercing familiarity. This 'Wait' almost always means 'Never.'" Soon after King was released from prison, the nation watched in horror on the nightly newscast as King and hundreds of activists, including young children, were brutally attacked with fire hoses and dogs by the police per orders issued by Bull Connor, the commissioner of public safety in Birmingham. The violence was so horrific that Kennedy was finally persuaded to overcome his fears of a backlash. On 11 June, he addressed the nation: "We are confronted primarily with a moral issue. It is as old as the scriptures and is as clear as the American Constitution." He then sent a proposal to the House of Representatives banning segregation in public accommodations. To build pressure, civil rights leaders organized a mass rally in Washington on 2 August 1963, which drew over two hundred thousand people. Americans who had

never seen the movement up close were awed by the stirring oratory in front of the Lincoln Memorial. Most memorable was King's historic "I Have a Dream" speech, which envisioned a world where white and black children could play together in peace. "Now is the time to make justice a reality for all of God's children," he said. Prinz delivered a speech as well. "Our ancient history began," the rabbi told the crowd, "with slavery and yearning for freedom. During the Middle Ages my people lived for a thousand years in the ghettos of Europe. Our modern history begins with a proclamation of emancipation."

By the end of 1963, the political landscape was shifting. The civil rights movement, according to the historian Manning Marable, had "grown from a modest group of black students demonstrating at one lunch-counter to the largest mass movement for racial reform and civil rights in the 20th century." Among supporters, the excitement over what the movement was accomplishing coexisted alongside the sadness about fallen casualties. In June 1963, for instance, a white supremacist had murdered the civil rights activist and World War II veteran Medgar Evers in his driveway in Jackson, Mississippi. On 22 November, tragedy reached the highest levels of power when Lee Harvey Oswald assassinated President Kennedy during his trip to Dallas, Texas. The president's shocking murder left Americans feeling that the era of grand expectations, when the postwar economy seemed to promote endless hope for middle-class growth, had come to an end. When Vice President Lyndon Johnson, a Texan and former Senate majority leader, took over the Oval Office, nobody knew what to expect. Many liberals feared that Johnson's heart was in the wrong place. With Kennedy's civil rights bill stuck in the House Rules Committee, they wondered whether this product of the conservative southern Democratic caucus would refuse to throw his presidential weight behind the cause. The challenges made Heschel doubly

determined to lean on his tradition as his way to ensure that the cause didn't die. He never minced words about the dangers that activists faced.[24]

President Johnson turned out to be better for liberals than many expected. Telling the nation, "Let us continue" by honoring the memory of Kennedy through the passage of a bold domestic agenda—including the deceased president's civil rights bill—LBJ worked with liberal Democrats in the House to wrench the legislation out of committee and move it through the full House.

Although Heschel had missed the March on Washington (he was scheduled to speak in New York), he engaged with the struggle to build support for this legislation. Everywhere his message to interfaith audiences was the same: to sit on the sidelines was sinful. "I often sit and wonder: perhaps our souls went up in flames along with their bodies in Majdanek and Auschwitz," he pondered in Yiddish during an event with King.[25] On 25 February 1964, Heschel spoke to a conference that included the mayor of New York, Robert Wagner Jr., as well as Cardinal Spellman, the archbishop of New York. Standing in the ballroom of the Americana Hotel, Heschel condemned white Americans for sitting silently as African Americans fought for their freedom. "Life could be so pleasant," he said, dripping with sarcasm. "The Beatles have just paid us a visit. The AT&T is about to split its stocks. Dividends are higher than ever. Castro is quiet and well-mannered. Khrushchev is purchasing grain from us. Only the Negroes continue to disturb us: What shall we drink?" As he had done in Chicago, Heschel turned to the relevance of Judaism. "The teaching of Judaism is the *theology of the common deed*. . . . The great challenge does not lie in organizing solemn demonstrations, but in how we manage the commonplace." In Heschel's mind, "the white man is on trial. . . . Shall the triumph of faith be defeated by a premature sense of accomplishment?" Heschel urged white people to realize that

"the strength of reliance on non-violence may not stand the test of long and bitter humiliation. Unless the Negroes come to realize that their struggle is a struggle for all Americans, unless they are joined in this struggle by white people, the spiritual gains of 1963 [referring to civil rights protest] may be lost."[26]

The next obstacle for the civil rights bill was the Senate, where southern Democrats launched a filibuster to stop the legislation dead in its tracks. Religious organizations mobilized to build pressure on senators to vote for cloture, which would end the talkathon. Many religious groups came to Washington to lobby elected officials and generate publicity for the cause. In the fall of 1964, Heschel joined a twenty-four-hour religious vigil at the Lincoln Memorial in Washington. "Civil Rights is basically a moral issue we are all protesters before God," read the banner that he held as photographers snapped his image for the papers.[27] In his statement to fellow protesters, Heschel argued that "failure to pass the Bill would be worse than a defeat; it would be a disaster." He continued: "How many disasters do we have to go through in order to realize that all of humanity has a stake in the liberty of one person; whenever one person is offended, we are all hurt. What begins as inequality of some inevitably ends as inequality of all." Heschel warned of the "deadly poison that inflames the eye, making us see the generality of race but not the uniqueness of the human face. Pigmentation is what counts." He ended his statement by reading from Isaiah 62: "Upon your walls, O Jerusalem, I have set watchmen; all the day and all the night they shall never be silent; You who put the Lord in remembrance, take no rest, and give him no rest, until he establishes Jerusalem and makes it a praise in the earth."[28]

For Heschel, racism cast a long shadow on all of America. How could his fellow countrymen sit by, in the aftermath of the Holocaust, and deny citizens rights that should be afforded to everyone regardless of race or ethnicity? How could so many

Americans remain quiet after seeing the horrendous images of southern police brutalizing young peaceful protesters marching for equality? As middle-class Jews nestled comfortably in their suburban homes, millions were suffering, not only in the United States but all over the world. As Heschel told his colleagues in the Rabbinical Assembly during a speech at their Golden Jubilee Convention in 1964, "The essence of a Jew is his involvement in the plight of other people, as God is involved."[29] An international human rights movement in the 1940s and 1950s was shining a bright spotlight on the ways that individuals in numerous countries lived in subjugation and with unequal status.[30] The scourge of discrimination was preventing too many persons from enjoying basic rights, from African Americans in Birmingham, Alabama, to ethnic communities living under governments that did not allow them to practice their religion.

Engagement with race relations magnified his concern about the human rights of fellow Jews living under the domination of the Soviet Union. Heschel never forgot that German Christians, America's elected officials, and even mainstream Jewish organizations had failed to mobilize when the Nazis engaged in mass genocide. His new home country had allowed refugees to languish. The experiences of rallying in Madison Square Garden and marching in the streets of Washington in the early 1940s were seared into his memory, as was the outcome that left six million Jews dead, including much of his own family. During the early Cold War, the Soviets were preventing the two to three million Jews living under their control from enjoying true freedom. The situation behind the Iron Curtain only worsened. Jews were not allowed to practice their religion, and anti-Semitism was a threat (despite its being classified as a crime against the state).[31] They were even prohibited from being buried in certain cemeteries. Local militia broke up informal prayer groups (minyanim) while the government shut

down the only kosher meat butcher in Moscow.[32] The Soviets went so far as to prevent the baking of the unleavened bread, matzah, eaten during Passover.[33]

The sense of urgency among American Jews about their Soviet brethren heightened with the trial of Adolf Eichmann in Jerusalem, which opened in April 1961. Eichmann was one of the highest-ranking Nazi officials who had been captured in Argentina by the Israeli Mossad. The testimony in the trial brought back to life the horrors of the "Final Solution," culminating in Eichmann's execution on 1 June 1962. After being reminded in vivid detail about what the world had allowed the Nazis to do, more American Jews felt determined to never let it happen again. This meant that in the early 1960s Soviet Jews needed to be saved before it was too late. In the United States, Jewish organizations started to work through back channels to convince politicians to pressure the Soviets into allowing Jews to emigrate. Three prominent figures, Senator Abraham Ribicoff of Connecticut, Senator Jacob Javits of New York, and Supreme Court Justice Arthur Goldberg, headed the cause.

Moshe Decter, a fiercely anticommunist Jewish rights activist and the former editor of *The New Leader*, published an article in *Foreign Affairs* in 1963 entitled "The Status of Jews in the Soviet Union." This was a perfect Cold War issue, something to lob at the Soviets, but it was much more than that. The concern about Soviet Jews spoke directly to the fears born out of the Holocaust as well as the questions that were being put front and center by civil rights activists. "During the past quarter-century," Decter wrote, "enlightened public opinion throughout the world has become keenly sensitive to the treatment of minorities as a barometer of moral decency and social sanity." Unfortunately, he noted, Soviet policies toward Jews were "tantamount to a policy of discrimination for it denies to the Jews such ethnic-cultural rights as are generally accorded to all other Soviet nationalities."[34] Inspired by Decter's article, the

newly formed Cleveland Committee on Soviet Anti-Semitism put together a booklet called "Soviet Terror Against Jews: How Cleveland Initiated an Interfaith Protest," which they mailed out to synagogues all over the country.[35]

Heschel became active. On 7 October, he and Rabbi Uri Miller, the president of the Synagogue Council, convened a meeting in New York with representatives from the major Jewish organizations. The meeting resulted in an agreement to launch a massive public relations campaign to promote this cause, including holding a national conference.[36] Recalling the laggard response to the Nazis in an interview with a Yiddish newspaper, Heschel lamented that "Russian Jews are an abstraction for Americans. They know about Florence, Naples, Miami, [the] Waldorf Astoria, but what do they know about Berdichev, Odessa, Vilna, and Warsaw! This exemplifies the indifference."[37] He met with the Cleveland group to strategize over public relations[38] and coordinated with Cardinal Richard Cushing, the archbishop of Boston, to plan an interfaith demonstration that could "stir the conscience of not only millions of our people who are not properly informed about this problem, but as well will have [an] incalculable effect on leadership in Russia."[39] It was time for American Jews to take up the cause of their fellow Jews just as he was urging them to do with civil rights for African Americans.

With Yom Kippur approaching, on 4 September 1963, Heschel called his fellow rabbis to action in a sermon at the JTS. He told his rabbinic colleagues that the plights of African Americans and Soviet Jews were intertwined: "We are all involved in the great battle for equal rights being waged in America and rejoice in the fact that millions of Americans are wholeheartedly taking part in the effort to eliminate the inequities that result from prejudice and discrimination." But the fight could not stop at the water's edge: "While the victorious drama has electrified all Americans, another drama is being enacted

which, though agonizing and heartrending, and perhaps more tragic than the story of the Negro people, is being ignored. I mean the plight of the Jews in Soviet Russia." Heschel implored his colleagues to arouse congregants and sway local officials. "There is no sustained action," he warned, "no program of informing or impressing upon our own people and the people all over the world of being witness to spiritual genocide." He took aim at rabbis and scholars who, he said, were "occupied with sublime issues, like doing research, composing books, arguing whether to cooperate with rabbis whose outlook or affiliation does not conform to certain standards. We are busy raising funds for new synagogues, celebrating Bar Mitzvahs and testimonial dinners. We are busy in the nineteen-sixties just as we were busy in the nineteen-forties." If American Jews understood the necessity of a civil rights movement then they certainly could grasp the urgency of a comparable campaign to save Soviet Jews: "If we are ready to go to jail in order to destroy the blight of racial bigotry, if we are ready to march to Washington in order to demonstrate our identification with those who are deprived of equal rights, should we not be ready to go to jail in order to end the martyrdom of our Russian brethren? To arrange sit-ins, protests, days of fasting and prayer, public demonstrations to which even Russian leaders will not remain indifferent?"[40] The speech received extensive media coverage. Thousands of Conservative rabbis incorporated his words into their sermons and reprinted them in congregational newsletters.

Heschel used his platform in the news media and joined other activists to spread the word about the plight of Soviet Jews. "Dr. Heschel has been quoted almost daily and in large stories in the Jewish Day and in the Forward [two major leftist Yiddish language newspapers] about Russian Jewish situation," noted Marc Tanenbaum.[41] In April 1964, he joined twenty-four American Jews in Washington to generate publicity. Senator

Ribicoff spoke about the challenges within the Soviet Union: "His ways of worship are severely limited. His synagogues are shut down, he is denied burial in Jewish cemeteries." Prinz likewise warned against complacency: "The terror is gone, but the policy of extinguishing every spark of Jewish consciousness and identity continues. Official Soviet practice today perpetuates the Stalin policy of depriving Soviet Jewry of both continuity with its past and of free expression in its present. Individual murder is no more. But cultural genocide continues."[42]

King saw the linkages as well. He cosponsored a meeting organized at the Carnegie Foundation by Moshe Decter which produced a statement called an "Appeal of Conscience for the Jews of the Soviet Union." When King spoke to the United Synagogue one month later, he blasted the Kremlin for an "attempt to liquidate the Jewish people in Soviet Russia." On another occasion, he sent word through his secretary that he approved of Heschel including the issue in an address he was making to the Southern Christian Leadership Conference since saving Soviet Jewry would "be in keeping with the theme of the convention."[43]

The budding Soviet Jewry campaign had a grassroots element as well. In 1964, Jacob Birnbaum, an Orthodox British émigré whose grandfather helped coin the term "Zionist," was inspired by the Student Nonviolent Coordinating Committee. Birnbaum established the Student Struggle for Soviet Jewry (SSSJ), which was committed to direct action. "Let My People Go!" became their rallying cry. On 1 May 1964, SSSJ organized a march to the Soviet Mission to the UN on 67th Street and Third Avenue that drew over one thousand college students, mostly middle-class Jews. "Forced assimilation of 3,000,000 Jews must stop," they chanted. "Free Americans cannot neglect our Soviet brethren." And "Let my people live."[44]

A few months later, Heschel was one of the leaders of an

even bigger march to the Soviet Mission, this time joined by political luminaries. Numbering over two thousand Jews (sponsored by twenty-six Jewish organizations), it started at Hunter College, marched around a few blocks, and then ended back at the Soviet Mission.[45] The former attorney general Robert Kennedy, who was running for the Senate, kicked off the event. The candlelight procession, which included the theologian Max Schenk and the Yiddish poet Jacob Glatstein, as well as Kennedy's opponent, Republican Senator Kenneth Keating, was halted by the police at Lexington and 67th Street. Heschel, along with Keating, Phillip Baum of Hunter College, Theodore Bikel of the AJC, and George Maislen of the United Synagogue of America were the only ones allowed to enter the building. After the rest of the marchers were refused admission, Heschel and the other leaders slipped a petition under the front door with a list of demands, calling for a "redress of wrongs and sufferings, the elimination of discrimination, and the full restoration of Jewish rights in the USSR." The *New York Daily News* printed a photograph of Heschel holding up a sign that read "Jews Demand Equal Rights in Soviet Union!"[46] The event, with Heschel's photograph, made it into the newspapers.[47]

Each experience of fighting for human rights, whether at home or abroad, whetted his appetite for greater involvement, and put him into more contact with like-minded preachers. As he awakened to the social struggles taking place all around him, Heschel displayed the same intensity in his journey into activism as he did in his scholarship. He only knew how to move at full speed. The rallies and meetings took him into new corners of injustice and increased his ambition as to what was possible and necessary. He started to rage about the world around him in the same tenor of the Prophets, refusing to be tamed by calls for pragmatism and moderation. For Heschel, the 1960s was turning into a global fight against racism and, for a Jew, that meant taking on the Catholic Church.

The accusation that Jews were responsible for the cruci-fixion of Jesus—the deicide—and the proclamation that they should be converted to Christianity had long been a center-piece of anti-Semitic thought. The idea persisted, according to leading Jewish organizations, that Christians portrayed Jews as frenzied killers and that certain aspects of the Roman Catho-lic liturgy and commentaries they "have traditionally elicited, contribute to anti-Jewish attitudes and behavior."[48] But by the 1960s, the demise of colonialism as well as the devastation wrought by the Holocaust challenged the standing doctrine of the church and made Vatican leaders rethink core issues.[49] Pope John XXIII called for a Second Vatican Council from 1962 to 1965 to reevaluate the church's positions toward other religions. The Catholic leadership understood the revolution-ary changes that had taken place since Vatican Council I, over ninety years earlier. "In short," one report noted, "the alert and forward-looking elements of the Catholic Church are clearly facing the problem of a world in which Christians are in a mi-nority and in which the prospects for growth and influence are diminishing."[50]

For American Jews, the potential change in Vatican policy presented a vital opening. If the church officially renounced its doctrine, the decision would constitute a massive pushback against anti-Semitism, finally placing the weight of the Vatican behind the Jewish world. The opportunities for Jews to be part of the decision-making process, however, were limited. The church hierarchy was extremely insulated and didn't provide many opportunities for outsiders to influence deliberations. For many Jews, the feeling was mutual. Prominent Orthodox rabbis, including Soloveitchik, whom Heschel met in person only during conversations held as part of an advisory group for AJC, adamantly opposed any kind of discussion with Christian leaders about theological matters.[51] Heschel didn't agree with that sentiment. His understanding of religion grew out of the

individual orientation toward the divine, rather than specific practices, and this gave him a way to see the possibility of inter-faith dialogue.[52] "The issues at stake were profoundly theolog-ical," he later said. "To refuse contact with Christian theolo-gians is, to my mind, barbarous. There is a great expectation among Christians today that Judaism has something unique to offer."[53] It was true that Christians and Jews could "disagree about the ways of achieving fear and trembling," he said, "but the fear and trembling are the same."[54] Other theologians were just skeptical that there was any real support for change within the church. Reinhold Niebuhr believed that nothing would come of the discussions since, as he told Heschel privately, the "reac-tionary prejudices of the Catholic prelates . . . were very deep."[55]

But Tanenbaum, who had become the director of the De-partment of Interreligious Affairs for the AJC under President Joachim Prinz, believed that reform was worth pursuing. As a voice championing the human rights of Jews, AJC took the lead in trying to influence the Vatican's deliberations, believing that any substantial change would fulfill its core mission. While AJC sought input from Jewish scholars all around the world, Tanenbaum, on the basis of their long friendship, believed that Heschel could be the most effective point person for this mission. Tanenbaum and others at AJC were pleased when the Vatican Council appointed Cardinal Augustin Bea to chair the secretariat. Bea was a German-born Old Testament scholar who had tremendous admiration for the Jewish community. The Je-suit priest had built a stellar reputation for his intellectual acu-men while teaching biblical studies and archeology at the Pon-tifical Gregorian University before becoming a cardinal of the church in 1959. Expressing his optimism about Bea's appoint-ment, Tanenbaum told Heschel that the window for change was real as there was a "growing acceptance on the part of impor-tant Roman Catholics of the concept and practice of religious pluralism."[56]

In November 1961, Tanenbaum arranged a meeting between Heschel and Bea at the Vatican. It went very well. Heschel admired Bea's work on the Song of Songs, and their conversation ranged freely from biblical texts to contemporary anti-Semitism. Heschel left feeling optimistic.[57] He said that he wanted to work more closely with AJC on the issue.[58] Bea walked away feeling good as well. The cardinal wrote Tanenbaum and Zachariah Shuster that Heschel was an "excellent interpreter of Jewish lore in modern terms, and a man imbued with a spirit of enthusiasm about ultimate values. . . . [H]e succeeded in creating a rapport with Christian leaders in a way few laymen and even religious leaders could have done."[59] According to Shuster, who witnessed the interaction up close, the practical results were that Bea wanted to cooperate, going so far as to provide the general outlines of a declaration which would include a condemnation of anti-Semitism.[60]

Heschel wrote a lengthy report for AJC entitled *On Improving Catholic–Jewish Relations.* "One wave of hatred, prejudice or contempt," he wrote, "may begin in its wake the destruction of all mankind." In the report, Heschel urged the council to understand that though there was not a single cause to explain the "ancient and complex evil" of anti-Semitic thought, it was clear that among the key sources was "the slanderous claim that 'the Jews' are collectively responsible for the Crucifixion of Jesus, that because of this the Jews are accursed and condemned to suffer dispersion and deprivation throughout the ages. This charge has been used by anti-Semites for centuries, to justify the most cruel and inhuman treatment of Jews; it has even been advanced to justify the fate of six million Jews during the Nazi holocaust."[61]

Heschel served as an unofficial ambassador between the AJC and the Vatican. At a private luncheon on 27 March 1963, in Boston, Heschel presented Cardinal Bea with a copy of *The Sabbath.* The men developed a friendship as they worked through

the thorny issues at hand. There were "bitter enemies of the Jews who are in Rome," warned Bea, including the "Arabs and the professional anti-Semites," seeking to undermine any progress. Yet Bea also made it clear that the pope personally saw change as vital, a way for the church to rehabilitate its image. "It is important for you to know that the Pope and I are completely united in these matters," reassured Bea. Heschel was firm. Any effort to improve Jewish–Catholic relations, Heschel said, required a clear statement condemning the charge against the Jews "of *deicide* as a heresy or as a blasphemy." Bea believed it was possible.[62] Most of their negotiations were done in secret and with the knowledge of only the high-level leaders at AJC. One of the few public encounters took place at a well-publicized dinner in Bea's honor at the Plaza Hotel in New York. Speaking before the attendees, Heschel urged the cardinal to remember what was at stake with these deliberations: "Our era marks the end of complacency. We all face the dilemma expressed by Moses: 'I have put before you life and death, blessing and curse. *Choose life.*' Religion's task is to cultivate distrust for violence and lies, sensitivity to other people's suffering, the love of peace. God has a stake in the life of every man."[63] Heschel was optimistic. The cardinal, Heschel wrote Buber, "told me confidentially that he had essentially accepted the content of my memorandum and [would] put it on the agenda of the council."[64]

The negotiations went slowly. But Heschel kept at it. On 3 June, Pope John XXIII died and under his successor Paul VI plans stalled. Conservative forces within the Vatican and opponents in the Arab world (including President Gamal Abdel Nasser of Egypt), where there were fears that changes by the Vatican would bolster Israel's standing, mobilized against Bea and the new pope, who supported reform, throughout the summer and fall.[65] Heschel flew to Rome in December 1963. In a meeting with Johannes Willebrands, the secretary of the Sec-

retariat for Promotion of Christian Unity, he warned that the passage that continued to hold some Jews responsible for the crucifixion put the entire declaration at risk. A declaration of love, Heschel said, should not impose any conditions. Heschel, according to Shuster, explained to Willebrands that Jews expected "recognition of their existence as a continuous and living body with its own faith and culture, and independent of any eschatological beliefs about the distant future." Heschel stressed that using the term "not all Jews" might be interpreted as meaning a majority of them were still responsible. Willebrands pushed back, saying that the declaration was aimed at Christians, not Jews, but he eventually conceded to Heschel's points.[66] Heschel expressed a sense of urgency to Father Gustave Weigel, one of the leading liberal Roman Catholic theologians in the United States, for "cleansing the hearts and minds of men, on how thick the spiritual darkness is that covers the lives of most men."[67] By the spring of 1964, there were ominous rumors that the council was gravitating toward a watered-down compromise that did not include a rejection of the collective guilt of Jews for Christ's crucifixion nor did it firmly denounce the imperative of conversion. Livid, Heschel released a condemnatory statement, published in the *New York Times* and *Time:* "As I have repeatedly stated to leading personalities of the Vatican, I am ready to go to Auschwitz any time, if faced with the alternative of conversion or death. Jews throughout the world will be dismayed by a call from the Vatican to abandon their faith in a generation which witnessed the massacre of six million Jews and the destruction of thousands of synagogues on a continent where the dominant religion was not Islam, Buddhism, or Shintoism."

There were other rabbis and Jewish leaders who supported the pursuit of Catholic–Jewish dialogue at this critical moment. Heschel frequently consulted Finkelstein throughout the negotiations that would take place. Rabbi Arthur Hertzberg, an

immigrant from Lubaczow, Poland, who came from a family of prominent Orthodox rabbis, was extremely critical of the role that the church had played in promoting anti-Semitism. He wrote in *Commentary* in April 1963, "The Jews must diagnose the Western tradition as not merely prone to the virus of anti-Semitism but chronically, or endemically, ill with it. For their own safety and for the future of their children, Jews must look to a radical change in the very foundations of Western civilization."[68] Hertzberg, who was also a civil rights advocate, saw discussions with the Vatican as a possible opportunity to start tackling the theological justifications that had been used to promote anti-Semitism as well as the historic failures of the church to combat attacks on global Jewry. When the New Orleans native Label Katz, the president of the international B'nai B'rith, met with the pope as part of a three-person delegation, he said upon leaving that "affirmations of interreligious friendship inherent in Ecumenical Council declarations have found wide acceptance and support." Katz reported that the pope conveyed his pleasure about the need for "cordial relationships and constructive cooperation" to occur between Catholics and Jews, "both in spiritual and temporal matters."[69] Katz, an early advocate for protecting Soviet Jewry, praised Pope Paul VI for fostering a "spirit of interreligious liberalism" through a "genuine trilogy of Catholic, Protestant and Jew."[70]

On the eve of Yom Kippur, in September 1964, Heschel met with Pope Paul VI in a dramatic last-ditch effort to convince the Vatican to follow through on its promise. AJC arranged for Heschel, along with Shuster, a top-secret visit with the pope. Church officials had switched the date from Saturday, 12 September, to 14 September after Heschel informed them that he could not meet on the Sabbath. Sitting in the Hotel Mediterraneo in Rome, Heschel wrote Sylvia and Susie that the pope's office had "expressed regret for having forgotten that I could not come on the Sabbath." He told his family

that the meeting with the pope had been declared "an extraordinary privilege" for Heschel but they should not "*speak to anyone about it.*" Explaining that he was working on a memo in the early morning hours to submit to the pope, he urged his wife and daughter, "Don't worry. Just be happy and pray."[71]

For Heschel, the times felt historic. Back in the United States he was fighting for African Americans. The struggle to save Soviet Jews was gaining steam. In Washington, President Johnson had pushed the Civil Rights Bill through Congress. The watershed legislation ended legal segregation in public accommodations and paved the way for an Equal Employment Opportunity Commission that was charged with combatting racism in the workplace. The president was not finished, as he promised a bold domestic agenda in his second term on the cusp of winning a landslide victory against Republican Senator Barry Goldwater. And now Heschel was sitting in a hotel in Rome, preparing to meet the pope, in an effort to eradicate a doctrinal foundation of anti-Semitism.

Heschel wasn't in Vatican City to bargain. He laid out his cards in his strong memo to the pope. Heschel wrote that the time had come for the Catholic Church to reform its ways: "Anti-Semitism is a satanic force, and its unique power found a manifestation in crimes unprecedented in the annals of history. . . . It is our hope that the Great Council will take the historic opportunity to *specifically* declare its condemnation of anti-Semitism in all its forms as sinful and evil. Such a position would open a new era in Christian–Jewish relations by disassociating, once and for all, Christian teaching and belief from anti-Semitism."[72] Heschel was a theologian who understood this moment against a backdrop of centuries of discrimination and a world that he hoped was changing. The thirty-five-minute meeting with the pope was tense. The pope explained to Heschel that excessive pressure would backfire. He reiterated that there were many powerful forces who opposed any doctrinal change.

Heschel had little success in softening his host. There were moments when he stumbled with his words, appearing to make the situation even worse. He departed from the room concerned about what would happen next, though he still followed up in a letter with pleasantries: "The deep understanding which Your Holiness indicated for the integrity and depth of the Jewish religious commitment to the God of Abraham, Isaac, and Jacob, and the Covenant of Sinai represent a beautiful illustration of what Your Holiness has in mind in expressing the vision of mutual esteem."[73]

Heschel became part of the story in October when the press broke the news that he had been engaged in secret negotiations with the Vatican. Some in the Jewish community did not understand how Heschel had met with the pope on the Jewish High Holidays (and while he was mourning the death of his sister Sarah, who died on 30 June 1964), or how he had become the self-appointed representative of their international community on a matter of such magnitude.[74] Orthodox rabbis disapproved that he had even met with the Catholics. The negative media coverage triggered comments that Heschel was himself responsible for the breakdown in the negotiations.[75]

The critics' fears were misplaced. The church itself was undergoing an important reform. On 20 November, the council overwhelmingly voted in favor of compromise language. The final wording did not contain a direct refutation of the deicide charge and still indicated a preference for conversion. But many prominent Jewish leaders saw the revised text as an important step forward in the fight against anti-Semitism. The chief rabbi of Israel, Isser Unterman, declared that "the fact that the great Catholic church has come to the conclusion that their attitude toward the Jewish people has to be revised is warmly welcomed by us."[76] Heschel himself was pleased with the document, which, he told the University of Judaism, includes recognition of the "religious dignity of the Jews."[77] In media

coverage, Heschel received praise for his role in the negotiations. The final decision would have to wait until the council met in October 1965.

Even after this progress, the situation almost blew up in his face. Around Christmas, the Israeli newspaper *Ma'ariv* published an interview in which he castigated the Vatican for its inaction during World War II and its continued adherence to doctrine that supported anti-Semitism.[78] Heschel's great strength was his ability to express moral indignation behind a cause; political tact was not always his strong suit. In the most controversial portion of the interview, Heschel stood by his comments about preferring to go to Auschwitz rather than be converted. These statements sounded to Vatican officials, the director of the AJC's European Office Zachariah Shuster noted, as if Heschel said they were Nazis.[79] Cardinal Bea lit into his friend by saying that the article caused him to spend the "most embarrassing three quarters of an hour I have been called upon ever to spend in the Eternal City" and threatened the "ultimate catastrophe" of their "dearest plans."[80] With the final decision in limbo, the AJC apologized to the Vatican and distanced itself from Heschel. "I am particularly dismayed and deeply hurt," Heschel noted to himself, "by the fact that some of the newspaper stories have been told in a way which is morally deplorable representing views and attitudes repulsive to me."[81]

Regardless of the fallout, by 1964 Heschel had established himself as a highly regarded public figure: part theologian and part activist. Heschel met with political leaders and understood the importance of grassroots activism on behalf of a global campaign of human rights. But as Martin Luther King was putting himself on the front lines every day, Heschel continued probing deeper through his writing and classroom teaching into the connections between his theological arguments and lived experience. In May 1963, Heschel received recognition for his intellectual contributions when Stanford University appointed

him to give the Raymond Fred West Memorial Lectures, a distinguished series that had included prominent thinkers like Reinhold Niebuhr and Julian Huxley.[82] Heschel delivered his three lectures, which became his book *Who Is Man?*, in the Dinkelspiel auditorium with hundreds of students and professors attending. In these talks, he called for a philosophy that addressed the challenges of modern man. "Philosophy cannot be the same after Auschwitz and Hiroshima. . . . Philosophy, to be relevant, must offer us a wisdom to live by—relevant not only in the isolation of our study rooms but also in moments of facing staggering cruelty and the threat of disaster," Heschel noted. "The question of man must be pondered not only in the halls of learning but also in the presence of inmates in extermination camps, and in the sight of the mushroom of a nuclear explosion."[83] To prevent a repetition of the Holocaust and tackle the ever-present remnants of racism required moving beyond the classroom, what he called a "depth theology." He distinguished humans from animals based on the fact that they had the capacity for self-introspection. "Animals," Heschel argued, "are content when their needs are satisfied; man insists not only on being satisfied but also on being able to satisfy, on being a need not simply on having needs. Personal needs come and go, but one anxiety remains: Am I needed? There is no human being who has not been moved by that anxiety."[84] In a world that was shifting rapidly toward activism, Heschel was providing a theological road map. Just a few months later, across the San Francisco Bay, students at the University of California at Berkeley launched the free speech movement by challenging campus regulations put into place during the McCarthy era. Mario Savio ignited five hundred students, along with campus representatives from the Congress of Racial Equality, the Student Nonviolent Coordinating Committee, and the Students for a Democratic Society, as they stormed the administration office to demand an abolition of the rules. "There is a time

when the operation of the machine becomes so odious," Savio declared, "makes you so sick at heart, that you can't take part, and you've got to put your bodies upon the gears and upon the wheels, upon the levers, upon all the apparatus, and you've got to make it stop." Heschel had already been laying the groundwork for this kind of thinking. "I am afraid of people who are never embarrassed at their own pettiness, prejudices, envy, and conceit, never embarrassed at the profanation of life," he told a rapt audience at Stanford.[85]

All of this work on human rights was building toward an experience in Selma, Alabama, that would bring Heschel to the realization that his life as an activist and as a theologian could no longer be separated. Heschel had become fully integrated into the civil rights movement that was driving American political debate, with religious figures at the head of the effort. He watched proudly from the crowd as JTS granted King an honorary doctorate for his campaign to "realize the scriptural injunction to love one's neighbor as one's self" (my grandfather, Rabbi Nathan Zelizer, sat on the stage with King to receive an honorary degree as well, and my father, Gerald Zelizer, sat with the students being ordained). Upon accepting the honor, King said to the graduating class, "This expression of support and confidence will give me strength to carry on in the struggle for freedom and human dignity."[86] Max Routtenberg, the president of the Rabbinical Assembly, implored his colleagues to show "vigorous leadership in the struggle for human rights," according to a reporter for the *New York Times*.[87] "You have demonstrated," the event's program stated, "how religious leaders may once more point the way to the solution of grave moral dilemmas and the eradication of injustice in this land."[88] The truth of the matter was that senior clergy were still catching up with younger Jews who were already putting their lives at risk through their protests. Indeed, not long after the JTS ceremony, two young Jewish activists named Andrew Goodman and

Michael Schwermer were abducted and murdered by Klansmen in Mississippi, along with their African American companion, James Chaney, all of whom had come to the state during Freedom Summer to support voting rights.

If religion was going to have its maximum effect on the campaign for human rights, Heschel was coming to believe, it would have to be an interfaith project. From his new position as visiting professor at the Union Theological Seminary in 1965, Heschel said, "The supreme issue today is not the *halakhah* for the Jew or the Church for the Christian—but the premise underlying both religions, namely, whether there is *a pathos*, a divine reality concerned with the destiny of man which mysteriously impinges upon history." This was part of the first public address at the seminary, titled "No Religion Is an Island."

The time was urgent for all humankind, regardless of religious affiliation, to embrace a commitment to social justice. From the Holocaust to the American South, modern man had to find common cause, as children of God, to right wrongs. "I speak as a person who was able to leave Warsaw, the city in which I was born, just six weeks before the disaster began. My destination was New York," Heschel said; "it would have been Auschwitz or Treblinka. I am a brand plucked from the fire, in which my people was burned to death." But Heschel saw a point of commonality between religions in that they were all dealing with the "tragic insufficiency of human faith." He lambasted anyone who believed that a single religion had a monopoly on the truth. "Thus any conversation between Christian and Jew in which abandonment of the other partner's faith is a silent hope must be regarded as offensive to one's religious and human dignity. . . . Is it not blasphemous to say: I alone have all the truth and the grace, and all those who differ live in darkness, and are abandoned by the grace of God?"[89]

The multiple demands of teaching, scholarship, and activism—as well as his deep devotion to family—took a physical

toll on the rabbi. Working on all cylinders made his health delicate. But Heschel wasted no time. He spent Sabbath afternoons discussing with friends what the Prophets would do about the injustice taking place in the middle of the 1960s. Heschel always was committed to Judaism as he had learned it in Warsaw, but since arriving at JTS he proved to be open to different denominations and forms of faith, at a personal and not just political level, even flexible to thinking differently about his own practice. Just as he criticized Reform and Conservative leaders, so did Heschel feel that the Orthodox could be too dogmatic about Jewish law, paying insufficient attention to the authenticity of their observance. Speaking of Orthodoxy in the 1960s, he complained toward the end of his life that "the demand of the hour is renewal, purification, vitality, but the extremist establishment stands like a medieval castle. Their leaders are busy erecting new fences and walls, instead of building a house for people to live in. As a result, Judaism looks like a jail to the young, instead of a foundation of joy and life."[90] Personally, he often prayed at the Hasidic synagogue near his Upper West Side home, but at other times with his colleagues. And when his daughter wanted to have a bat mitzvah on the Sabbath morning, including reading the Haftorah, Heschel said yes, even though Conservative practice allowed this ceremony only for boys.[91]

Nothing had prepared Heschel for what he experienced in 1965 while marching alongside the most influential civil rights leaders in the country. On 7 March, Alabama police brutally attacked peaceful protesters whose only sin was to march across the Edmund Pettus Bridge between Selma and Montgomery to show their support for African American voting rights. Like most Americans who watched what came to be called Bloody Sunday, when the ABC network cut away from a film called *Judgement at Nuremberg* about the Nazi war crimes trials, Heschel was outraged by what he saw. The police cracked open the skull

of one of the protesters, John Lewis of the Student Nonviolent Coordinating Committee (SNCC), with a baton. Heschel was stirred to action. Two days after Bloody Sunday, Heschel joined eight hundred protesters who marched to the FBI headquarters in New York.

On 15 March, President Johnson gave a powerful address to a joint session of Congress in which he called on legislators to send him a voting rights bill. Johnson had been trying to hold off on this bill, fearing that moving too soon on a second civil rights bill would trigger a political backlash in the South and stifle the rest of his domestic initiatives. But the traumatic images from Selma were too much for him and for much of the nation to bear. The president insisted that the House and Senate had to move on a voting rights bill and to do so right away. He proclaimed in dramatic fashion, "We Shall Overcome!" embracing the mantra of the civil rights movement, which many of the legislators in the chamber still considered to be radical.

King, who cried upon hearing Johnson's remarks, believed it was essential to keep the pressure up. On behalf of the activists, he sent an invitation to priests and rabbis to come join another march from Selma to Montgomery on Sunday, 21 March. His goal was to place the moral authority of these leaders on display. King wanted to demonstrate that the religious world was on the side of the protesters. Bringing enough preachers and rabbis to the streets of Selma would be an answer to the concern that he discussed in his "Letter from a Birmingham Jail," a missive that was aimed at fellow preachers: "Perhaps I have once again been too optimistic. Is organized religion too inextricably bound to the status quo to save our nation and the world?" If enough persons accepted his invitation, it would be proof that organized religion did not in fact always serve a broken status quo.

With the federal protection of voting rights at stake, King sent word that he wanted Heschel to join him. The danger was

very real. On 9 March, a white Unitarian minister who had participated in the Selma protests, James Reeb, had been severely beaten by a group of white racists after dining in an integrated restaurant. The minister died on 11 March. "We weep over the death of the Rev. James J. Reeb, and we weep over the death of justice in Selma," remarked Rabbi Robert Marx, the director of the Union of American Hebrew congregations, upon hearing the news.[92] Despite fearing for his own safety, Heschel decided to go. He felt as if he had no option. His work on the Prophets and experience with the Holocaust convinced him that remaining silent, the sin of indifference, was not possible. When the Sabbath ended on the evening of 20 March, he embarked on this journey. "He kissed me goodbye. And I remember thinking 'I don't know if I'll ever see him again,'" Susannah recounted, as she too was aware of the great risks that her father faced by setting foot in the violent streets of Alabama.[93] Heschel and Kelman flew to Atlanta together, where they spent the night in a hotel.[94] "Our move [*sic*] was one of great expectation," Heschel noted. "The awareness of the importance of the cause."[95]

When the rabbis arrived at Selma via Atlanta, Andrew Young, the executive director of the SCLC who had studied Heschel's work in seminary during the 1950s, picked them up. Young was accompanied by the director of the Washington office of the American Jewish Committee, the World War II veteran Brant Coopersmith, who, as Heschel noted in his diary, "with tears in his eyes expressed his great joy of the fact of my going to Selma."[96] Young, one of King's top lieutenants, had become a devoted reader of Heschel and considered him to be an "intellectual father." *The Prophets* inspired him through the ways that Isaiah retained his faith in humanity at one of the worst moments for the people of Israel. Like many civil rights leaders, Young carried around his copy of the book wherever he traveled.[97] They slept at the home of Sullivan Jackson, a

dentist, and his wife, Richie Jean Jackson, a teacher. King and other activists usually slept in the Jacksons' home and used it as an informal headquarters when they were in town.

The protesters prepared for their march at nine o'clock in the morning at Brown Chapel African Methodist Episcopal Church, where hundreds of activists spent the night. "It seemed like a life-time waiting in the Church," Heschel noted.[98] Clergy from different religious backgrounds filled the room, all convinced that Selma was "where the church must be."[99] There were many other rabbis in attendance, most of them from the Reform movement. Those who were in Selma before the weekend began had conducted Sabbath services, singing the hymn "Adon Olam" to the tune of "We Shall Overcome."[100] The Northern Californian David Teitelbaum, who arrived with four colleagues, recalled, "I was living out what Judaism has been teaching all along, that you have to help the oppressed and underprivileged, and not stand idly by the blood of your neighbor."[101] Rabbi William Braude, a graduate of the HUC, explained, "When I was a little boy and came to the United States, for the first time I saw policemen who not only didn't harm me but would help me. Little Jewish boys in Russia were afraid of policemen, as little Negro boys are in the South. I wanted to change a situation where boys in America are afraid of policemen, to do what little I could."[102] When asked by a *New York Times* reporter why he had traveled down south to the protests, Heschel replied, "I believe I must recall what is the most important challenge I face, and that is realizing that I am involved in the fate and dignity of my fellow man."[103] The danger, though, was palpable. During their orientation on Sunday morning, the clergy were told, "Selma is tense. Sale of firearms is up . . . and they do not sell to Negroes. In case of trouble the FBI will not step in."[104]

As they waited for King, one of the ministers asked Heschel to read from the Old Testament. Choosing Psalm 27, a decla-

ration of belief in God and salvation, Heschel recited these inspiring words: "When the wicked advance against me to devour me, it is my enemies and my foes who will stumble and fall. Though an army besiege me, my heart will not fear; though war break out against me, even then I will be confident." When King showed up at eleven, he conducted a service with the marchers, speaking for twenty minutes, comparing the protest to the Israeli exodus through the Red Sea. "The weather was magnificent. The sight of the thousands of people in front of us was inspiring. There was a spirit of exultation about the Service. It was almost exclusively in the spirit of the Hebrew Bible," Heschel recorded in his diary.[105]

Heschel asked King if he could be stationed in the first row. Both had a practical motivation for the two of them to be up front, King knowing the impact that it would have for Americans to see photographs of this prophetic-looking rabbi beside him and Heschel understanding what it would mean for a Jew to be at the front of the line. Heschel's involvement was symbolically important for a civil rights movement that was trying to stress its universalism and ecumenicism at a time when white racists were coming down hard on them for being radical communists seeking to destroy the fabric of the nation. The landscape had been changing dramatically as the participation of rabbis and middle-class students like Schwermer and Goodman were showing the world that civil rights activism was drawing from the mainstream.

While Jewish Americans associated with radical groups had been going down south for many decades to defend African Americans, by 1965 the movement attracted a broad array of inspired citizens. Heschel's prominent presence and that of other preachers was a way to emphasize this important point.

But the decision had more to do with practical considerations. Over the years, the men had come to trust one another and be inspired from working together. Reverend James Law-

son, a leading civil rights activist, recalled that "King was impacted by Heschel's analysis of the Prophets. Heschel made the conviction of the Prophet that God is here in our immediate struggle and that God's struggle is a struggle to help those who are voiceless to find voice, those who are blind to find sight. That it's in that unique dimension, that God is most present."[106] "My father and King were deeply moved by each other," Susannah recalled.[107]

When Heschel moved toward the front, one onlooker shouted out, "There goes *God!*"[108] For much of the march, the participants were silent. They had been instructed to avoid saying anything that could trigger violence: "There was a spirit of pleasantness and solemnity," Heschel said. "No militants, no bitterness. A feeling of solidarity prevailed many hearts, somehow transcending the difficulties and the problems of the moment. It was as if we were moved by a vision."[109]

He walked along US 80 arm in arm with Reverend Fred Shuttlesworth and Ralph Bunche, standing just a few persons over from King, with three thousand peaceful protesters behind them. Heschel was dressed in a black overcoat and wore a Hawaiian lei around his neck, a symbol of love (all the marchers in the front row had a lei). His long, tousled hair was overflowing. One rabbi, Maurice Davis, recalled that during the protest Heschel "never wilted, and never showed anger, even when the police drove by taking movies of us, as if to tell us that they had our faces on record."[110] The procession brought back memories, reminding Heschel of the walks he had taken with Hasidic rabbis in Warsaw who "felt a sense of Holy in what I was doing."[111]

Remaining silent in those fraught hours of the march was not easy. The notorious Sheriff Jim Clarke, who had directed the brutal crackdown of a few weeks earlier, stood in intimidating fashion, wearing his "Never" lapel on his blue police suit. White onlookers brandished Confederate flags and screamed,

"Nigger King go home" and "Meredith, Miss., Hates Niggers." Others interlaced their racism with anti-Semitism. "Koons, Kikes, and Niggers, Go Home!" blared the words on one sign.[112] Heschel was shocked to see white southern women spitting on the nun who was walking near him.[113] As Rabbi Saul Leeman, a Conservative rabbi from Rhode Island, recounted, "We could say we were not extended any Southern hospitality. As we marched, there were federal troops on each side of the road, with their rifles in hand. There were some helicopters hovering above. We felt as if we were in enemy territory."[114]

The march took place without incident. Despite the hostile crowds, over eighteen hundred Alabama National Guardsmen and approximately two thousand soldiers, federal marshals, and FBI agents protected the marchers.

Although the march would go on for fifty-four miles and five days, reaching twenty-five thousand participants, Heschel and a number of the most prominent figures who were there on day one took buses back to Selma or Montgomery to fly home. Heschel felt that he had been involved in something much grander than himself. He noted the hundreds of African Americans whom he saw wearing yarmulkes, which they called Freedom Caps. He was touched by the response of Jews whom he met along the way. A young Reform Jew from King's organization who drove Heschel and Kelman to the Montgomery airport told them that before the march he didn't identify at all with his religion; now his eyes had been opened. Upon hearing this story, Heschel thought to himself, "Jewish religious Institutions have again missed a great opportunity—namely, to interpret a civil rights movement in terms of Judaism. The vast number of Jews participating actively in it are totally unaware of what the movement means in terms of the prophetic traditions."[115]

Heschel's excitement was tempered by the behavior of white southerners he witnessed. In his diary, he recorded that the waitress at the airport dismissively referred to him and Kel-

man as "you people." The waitress said that her mother told her Santa Claus existed, but she had never believed her until seeing Heschel. "I ordered tea, I received half a cup. I ordered a hard-boiled egg—it could have been out of archeology. The piece of cheese was like thin paper and stale."[116] Still, he managed to find humor to lighten the situation. When the waitress glowered at him, asking "What favor did you do me?" Heschel responded, "I proved there was a Santa Claus," which led her to burst out laughing.[117]

Selma was cathartic for Heschel, whom civil rights activists were now calling Father Abraham, as he came to realize that "many human beings are serving as one in a sacred cause."[118] Andrew Young recalled that the march "put him in the category of himself being one of the prophets, and not just an academic. That he was a scholar, but actually, I mean it was quite significant for somebody of his stature. . . . [G]enerally academics are not committed to action, yet time and time again he was."[119]

These hours marching tilted the balance in his life toward fully embracing the new role he had been undertaking in the first half of the 1960s as an intellectual-activist: "I felt that anyone who participated in this March will never be the same. It was a great day in my life."[120] Heschel famously recounted, "I felt my legs were praying."

He left Alabama more committed to the networks of grassroots activism that were spreading like wildfire by mid-decade and prepared to dive deeper into the organizational work of movement building. On 29 March, Heschel wrote King, who now called his friend "my Rabbi," to describe the majesty of the experience: "The day we marched together out of Selma was a day of sanctification. That day I hope will never be past me— that day will continue to be this day. A great Hassidic sage compares the service of God to a battle being waged in war. An army consists of infantry, artillery, and cavalry. In critical moments cavalry and artillery may step aside from the battle-front. In-

fantry, however, carries the brunt. I am glad to belong to infantry! May I add that I have rarely in my life been privileged to hear a sermon as glorious as the one you delivered at the service in Selma prior to the march."[121] When Heschel read about a Republican disparaging the marchers as troublemakers and sexual deviants, he sent a strongly worded response to the editors of the *New York Times:* "It is slanderous to impute immoral behavior to hundreds of dedicated young men and women who left their homes to face danger in their effort to demonstrate peacefully on behalf of equal rights for all men."[122]

Selma turned Heschel into a more visible presence in the civil rights movement. Newspapers and weekly magazines throughout the country printed Associated Press photographs of this theologian locking arms with African American leaders to demand voting rights. The photographs appeared in the *New York Times*, the *Atlanta Constitution*, *Daily Telegraph*, the *Chicago Tribune*, and elsewhere. One of the most moving images, taken by *Look* magazine's James Karales, a photojournalist who had become determined to use his camera to promote social justice, captured King in a contemplative mood as Heschel stood near him visibly swept up by the historical weight of the moment.

The outcome of the protest stiffened Heschel's spine when thinking about activism, no matter the risks. As a result of the marches in Selma, President Johnson sent the Voting Rights Act to Congress and signed the bill into law on 6 August, which guaranteed that the federal government would intervene in states that were shown to restrict voting.

A few months later, Heschel was relieved when the Vatican took a major step forward in the fight against anti-Semitism. On 25 October, Vatican II officially adopted the "Nostra Aetate" as part of the "Declaration on the Relationship of the Church to Non-Christian Religions." The compromise text, passed by a vote of 2,221 to 88, called for "mutual respect and understanding" as well as "biblical and theological studies" between Cath-

olics and Jews, both interpreted as victories by the media. Though short of a repeal of deicide, the final declaration stated that the crucifixion of Christ "cannot be charged against all the Jews, without distinction, then alive, nor against the Jews of today" and that the church "decries hatred, persecutions, displays of anti-Semitism, directed against Jews at any time and by anyone." The new text anticipated an age when "all peoples will address the Lord in a single voice and 'serve him shoulder to shoulder,'" a dramatic statement about granting Judaism equal standing under God. Although the language did not officially renounce the deicide, the declaration explicitly rejected anti-Semitism for the first time in church history. "The Church . . . moved not by political reasons but by the Gospel's spiritual love, deplores hatred, persecutions, displays of anti-Semitism directed against Jews at any time by anyone." The compromise was considered a breakthrough in Catholic–Jewish relations. The declaration, stated Morris Abram, the president of the American Jewish Committee, marked "a turning point in 1900 years of Jewish–Christian history" and the "climax to an unprecedented effort to bring about a new era in relations between Catholics and Jews."[123]

The three years that followed the publication of *The Prophets* had been transformative for Heschel, who emerged as an important voice in the struggle against anti-Semitism and racial oppression. This immigrant from Warsaw had evolved from being a bookish theologian sitting in his smoky seminary office and writing about the relationship between God and man to a nationally well-known activist. Nor was Heschel close to finished with this phase of his life. The movement gave him a taste of what it meant to be spiritual by taking a physical stand against reactionary forces. He didn't just need to write about how the Hebrew Prophets decried the injustice around them because now he was doing that himself. Social justice activism infused new meaning into Judaism within the world in which he lived.

The raw power of marching on the front lines in Selma, which ultimately produced one of the most historic pieces of civil rights legislation in American history, had illuminated the intrinsic connection between his theological beliefs and progressive activism. Continuing to be part of the fight for civil rights, he redirected his newfound energy toward the ravages of war.

6

Washington

"Violence is obscene," argued Heschel in *The Prophets.* Writing years before America's escalation of the conflict in Vietnam, Heschel made clear what he saw as the dangers of military force: "When the prophets appeared, they proclaimed that might is not supreme, that the sword is an abomination. . . . The sword, they said, shall be destroyed. . . . The prophets, questioning man's infatuation with might, insisted not only on the immorality but also on the futility and absurdity of war."[1] These words were on the rabbi's mind as he watched the United States become deeply entangled in a disastrous war.

By the mid-1960s, Heschel had become intensely active in social protest movements worldwide. Vietnam would prove no exception. Along with the rest of the country, Heschel watched as a president who played a vital role in the passage of civil rights and antipoverty programs diverted precious resources toward an unwinnable conflict in Southeast Asia. Lyndon John-

son inherited from John Kennedy a policy of economic and military assistance to the western-friendly, corrupt government of South Vietnam in its battle against the communist North. By the time LBJ took office, there were approximately sixteen thousand military advisors in the theater of war. Following decades of colonial rule under Japan and then France, Vietnam, under the Geneva Accords of 1954, was divided into two countries along the 17th parallel. South Vietnam was headed by Ngo Dinh Diem, whose corrupt, autocratic regime allied with the United States and other Western interests. North Vietnam was led by Ho Chi Minh, who sought to reunify the nation under a communist regime. Ho was enormously popular throughout the country and relied on a military organization in the South known as the Viet Cong. In the same month that Kennedy was assassinated, Diem was arrested and killed in a CIA-backed coup. From that point forward, the South Vietnamese government was highly unstable. While the Vietnamese perceived the conflict to be a postcolonial civil war, American policymakers viewed it as integral to the global Cold War; the outcome, they believed, would determine the future of the entire region. According to the so-called domino theory, to which the president and his advisors subscribed, if one country fell to communism, no matter how small, the others around it would follow. With this mindset, Johnson decided to escalate America's involvement into a full-scale military operation. In August 1964, he persuaded the Democratic Congress to pass the Gulf of Tonkin Resolution granting him authority to use military force in Southeast Asia. The language was so broad, Johnson joked, that it was "like grandma's nightshirt, it covered everything." A year later he launched an intense bombing campaign against North Vietnam, and soon he sent tens of thousands of ground troops into combat. Johnson understood all the risks involved, privately admitting to advisors that the conflict might be unwinnable.

It was not long before a small antiwar movement started to

take shape. Activists who had campaigned against nuclear weapons, as well as college students who were inspired by civil rights, turned their sights to Vietnam when the administration launched Operation Rolling Thunder in March, a ferocious bombing campaign against the North. That month the Students for a Democratic Society at the University of Michigan organized the first "teach-in." One faculty member, the anthropologist Marshall Sahlins, blurted out to his co-organizers, "They say we're shirking our responsibilities. Let's teach in instead of teaching out. We'll take over the buildings after classes and talk about Vietnam all night. A teach-in." More than three thousand students, faculty, and staff showed up. They packed into four auditoriums for twelve hours of classes and speeches about the looming dangers overseas. Within days the event inspired others. At Columbia University in New York, one economist said, "The students of the universities are coming out of a long sleep." The Vietnam Day Committee put together a thirty-three-hour teach-in at the University of California at Berkeley that drew over ten thousand people. "The white man cannot settle the internal problems of Asia," the Democrat Ernest Gruening, one of the two senators to vote against the Gulf of Tonkin Resolution, told the students. President Johnson initially dismissed all of these gatherings as insignificant. "Don't pay any attention to what those little shits on the campuses do," the president told Undersecretary of State George Ball, "The great beast is the reactionary element in the country." Johnson's main political concern was looking soft in the eyes of conservative Republicans, like Senator Barry Goldwater. Others in the administration, however, took the Left more seriously early on. Attorney General Nicholas Katzenbach speculated to reporters that communists had been involved in organizing the protests, a familiar tactic in the Cold War by politicians who wanted to smear their opponents.[2]

Heschel jumped right into this brewing battle. His involve-

ment with civil rights, Soviet Jewry, and anti-Semitic Catholic doctrine had drawn him deeply into the world of social activism, and the situation in Vietnam seemed like the logical next step. "Worse than war is the belief in the inevitability of war," he noted.[3] Heschel followed the events in Southeast Asia on the nightly news with growing concern. He had been sensitized to the catastrophe of war after having experienced the impact of two worldwide conflicts. As he said during an interview at the University of Notre Dame with his friend and fellow civil rights advocate President Theodore Hesburgh, "I am really a person who is in anguish. I can't forget what I have seen and been through. Auschwitz and Hiroshima never leave my mind. Nothing can be the same after that."[4] He saw in the students who were starting to mobilize against the war the same spiritual crisis he had been warning against for many decades. "Our young people are disturbed at parents who are spiritually insolvent," he told the General Assembly of the Council of Jewish Federations and Welfare Funds. "They seek direction, affirmation; they reject complacency and empty generosity."[5]

When dozens of his fellow clergy spoke out about how antiwar critics were being harassed and threatened, Heschel did not hesitate to participate even though opposition to the war was a mere blip on the national radar. On 25 October 1965, he joined approximately one hundred preachers at the United Nations Church Center in New York who gathered to support the right to protest the war, taking aim at Katzenbach's insinuation about communists. Like Heschel, many of the other preachers in the room had been active in civil rights. The proclamations of the Second Vatican Council and the experience with the civil rights movement had laid the groundwork for further interfaith cooperation.[6] He had previously worked with Union Theological Seminary President John Bennett, for instance, during a push for racial integration in New York City schools; they had also cosigned a press release condemning Republicans who

tried to take political advantage when one of Johnson's top advisors, Walter Jenkins, was arrested in October 1964 for having sex with another man in a YMCA bathroom.[7] Richard John Neuhaus, a Lutheran from Ontario who had been ordained at the Concordia Seminary and served as the pastor at St. John the Evangelist Church in Williamsburg, was arrested during a sit-in at the New York City Board of Education demanding racial integration. The Jesuit pacifist Daniel Berrigan, a poet, had gone with his brother Philip to the March on Washington in 1963, and there he felt an "immense profound spiritual force" that was "moving through the hearts and minds of the marchers, like a single bloodstream, animating, nourishing, communicating to all a strong purpose and a sacred sense of the meaning of the day."[8] The Yale University chaplain William Sloane Coffin served in Europe during World War II and worked for the CIA in the Korean War. After studying to become a minister, Coffin had been arrested for acts of civil disobedience, once when participating in the Freedom Rides.[9] All of these men, except for Bennett, regarded the older Heschel as a mentor. As Berrigan put it, Heschel "was a father to me, in more senses than one. . . . The rabbi was an ancestor of the spirit."[10]

The preachers shared Heschel's view that the war was the next major cause moral leaders had to commit themselves to. There was no backing down. When the group held a press conference, Heschel placed his hand on Berrigan's shoulder: "Are we then finished, do we go home content, and the war goes on?"[11] Then, answering his own question, Heschel told reporters that they would continue to organize.[12] Without much discussion, Heschel had essentially vowed to build a national organization. In his "disingenuous little boy way," Neuhaus recalled, Heschel responded, "Oh, well I hope I haven't created any problems."[13] The founders named their committee the Clergy Concerned About Vietnam. "With humans being killed and wounded," Heschel and his colleagues said, "religious lead-

ers must, in principle, issue a clear call to see the way toward peace." They positioned themselves as an alternative to abdicating moral responsibility "in favor of the government or the extremist groups which would exploit the present confusion for their own questionable purposes."[14]

Every day, the news from the war sounded worse. Heschel and his colleagues were early critics of administration policy, shifting their focus from the protection of the right to protest to condemning the war itself. Heschel admitted to another gathering of clergy that for the first time he was starting to lose confidence in the good intentions of elected officials: "For many years I felt that the Federal government had all the facts and was competent to make the necessary decisions. But in the last few weeks I have changed my mind completely. I have previously thought that we were waging war reluctantly, with sadness at killing so many people. I realize that we are doing it now with pride in our military efficiency."[15] When Johnson issued a temporary ban on bombing in North Vietnam in late 1965, they called for it to become permanent. In a telegram to Johnson, the committee said, "We are appalled by the inhumanity of the war in Vietnam, and the extension of hostilities to neighboring countries. Impending national decisions about Vietnam will fundamentally influence the political, military, and above all—moral—future of our nation and world."[16] Yet it was not long before Johnson resumed the bombing.

Perhaps because they were all comfortable working through established institutions in their professional lives, the group proved to be remarkably effective at building an organization of their own. They established local committees in every state. Heschel and his colleagues, who were working without the formal support of the national religious organizations to which they were each connected (most of which endorsed the war or did not want to take a controversial stand on the conflict) used their church bureaucracies and mailing lists to grow the mem-

bership. They took home lessons learned from the civil rights movement by sponsoring church resolutions at national conventions and placing ads in newspapers calling for a negotiated end to the war.[17] Relying on volunteers from the seminaries in Morningside Heights, Coffin worked the phones to put together an extensive network of contacts. They turned to independent journals like *Christian Century* to disseminate their ideas. By the end of the year, despite meager financial resources (a little over six thousand dollars in contributions), the committee claimed sixty-eight chapters and a forty-one-person national committee.

To go up against Lyndon Johnson and the war was risky. Not only was Johnson known to be one of the most vindictive people to hold the office, but also most Americans backed the president's policies. The antiwar movement was barely visible. The leadership of most major religious associations, including those from the world of Judaism, stood by the president. When Daniel Berrigan emerged as a vocal opponent of Johnson's policies, Cardinal Spellman of the Archdiocese of New York and his superiors essentially exiled him to Latin America. "The removal of Father Daniel Berrigan from our work in the Clergy Concerned for Viet Nam has been a source of great sadness for many of us," Heschel wrote in private correspondence.[18]

Heschel and his fellow clergy were out front on this issue, long before a full-blown movement had taken form.[19] Their early involvement was important as it helped bring legitimacy to the cause. In early February, Clergy Concerned About Vietnam led a Peace Mobilization in Washington attended by two thousand Roman Catholic, Protestant, and Jewish clergymen from forty-five states. The group met with Walt Rostow, the president's hawkish national security advisor, and announced a three-day Fast for Peace, which would be an "act of penitence" for the war in Vietnam. Benjamin Spock, who headed the medical committee, said fasters could subsist on rice and tea or fruit

juices or water.[20] One of the protesters was Edward Kaplan, a doctoral student at Columbia University, who was feeling such "disgust and hopelessness" about the war that he spent sleepless nights walking through the streets of the city. He wrote Heschel that he had gone to Washington hoping to be inspired but realized the struggle for peace was different from the protests for civil rights. Whereas civil rights was about "marching together in a sort of joyous fellowship," the antiwar effort aimed to increase the sense of anguish about the war.[21] They had a long way to go to arouse the sympathies of fellow Americans, most of whom didn't know or care about the conflict. Heschel did not despair. "There still is time," wrote Heschel on the pages of the *Long Island Jewish Press*, as he urged Jews to pray for Johnson's success in undertaking diplomacy.[22]

There had been a slight shift in the political winds in February 1966. Senator William Fulbright of Arkansas, a mainstream liberal internationalist in the Democratic Party and ally of the president, convened televised hearings in which he grilled administration officials before the Foreign Affairs Committee about the problems with Vietnam. Foreign Policy Advisor George Kennan admitted that the United States should withdraw "as soon as this could be done without inordinate damage to our prestige or stability in the area." For many middle-class Americans, it came as a surprise to see someone of Fulbright's stature convene hearings that contained such critical conversations about the war. But Fulbright's hearings didn't reflect bipartisan opinion, which still lined up squarely behind Johnson.

Heschel pushed for an expansion of the antiwar movement. Two months after Fulbright's hearings, he and his brigade of renegade preachers strengthened their organization. They renamed themselves the Clergy and Laity Concerned About Vietnam (CALCAV) with the hope of enhancing their appeal beyond clergy. They hired as a full-time executive secretary Richard Fernandez, an ordained minister from the United Church

of Christ who had been arrested in civil rights protests. When the thirty-one-year-old Boston seminary student attended his first meeting, he was struck by "this person at the end of the table that looked like he fell out of a book on the Prophets." Fernandez, who had read Heschel's work in seminary, had never met a Hasidic rabbi. "I found it ironic," Fernandez recalled, "that the prophets he wrote about he looked like."[23] To create "a public climate in which the Administration can and must seek alternatives to current policy," CALCAV established three divisions. The Literature Division handled the distribution of publications; the Action Division organized vigils, services, and demonstrations; the Educational Division maintained a speakers program and outreach to schools and churches as well as developing films and public displays.[24]

On 4 July the group of clergy and lay allies led a morally charged march over the George Washington Bridge to the Community Church, where they gathered to "End the War, Most Barbarous in History." Reverend Theodore Seamans, a Methodist minister from New Jersey, told reporters that "we should be waging war against poverty, ignorance and disease."[25] Student protesters were starting to burn their draft cards and engage in other forms of dramatic actions. David Paul O'Brien and three friends had stood in front of the South Boston courthouse and lit their cards on fire in front of a crowd that included undercover FBI agents. In contrast, CALCAV would act lawfully, and they would not endorse any kind of no-confidence vote in President Johnson. Whereas a few of them, namely, Berrigan, were clamoring to employ more radical forms of civil disobedience, Heschel and the others insisted on sticking with legal means.

In their minds, the radicalization of certain parts of the civil rights and antiwar movements threatened to undercut their legitimacy among mainstream Americans and elected officials. The antiwar mobilization lacked the kind of centralized

cadre of leaders that the civil rights movement had. While this fragmentation offered the clergy an opportunity to quickly gain influence, it also meant that more radical elements were likewise able to gain power.[26] During the early Cold War in the 1950s, liberal leaders, including those of mainstream religious organizations that were on the front lines of civil rights, had worked hard to separate themselves from the far left and to purge extremists from their ranks so as to insulate themselves from conservative attack. On foreign policy, mainstream Democrats had embraced a vision of liberal internationalism that entailed a strong stance against communism, often moving to purge leftists from their ranks. Getting too close to certain parts of the antiwar movement in the 1960s threatened to undercut their hard-earned standing. By focusing on moral appeals and peaceful rallies as well as coalitional work with reputable political organizations, the presence of preachers and rabbis, CALCAV believed, could bolster the antiwar cause among elected Democratic officials in ways that long-haired students could not. "We came into being specifically to provide a religious comment on the war," Heschel said about CALCAV, "that would not be allied to the traditional peace movement and that did not stem from a body . . . committed to its own continuation beyond the cessation of the present crisis."[27] All the work of CALCAV would be suffused with religious themes to give it a kind of moral grounding.

The antiwar clergy reached out to the Buddhist leadership in Vietnam to forge an international front. This was not a surprise given that, for Buddhists, religious persecution was an integral part of the Vietnam saga. Between May and November 1963, the South Vietnamese government had cracked down on Buddhist monks who were protesting the oppressive treatment of their religion. The photograph of a monk immolating himself to protest persecution under Diem had become one of the most iconic images of the moment. Buddhist activists had con-

tinued to fight for their rights as well as for a negotiated settlement with the communists. The CALCAV clergy assured the Buddhists "of our sympathy and prayers in your efforts to heal the wounds of your troubled country. We are painfully conscious of the terrible responsibility borne by America." In another letter, Heschel's cabal reached out to Roman Catholic leaders who had tended to be more allied with the South. They apologized to both factions for the "failure on the part of some Americans to distinguish Vietnamese patriotism from Communist influence," which they called "a grave error and injustice," assuring them that as religious Americans they "deplore the intensification of violence in the form of increased bombing and casualties at a time when the policy behind the violence is increasingly confused."[28]

The Holocaust, which had come to an end only twenty-one years earlier, was never far from Heschel's mind. Indeed, the Holocaust was still fresh for most American Jewish families who constantly retold the stories in familial and communal settings, and whose nightmarish memories had worsened with the gruesome trial of Adolf Eichmann, as the term "Holocaust" came into popular usage.[29] "Auschwitz is a manifestation of what a world without God is capable of doing," Heschel scribbled to himself.[30] In an address to the National Convention of Religious Education Association, Heschel described Vietnam as an "ecumenical nightmare, Christians, Jews, Buddhists, dying together, killing one another. So soon after Auschwitz, so soon after Hitler." The response to the "Nazi atrocities" should have been a "revival of the conscience." Instead, the world felt broken. "Today is the anniversary of the death of President Kennedy. His assassination shook the world. Yet it made no impact on our laws and customs. No lesson was learned, no conclusion was drawn. Guns are still available c.o.d. Mass killing in Chicago, in Houston, Texas, in Arizona, and elsewhere, is becoming a favorite pastime of your boys. The Pentagons of the world

are Temples," he said, where decisions were made about "how many shall live, how many shall die," a reference to the Unetaneh Tokef prayer that Jews chanted on Rosh Hashanah and Yom Kippur while contemplating the fate of every individual in God's final judgment. "Religion cannot be the same after Auschwitz and Hiroshima," he insisted. "Its teachings must be pondered not only in the halls of learning but also in the presence of inmates in extermination camps, and in the sight of the mushroom of a nuclear explosion."[31]

In a post–World War II world, individuals had to fight for social justice, correct past wrongdoings, and refuse to commit new sins. Alongside his antiwar activism, Heschel continued to pursue the cause of Soviet Jewry. "In the darkness of the nights I often wake up by a voice that cries out of me slashing my throat: *They have killed my people!*," he wrote in his notes. "It is nightmare so gruesome, a grief so infinite—*They are destroying my people.*"[32] Heschel's resistance to political considerations frequently brought him into conflict with natural allies. During an address to the Rabbinical Assembly in May 1966, Heschel caused a stir by criticizing the five hundred rabbis sitting in the convention ballroom for ignoring the crisis: "Over and above the noise of our banquets and testimonial dinners I hear the cry of Russian Jews: 'The Jewish people forsakes us. The Jewish people has forgotten us.' Their dismay is mixed with disdain for those whose voice is loud but whose hearts are made of stone." Heschel directed his criticism toward the Conference of Presidents of Major Jewish Organizations, the umbrella organization of twenty-four groups leading the fight for Soviet Jewry, on the grounds that they had "consistently frustrated efforts of many of us to cry out for our anguish over the plight of Russian Jewry."[33] He and Elie Wiesel, who credited Heschel with awakening him to the plight of Soviet Jews,[34] spent many afternoons lamenting how few Jewish adults would show up to synagogue meetings and marches about this issue.[35] Heschel

had become very close to Wiesel, the survivor of Auschwitz whose novels and essays had done more than almost anything else to convey the horror and tragedy of the Holocaust to the American public. The lack of urgency about Soviet Jewry seemed like an extension of the general problem of cultural assimilation, with Jews having lost any connection to brothers and sisters living overseas, part of their essential roots. Their friendship had convinced Wiesel to undertake an assignment in Moscow for the Israeli newspaper *Haaretz*, which provided the material he used to publish his book *The Jews of Silence* (1966), a classic treatise on the situation.[36]

Heschel believed that Jews had to speak out about Vietnam too. In the fall of 1966, Heschel urged Jewish intellectuals to support an antiwar statement in the *New York Times*. In a letter to prospective supporters, Heschel and Leo Pfeffer, a legal advisor to the AJC who had been a strong civil rights advocate, wrote that it was "sad testimony to the decay of conscience that we go on pursuing our own work, enjoying our prosperity and at the same time remain oblivious to the human situation in Vietnam. We should at least be aware of the destruction and suffering of the innocent. . . . Our dreadful share in causing so much anguish is multiplied by our own indifference. Our sinfulness increases daily. We must repent if we are not to forfeit the privilege to pray."[37] Their letter claimed that Jews had distinct concerns about the war that arose from thousands of years of persecution: "Within our own lifetime more than one out of every three Jews have been put to death because we did not possess the Nordic blood of Adolf Hitler. . . . Through bombs and napalm, through fire and famine, we are killing husbands and fathers and then kill those we have made their widows and orphans."[38]

The religiously infused rhetoric that Heschel and his colleagues employed didn't sit well with many participants in the antiwar movement. Unlike the civil rights movement, where

African American preachers and churchgoers were at the forefront of activism from the very start, the antiwar movement was largely secular in its orientation. The rallies and marches were filled with young Americans who didn't care about what the Hebrew Prophets had to say. Many of them had seen how religious moralism often tilted in a politically conservative direction during the early Cold War, such as those who supported Governor Ronald Reagan's war against the student activists at the University of California, Berkeley.

In fact, most mainstream religious organizations—their leaders and their members—were not on the side of the protesters. Within the Jewish community, for instance, Heschel's antiwar positions were highly controversial and unpopular. Polls showed that, like much of the rest of the country, American Jews were deeply divided over the war in the fall of 1966. According to Gallup, 43 percent of Jews backed Johnson's policies, compared to 40 percent who were against him and 17 percent who said they had no opinion on the issue.[39] Another poll, slightly more unfavorable for the administration, still found only 48 percent of Jews opposing involvement in Vietnam.[40]

A sizable number of Jewish leaders were uncomfortable about being part of any kind of "Jewish" response to Vietnam.[41] Abraham Sachar, the president of Brandeis University, respected what Heschel thought, but felt "[it] will be a tragic day in American history when foreign policy issues get debated and decided on the basis of racial or religious groupings." He urged Heschel to continue his personal protests, but "in Heaven's name, do so as a troubled American, and not as a Jew. You have no right to speak for me and for millions of my co-religionists and, in arrogating this responsibility to yourself, you are creating terrifying problems that may haunt us in the future."[42]

With regard to Vietnam, there were particular concerns within the Jewish community about the political risks of Heschel's outspoken opinions in relation to President Johnson's sup-

port for Israel. This was one of the foremost reasons that so many Jewish organizations avoided taking a strong stand on the war despite their having committed to civil rights. They either stood by the president or were silent. Their fears were stoked on 6 September 1966, when the president met with the newly elected national commander of the Jewish War Veterans, Malcolm Tarlov. According to Tarlov's account, Johnson interrupted the veterans in the middle of their opening statement to say how unhappy he was that there were so many Jews opposing the war.[43] Upon hearing the story, Heschel, immediately assuming he had been one of the Jews to whom Johnson was referring, defiantly told the press that "if Abraham had no hesitation about challenging the judgment of God over Sodom and Gomorrah, lest it would sweep away the innocent with the guilty, should not an American have the right to challenge the judgment of our President when horrified by the war in Vietnam!" He lamented that Vietnam had put him in conflict with a president whose civil rights record was so admirable. "Amicus Plato sed magis amica veritas," Heschel recited in Latin: "Plato is my friend, but truth is a better friend."[44] Johnson tried to contain the fallout from these stories by vehemently denying Tarlov's account and instructing UN Ambassador Arthur Goldberg to assure Jewish leaders of their freedom to disagree with him on any issue.[45]

The Rabbinical Assembly opposed Heschel. In January 1967, the assembly declared their full support for the military operations and criticized clergy like their colleague for exercising "poor judgement": "We deplore the efforts by the so-called 'Guardians of the Faith' organized under the name Clergy and Laymen Concerned About Vietnam, to embarrass our government and elected officials, having pre-judged and condemned our Government and its policies beforehand." Nor did many of his colleagues on the faculty support Heschel's outspoken positions on the war.

The attacks didn't slow Heschel down one bit. He felt closer to the Hebrew Prophets who raged about the world's injustice even when everyone around them was indifferent. Wiesel sought Heschel's counsel after receiving a call from someone in Israel who warned that his opposition could endanger political support for the Jewish state. When Heschel and Wiesel took a stroll on the Upper West Side to discuss whether the Israeli friend might be right, and whether they should be more quiet about their feelings, Heschel stopped in the middle of the street and said, "Listen, there are people in Vietnam who have been bombarded for years and years and years, and they haven't slept a single night. How can we simply go on, and not try to help them sleep at night?" The image Heschel conjured would stay with Wiesel for years as he persisted in his opposition to the war.[46]

Heschel found solace in the fact that a few prominent Jewish leaders and a handful of groups, though mostly from the Reform movement, agreed with his unpopular stand. Rabbi Jacob Weinstein, the president of the Central Conference of American Rabbis, had been called on by Presidents Kennedy and Johnson to advise on the labor issue. In January 1966, he cosigned a statement condemning the president of the Jewish War Veterans for being supportive of Johnson's efforts overseas and critical of protesters, saying, "Bomb-rattling jingoism is no more tolerable from a Jewish source than from a militaristic general demanding that we bomb the 'enemy back to the stone age.'"[47] Rabbi Maurice Eisendrath was a prominent Reform rabbi, ordained from the HUC in 1926, who had served as president of the Union of American Hebrew Congregations and founded the national center of Reform Judaism in New York City. Eisendrath fought for reforms within Judaism, such as expanding the number of female rabbis, and was an outspoken advocate of civil rights as well as a fierce opponent of the war in Vietnam. "What religion worth its salt will not find itself in

trouble in days such as these?" Eisendrath asked. "What religion and especially what kind of Judaism can run for cover when tyranny and the spirit of oppression are in this land? What prophets of any faith fail to get into trouble?" The charismatic and telegenic Rabbi Balfour Brickner, a World War II veteran from Cleveland, had moved to New York in 1961 to serve as the rabbi of the Stephen Wise Free Synagogue and to work on the staff of the Union of American Hebrew Congregations. Brickner, imprisoned while protesting for voting rights, had grown up in a family deeply committed to Zionism (he was named after the foreign secretary who announced support for the creation of a Jewish state in 1917). The rabbi had nothing good to say about America's involvement in Vietnam and expressed profound frustration that so many Jews were remaining silent about the war. "When a church starts to do its job," he said, "people dislike it."[48]

The United Synagogue Youth of America and the National Federation of Temple Youth (the Conservative and Reform youth groups) stood firmly in opposition to Johnson. So too did the AJC, which had worked closely with Heschel on Vatican II. A sizable number of Jews were involved in the secular antiwar organizations of the New Left at the grassroots level. There was one moment in the 1960s when the presidents of the Students for a Democratic Society on five major campuses were Jewish, while the publishers and editors of numerous progressive outlets, like *Studies on the New Left* and *Ramparts*, were as well. Several well-known intellectuals and activists, including Abbie Hoffman, Paul Goodman, Noam Chomsky, Herbert Marcuse, and others, were of Jewish origin.[49] One study at the University of Chicago found that 45 percent of the students who protested the draft in 1966 were Jewish.[50] Compared to Catholics and Protestants, Jewish citizens polled became less supportive of the war over the decade.[51]

Bridging his worlds of writing and activism, Heschel wrote

a large number of scholarly publications in the mid-1960s that dealt with common issues. He published an important collection of essays, entitled *The Insecurity of Freedom*, with pieces he had written about contemporary topics.[52] In the book, he attempted to bring together the four strands of his life—Judaism, religion, philosophy, and politics. Starting with the title, Heschel put forward his claim that humans were granted the freedom to choose whether to live a religious life and open themselves to God. Freedom, according to Heschel, was a "burden that God has thrust upon man." He posited that the defense of freedom was the primary means through which individuals could protect their humanity in the age of skyscrapers. His work started to bring full circle the existential spiritual concerns he had expressed in books like *God in Search of Man* with his activism. In essays he had written in the 1950s and early 1960s, Heschel wanted to show how religious thinking was "a source of cognizant insight into the ultimate issues of human existence. Religion is more than a mood or a feeling. Judaism, for example, is a way of thinking and a way of living." The collection, according to one reviewer, was "so powerful a repository of high wisdom that it can—and should—serve as a constant source of enlightenment to anyone who thinks, regardless of what he believes."[53]

More difficult than the hostility of colleagues was the fact that Johnson's policies didn't change. The realization that Heschel had about Vietnam was that the war would not be ending anytime soon absent more intense pressure on the political elite. Words alone would not sway an administration that was sticking to a mistaken path. Troop numbers kept rising along with draft calls. In 1966, 385,000 troops were deployed; 382,010 people were drafted. "And if we are wise now, we will not repeat our mistakes of the past," Johnson said in one of his speeches. "We will not retreat from the obligations of freedom and security in Asia." Johnson's refusal to undertake substantive steps

toward negotiations in Vietnam pushed Heschel and his fellow clergy toward mobilizing rather than just sermonizing.[54]

Whereas Heschel had been something of an interloper in the civil rights protests in Selma in 1965, he took on a leadership role in antiwar demonstrations. With CALCAV, he had entered into the movement at the ground level before the opposition to Vietnam really had any kind of national presence. The antiwar mobilization had just started to materialize in a substantial way in the spring of 1967. Two months before an antiwar demonstration was to take place in several cities across America—it was anticipated to be the largest showing thus far and aimed to bring together all of the organizations that had emerged to protest the war—CALCAV put together its own national mobilization in Washington from 31 January to 1 February 1967. One of the flyers used to promote the event, entitled "VIET-NAM: The Clergyman's Dilemma," began by saying, "Scripture warns that 'where there is no vision the people perish.' The failure of vision regarding Viet-Nam is a blindness to realities no less than to ideals. The threat of this moment is a preoccupation with the enemy that destroys our society's power to understand itself or its foes. In such a time leaders in the religious community of the nation must risk the displeasure of the powers that be in order to challenge dogmatisms that imperil ourselves and our world."[55] The Executive Committee released a statement to the press, which circulated among participants: "A time comes when silence is betrayal. That time has come for us in relation to Vietnam. As members of American churches and synagogues, we voice not only our own convictions, but seek also to articulate the unexpressed fears and longings of millions of Americans."[56] Still intent on distinguishing themselves from the increasingly radical elements of the antiwar movement—those who were burning their draft cards and calling Vietnam Johnson's War—Bennett, Heschel, John McKenzie, the president of the Catholic Biblical Scholars

Association, and Philip Scharper, a Catholic publisher, wrote the president that the mobilization "is not to be construed simply as a protest but rather as a cry of anguish and a sincere effort to support you in seeking a peaceful speedy end to the war in Vietnam."[57]

Heschel had been in Washington several times before, but this moment was different. He was arriving to the nation's capital as a leader in an influential organization that was at the very center of a movement shaking American politics. He and his allies were forcing the president of the United States into a defensive crouch about his policies in Vietnam. His first time in Washington had been with the rabbis' march in 1943 to protest President Roosevelt's apparent indifference to the murder of Jews by Nazi Germany. Now, more than two decades later, he was standing in the middle of what had the possibility of becoming the kind of grassroots juggernaut he could only have dreamed of twenty-four years earlier. While he came to Washington to protest for civil rights, this time his target was very different. In 1963 and 1964, Heschel had sought support from elected officials to support civil rights legislation that would stop white racists from oppressing African Americans. With Vietnam, Heschel was no longer asking for their help. The focus of his protest was now the nation-state itself for enacting a foreign policy that resulted in mass death and destruction.

Heschel was among the more than two thousand clergy and religious laypeople who traveled to Washington. The New York Avenue Presbyterian Church, a congregation from 1803, served as the headquarters. On the morning of 31 January, the basement and the hallways, one reporter recounted, "were cluttered with bedrolls, sleeping bags, box lunches and general bedlam. But the confusion was organizational, physical, external; the participants, so far as their main objective was concerned, were not confused."[58] The participants drank coffee, ate cookies, socialized, and registered. Many of them chose to

fast, subsisting on water and fruit juice, to emphasize the religious character of their protest.[59] "As members of American churches and synagogues, we voice not only our own convictions, but seek also to articulate the unexpressed fears and longings of millions of Americans," proclaimed the position paper released by the Executive Committee of CALCAV. Though the statement about the millions was merely speculative (a majority of Americans didn't agree that the war was a mistake), high-profile antiwar activities created the sense that the discontent was heating up. Senator Fulbright's hearings had showcased legislators who were critical of the war. Eight hundred students mobbed Secretary of Defense Robert McNamara, screaming "murderer" and "fascist," forcing him out of his car and onto the hood when he came to speak at Harvard University. In late December, the Student Mobilization Committee formed to coordinate the disparate opposition activities taking place among high school and college students. But senior leaders with organizational connections and clout had a responsibility to make certain that all of these budding protest efforts turned into something bigger. "We are not here just to wring our hands and say, 'Isn't war too bad?'" one of the delegates, Reverend George Hill of Hartford, said.[60]

The first stop was the White House. They led a vigil, filling two city blocks. Angry counterprotesters hurled insults and waved blistering signs.[61] Jozef Mlot-Mroz, an anti-Semitic Polish immigrant with fascist sympathies who was a known counterprotester at left-wing events, chained himself to the fence and, throwing anti-Semitism into the mix, grasped a poster reading, "Communism is Jewish" before police took him away. The protesters refused to engage.[62] Taking a page from civil rights marches in Birmingham and Selma, CALCAV instructed all participants to remain orderly by ignoring "counter demonstrations and individual hecklers." The key to a successful demonstration, they said, was to "persuade a large audience

watching in person or through the news media of the point of view you support and of the desirability of sharing this point of view."[63] Hoping to convey a solemn, spiritual tone, they didn't sing or talk or even hold up signs.

Next they moved on to Capitol Hill, where the members broke up into state delegations to lobby their respective representatives and senators. About one hundred members from Illinois confronted Senate Minority Leader Everett Dirksen, a Republican who had supported civil and voting rights but was a firm backer of the war. When the senator told CALCAV that "you can't surrender. You can't retreat," they interrupted him in midsentence to ask, "Why? Fulbright [J. William Fulbright, the chairman of the Senate Foreign Relations Committee whose televised hearings on the war galvanized antiwar opponents] says stop the bombing and start negotiations with the Viet Cong!"[64]

Some senators were wavering in their support for the war. Senator Ted Kennedy greeted the Massachusetts delegation, seventy strong, dressed in a blue shirt and a tight suit. "He looked like a Bar Mitzvah boy freshly scrubbed and sent to the reception line," one of the Jewish participants observed. Speaking for fifteen minutes and then taking fifteen minutes more to answer questions, Kennedy explained that he wanted to stop the bombing and recognize the Vietcong. But the senator stressed that there were political limits as to what he would do on his own, and he would vote for the supplementary appropriations bill for the war because he could not partake in "undue militancy." Neither he nor his Massachusetts colleague Republican Senator Edward Brooke, who also expressed concerns about the war, promised substantive action because they didn't believe there was sufficient support for any kind of legislation.[65]

And others were in full retreat. Senator Fulbright met with CALCAV leaders and said that Johnson operated under the unrealistic assumption that greater military strength could win

the war, an assessment that, unbeknownst to the public, many administration officials agreed with.[66]

Heschel was hitting his stride. That evening, as the clergy reconvened at the Presbyterian Church, Heschel took to the pulpit as one of the keynote speakers after the singing of a few Christian hymns. Feeling the urgency of the moment, Heschel tossed aside restraint and let out a litany of harsh words: "This is an assembly of shock, contrition and dismay," he proclaimed. "Who would ever have believed that we peace-loving Americans are capable of bringing death and destruction to so many innocent people?" Instead of projecting power through military might, the United States should be offering assistance to those suffering. He asked, "Must napalm stand in the way of our power to aid and to inspire the world?" Heschel understood the difficult challenges that government leaders faced. But the war had to stop, and any pious person needed to realize that "to speak about God and remain silent on Vietnam is blasphemous." He lamented that "the sword is the pride of man: arsenals, military bases, nuclear weapons lend supremacy to nations. War is the climax of ingenuity, the object of supreme dedication—men slaughtering each other, cities battered in ruins. Such insanity has plunged many nations into an abyss of disgrace."[67]

Heschel spoke with the conviction of a religious leader driven to action. Paraphrasing the words of the Prophet Isaiah (62:1), he said, "For Vietnam's sake I will not keep silent, For America's sake I will not rest, Until the vindication of humanity goes forth as brightness, and peace for all men is a burning torch." He shared his memories of learning the story of Abraham almost sacrificing his son Isaac. Heschel concluded with the story of a seven-year-old boy who, reading about the time when Abraham had lifted his arm in preparation of killing his son, broke down in tears. His rebbe asked him why. The boy responded, "What if the angel had been late?" According to

the rebbe, "An angel cannot be late." Heschel then looked toward the antiwar activists, who were sitting on the edge of their seats listening to his every word with bated breath, and reminded them that, "man, made of flesh and blood, may be late." Heschel made it clear that for a pious person there could be nothing more vital at the moment than bringing an end to this horrendous war: "At this hour Vietnam is our most urgent, our most disturbing religious problem, Biblical problem, a challenge to the whole nation as well as a challenge to every one of us as an individual."[68] The evening concluded with Senators Wayne Morse and Eugene McCarthy, two leading congressional opponents of the war, outlining why Johnson's policies were so misguided—along with a message from Niebuhr, read by Heschel.[69]

The next day, Heschel went right into the belly of the beast. As one of the CALCAV leaders, Heschel met with Secretary of Defense Robert McNamara, the mathematically minded former Ford Motor Company president whom activists considered the architect of Johnson's War. Driving over in an old, beat-up VW van, Heschel and the other clerical leaders planned their strategy. They would present the secretary with a twelve-page statement of their views. After the preachers met with military officials, a colonel walked them down the sterile corridors into an elegant briefing room in the corner of the Pentagon. The room was decorated with teak tables and a large map of Vietnam on the wall. At a quarter after four, the secretary entered. "It's so good to see you," McNamara said. "You are absolutely right to be concerned about war and peace. I just wish you clergy had more to say on civil rights," a statement showing how tone-deaf he could be given the background of his visitors. As Coffin summarized their views, McNamara barely said anything. Growing impatient, Heschel could not contain his fury. He stopped his colleague in midsentence by repeating his charge that the entire operation was blasphemous. Coffin

recalled, "Heschel just erupted; he started sounding like Jeremiah. It wasn't the neat, clean logical stuff they are used to handling at the Pentagon; it was just right out of Scripture, pouring out of him as if he were in a trance."[70] A stunned McNamara listened attentively and expressed sympathy when the rabbi was done, admitting that he saw the legitimacy of their protests and had similar concerns. But that was it. After fifteen minutes, the meeting ended.[71] Coffin and the others left more troubled than when they entered, disconcerted by how such a decent person could do "so much evil."[72] More problematic, they had failed to obtain assurances of concrete policy changes.[73]

But realistically, the president, still more worried about conservative Republicans than about the Left, wasn't going to change course because preachers told him to do so. CALCAV was savvy enough to understand this, most of them having cut their teeth in the early civil rights protests. Their main goal was to keep building awareness of the problems with the war and to keep putting pressure on political leaders who were digging in. Heschel and his allies wanted to supply the antiwar movement with figures whom elected representatives would feel comfortable talking to and whom they, as well as their voters, respected. By continuing to grow the membership of CALCAV, even if many local chapters were not especially active, Heschel and Coffin could legitimately claim to have real numbers behind them when they walked into the corridors of power.

Eager to recruit other well-known figures to join their cause, the group went right after the nation's most prominent activist, Martin Luther King Jr., by inviting him to speak at Riverside Church on 4 April. The magnificent 392-foot-high ecumenical church sat in Morningside Heights, one of the highest points in the city. Since his first appearance at the church in August 1961, in the middle of the Freedom Rider protests, King had given several sermons about civil rights at this landmark building. Heschel, along with Coffin and Brown, had been

urging King to take a public stand against the war.[74] His endorsement would have an extraordinary impact as the umbrella organization of the antiwar movement, the National Committee to End the War in Vietnam, prepared to hold major demonstrations in New York and San Francisco on 15 April.

Upon receiving the invitation, King worried about alienating himself, and in the process the civil rights movement. The opposition to the Vietnam War was certainly intensifying, but in early 1967 it was perceived by much of the political establishment, and among most mainstream American middle-class voters, as something radical. When Gallup asked Americans if they had been part of a peace rally on Vietnam, 99 percent said they had not; only 9 percent said they would like to.[75] Prowar voices were still dominant. The midterm elections of 1966 had gone well for Republicans, with GOP campaigns centering on Johnson's unwillingness to be tough enough in Vietnam (as well as campaigns that castigated the president's proposal for a bill to prohibit discrimination in the sale or rental of property). Polls found that support for the operations in Vietnam stood at about 70 percent. Among African Americans surveyed, approval reached 50 percent.[76] Andrew Young and other civil rights leaders believed that the antiwar movement was far more extreme than anything they had encountered in the South.[77] The pacifist Bayard Rustin feared the implications of connecting civil rights to the antiwar effort.[78]

But King reached his breaking point. African Americans were bearing a disproportionate burden of this war. Just as he turned his attention to economic equality, King understood that Vietnam itself was one of the most damaging developments for African Americans. The ratio of black to white combat troops was double that of the national population. In October 1966, Secretary McNamara had launched the controversial Project 100,000, which sought to bring into the services recruits who had failed to qualify, justified by the argument that the military

could afford disadvantaged Americans the discipline they needed to succeed in society. A disproportionate number of recruits were African Americans and lower-class youth, which civil rights leaders decried as a way for the administration to find needed troops by taking advantage of those who were in need. One of the recruits, the heavyweight boxing champion Muhammad Ali (who failed his qualifying test in 1964), refused to be inducted. He told the press, "I ain't got no quarrel with them Vietcong. . . . No Vietcong ever called me nigger." King had also been profoundly impacted by Niebuhr, whose work he so respected. The year before, Niebuhr had come out against the war despite his well-known criticism of pacifism and isolationism. "We are making South Vietnam into an American colony," Niebuhr wrote, "by transmuting a civil war into one in which Americans fight Asians while China, the presumed enemy, risks not a single life."[79]

As the death toll kept mounting for Americans and Vietnamese, King decided that he could no longer remain silent. Before a rapt audience of three thousand people on 4 April, with a speech drafted with the assistance of CALCAV staffers, King denounced the war as immoral. Heschel sat in a seat to the right of him, next to the lectern. "If America's soul becomes totally poisoned," King warned, "part of the autopsy must read 'Vietnam.'" The civil rights leader expressed sympathy for the Vietnamese who "languish under our bombs" and urged that "this madness must cease." In one of his most provocative moments, King asked, "What do the peasants think as we ally ourselves with the landlords and as we refuse to put any action into our many words concerning land reform? What do they think as we test out our latest weapons on them, just as the Germans tested out new medicine and new tortures in the concentration camps of Europe?" He described the war as being symptomatic of the "deadly Western arrogance" that consistently placed U.S. policies on "the side of the wealthy, and the secure, while

we create a hell for the poor." The speech was, one reporter wrote, "King's most dramatic and explicit statement of disaffiliation from Administration policy in Vietnam—one which is likely to have substantial impact in the ranks of the civil rights movement."[80] King agreed to serve as the national co-chairman on the Executive Committee. CALCAV had promoted the event as "Dr. Martin Luther King Speaks on 'Vietnam: A Crisis of Conscience.'"[81]

Heschel spoke out too, condemning the war as "a supreme example of extreme absurdity. . . . The longer we stay in Vietnam the more we lose morally." He said that "the blood we shed in Vietnam makes a mockery of all our proclamations, dedications, celebrations." Drawing on his theological writing, Heschel warned that nobody could escape being culpable of "the agony and merciless killing done in our name. In a free society, some are guilty, and all are responsible."[82]

The CALCAV event was historic for King and the antiwar movement. Securing King's support was a huge accomplishment. King was now officially part of the antiwar movement that had come to consume so much of Heschel's life. In the words of the historian Peniel Joseph, "Riverside marked King's transition from a civil rights leader into a political revolutionary, one who refused to remain quiet in the face of domestic and international crisis."[83] When pressed by a reporter if he was offended, as some Jewish leaders were, by King's comparing the policies in Vietnam to Nazi Germany, Heschel replied, "I am not aware that Dr. King made such an analogy. He only made reference to concentration camps, which apparently in the mind of this listener conjured up such an analogy."[84] The strongest support for King came from liberal Protestant magazines, including *Christian Century* and *Christianity & Crisis*, a fact which revealed the expanding sentiment against the war.[85]

The predicted controversy followed. Numerous civil rights

leaders and newspaper editorial boards criticized King's decision to deliver the speech. "Dr. King makes too facile a connection between the speeding up of the war in Vietnam and the slowing down of the war against poverty," *New York Times* editors argued. Worse still, as one of the most important civil rights leaders, "[his] linking these hard, complex problems will lead not to solutions but to deeper confusion."[86] *Life* magazine branded the criticism as "demagogic slander that sounded like a script for Radio Hanoi."[87]

Notwithstanding the attacks, the rhetoric of religious leaders like King and Heschel offered something vital to an antiwar movement that was still perceived by large swaths of the population to be extremely radical. As they did with civil rights, these preachers framed the mission in dramatic terms that drew out the ethical dimension of the cause with great clarity. Their language had the ability to mobilize activists (like the charismatic speakers who were not religious), and, because of the speakers' public standing in even the most moderate communities, their words seeped into media coverage so that broader groups of Americans were exposed to the description of the protests in these favorable terms. In a country where many middle-class citizens still attended churches and synagogues, Heschel's arguments, though highly sensational and sometimes histrionic, connected the campaign to end the war in Southeast Asia to the moral lessons learned in services—far from the dangerous leftist images that conservatives talked about.

Starting with King's address, April 1967 turned out to be a turning point for the antiwar movement. Eleven days after Riverside, King stood alongside almost three hundred thousand people in the New York demonstrations at the Spring Mobilization to End the War in Vietnam. He marched with protesters from Central Park to the United Nations in what the *Boston Globe* called the "most dramatic demonstration of dissent since

New York was torn by anti-draft riots in the Civil War."[88] Maurice Eisendrath joined Martin Luther King to create Negotiation Now, which lobbied for a diplomatic end to the conflict.

When CALCAV, which was being secretly monitored by the FBI, published a book entitled *Vietnam: Crisis of Conscience* with essays by Heschel and King, the paperback sold over fifty thousand copies within a year and made the front page of fourteen major newspapers. Booksellers all over New York, Richard Fernandez recalled, were calling to ask, "Where's the book? Where's the book?" One of Heschel's friends, a businessman named Harry Wachtel in Long Island who worked with the civil rights movement paid to have it sent to every member of Congress.[89] Heschel's chapter, "The Moral Outrage of Vietnam," expanded on his Riverside speech and offered the clearest written articulation of his prophetic views of the war. "It is weird to wake up one morning and find that we have been placed in an insane asylum," he wrote. "It is even more weird to wake up and find that we have been involved in slaughter and destruction without knowing it." While Heschel avoided radical forms of protest, the words that he used were becoming as provocative as anything else being heard on the college campuses where students were now publicly burning their draft cards and aggressively confronting campus visits by companies like Dow Chemical, which manufactured the toxic gel Napalm. Heschel offered the movement perfect prose that captured the feeling of total disillusionment. Openly questioning the premises of American exceptionalism, the notion that the United States was different from and better than democracies in Europe, he wrote, "The absurdity of this war is tacitly admitted by almost everyone. . . . Is this a way to bring democracy to Vietnam: more explosives, more devastation, more human beings crippled, orphaned, killed?" He characterized Vietnam as a country that had been the "victim of colonial demoralization." Citing the Jewish liturgy, he ended by saying, "It is not for man to decide

who shall live and who shall die, who shall kill and who shall die. May no one win this war; may all sides win the right to live in peace."[90] "The combined authorship of this book," one reviewer noted, "is itself a testimony to the role of the religious community in the face of the Vietnam conflict. . . . The results of the political analysis are then judged by values based on Biblical faith."[91]

For Heschel, the antiwar movement took on deeply personal as well as theological meaning. One Sabbath, as the day of rest was coming to an end, Coffin and Martin Luther King visited Heschel at his apartment. "Just in time, you are just in time for the last bit of disengagement from the world we have to change . . . Shabbat!" Heschel said to his friends as he opened the door. He let Coffin hold the ritual spices and King the candle while they chanted the prayers, smelling the spice box and collectively drinking a sip of wine. When they were done, the men sipped schnapps and smoked cigars. Heschel told Coffin and King the story of the wise men of Chelm who deliberated over whether people grew the feet up or the head down. Heschel delivered the punch line, explaining that the answer was neither. Quoting the *va-yetel el echav*, he said that individuals grew from within and eventually moved beyond their egos toward other people. To conclude, Heschel lifted his glass and said, "Here's to the world's outgrowth of selfishness towards the humanities. . . . L'Hayim!"[92] On another occasion, Heschel invited Berrigan to his seder, an experience the preacher never forgot. "The food was excellent; the prayers of intercession—for an end to war, for the peace that passes all understanding, for the victims of the war, in our country [the dead were being conveyed home in increasing numbers month by month], for the victims everywhere; these were Heschel's fervent prayers—and mine also. This, I thought exultantly, was an ecumenicism I could take seriously." Berrigan recalled that Heschel led the service with the "solemnity befitting the occasion. His great

bearded head bowed and rose in prayer. He was, I thought, wrapt into the 'Shekhinah, the mysterium tremendum' [a reference to the Kabbalah]. I know no better way of putting it; he knew how to pray. Gathered with family and friends around a table or attending the majestic assembly of the Second Vatican Council, it made little difference. He lived before God."[93]

Heschel opposed the Vietnam War and believed the operations in Vietnam to be a horrendous decision, but he was not a pacifist. Sometimes he felt that force was justified. Just as Heschel challenged Johnson's use of military force in Vietnam, he defended Israel. There had been ongoing clashes between Israel and Palestinian groups that were based in neighboring countries. Israel's Arab neighbors refused to recognize the country's right to exist, and in the summer of 1967 Syria, Jordan, and Egypt appeared to be on the verge of a full-scale attack. On 5 June, Israel launched preemptive strikes, and after six days, Israel, with the U.S. Department of State announcing a policy of American neutrality, was victorious. The UN brokered a ceasefire after Israel had captured control of the Sinai Peninsula, the Gaza Strip, the West Bank, the Golan Heights, and the reunification of the Old City of Jerusalem. After the war ended, speaking for the New York Board of Rabbis, Heschel released a statement: "*Terror* and *dread* fell upon Jews everywhere. *Will God permit our people to perish?* Will there be another Auschwitz, another Dachau, another Treblinka?"[94] For him, Israel had to be seen in the context of the preservation of his people. When a friend had asked Heschel why he was "so dreadfully upset" before the war began, Heschel, according to *Time*, responded: "Imagine that in the entire world, there remains one copy of the Bible, and suddenly I see a brutal hand seize this copy, the only one in the world, and prepare to cast it into the flames."[95]

The territorial acquisitions that came with the victory generated friction between Heschel—who perceived the Six Day War and the aftermath to have been a morally legitimate use of

force—and many Christian peace activists—who characterized Israel as an extension of Western imperialism. They didn't think the preemptive attacks were warranted; Israel had just used the tensions as an excuse to expand territorially, they said. U.S. support of Israel, according to progressive critics, was no different than the country backing the corrupt South Vietnam. Benjamin Spock, who led the National Committee for a Sane Nuclear Policy, released a statement insisting that Israel must "renew its pledge to the U.N. not to seek to increase her territory, despite a continued policy of open immigration."[96] Daniel Berrigan, who had returned from Latin America more radical than when he left, was extraordinarily upset with his friend's fervent support of Israeli militarism, which he believed contradicted their stand in Vietnam. Heschel was "roughly handled," one civil rights lawyer observed.[97]

Not everyone in the antiwar camp opposed Israel's decisions, which gave Heschel solace. John Bennett wrote a letter in solidarity with Israel that was published in the *New York Times*, signed by a number of prominent figures from the Left, including Martin Luther King. In the broader U.S. public, Israel was still perceived to be a vital ally in the Cold War, and there was widespread agreement that the Arab countries had been the aggressors to an embattled Jewish state. When Gallup asked whom Americans sympathized with in June 1967, 56 percent said Israel and only 4 percent backed Arab nations/the Palestinians. Most prominent liberal Democrats, such as Senator Robert Kennedy, stood squarely behind Prime Minister Levi Eshkol of Israel.

Heschel would aggravate tensions with antiwar activists when Farrar, Straus and Giroux published his *Israel: An Echo of Eternity* the following year. The book was commissioned by the Anti-Defamation League, an organization created in 1913 to fight anti-Semitism, which hoped to put out a publication that explained the importance of Israel to the non-Jewish public.

"We are tired of expulsions, of pogroms; we have had enough of extermination camps," Heschel wrote in his effort to explain why Israel mattered so much. "We are tired of apologizing for our existence. If I should go to Poland and Germany, every stone, every tree would remind me of contempt, hatred, murder, of children killed, of mothers burned alive, of human beings asphyxiated." Heschel explained that "the Jews go to Israel not only for physical security for themselves and their children; they go to Israel for renewal, for the experience of resurrection."[98] He described the Israeli victory in 1967 in biblical terms and argued that the tensions in the region were a result of Arab extremists. Heschel went so far as to reiterate a classic trope from imperial discourses by arguing that the Arab people would be better off economically, culturally, and socially as a result of Israel's presence in the region. Whereas the unification of Jerusalem had become a point of bitter contention, Heschel saw the city as a beacon of justice: "Let Jerusalem inspire praying, an end to rage, an end to violence. Let Jerusalem be a seat of mercy for all men."[99] To be sure, there were clear limits to how much he tolerated the use of force: "We all must ask the nations of the Middle East: Drop your antagonisms and your antipathies, your hatred and your fears, and seek to think in terms of one family. The alternative to peace is disaster. The choice is to love together or to perish together. Let the love of life have the final word."[100]

The fissures over Israel were not nearly strong enough to sever his commitment to the antiwar movement. Vietnam endured as his overriding concern. "Heschel was obsessed with Vietnam. It was almost pathological," one friend recalled.[101] In October 1967, Heschel spoke about the war to an interreligious conference at the Ambassador Hotel in Los Angeles. Sponsored by the Council of Churches in Southern California and the Board of Rabbis of Southern California, the speech unpacked the problems with the war in Vietnam on moral grounds.[102] At

the UN in New York he helped to co-organize a CALCAV human rights vigil, calling for a "cessation of military hostilities around the world."[103] More members of CALCAV were starting to engage in radical forms of protest, burning draft cards, and the clergy turned their attention to supporting conscientious objectors who resisted induction.[104] Increasingly open to the value of civil disobedience, Heschel continued to feel that being arrested was counterproductive. When William Coffin argued that the only place for an honest man was jail, Heschel responded, "But will it stop the war?" After Berrigan said, "That's not the question," Heschel shot back, "Pardon me, that's the *only* question."[105] Nonetheless, Heschel cosigned a statement drawing on religion as a justification for individuals who refused to serve: "We hereby publicly counsel all who in conscience cannot today serve in the armed forces to refuse such service by non-violent means. . . . [I]n the sight of the law we are now as guilty as they."[106] By the end of 1967, Bennett and Heschel believed that the committee was having a serious impact: "Public opposition to the war in Vietnam is mounting. Recent polls indicate that the reservoir of American tolerance for our military intervention in Southeast Asia is running dry."[107] They took note of the expanding size and intensity of the protest movement. On 21 October, one hundred thousand people marched to the Lincoln Memorial in Washington to demonstrate against the war, and fifty thousand illegally broke off to head toward the Pentagon despite court orders against doing so.

Heschel returned to Washington in February 1968 for CALCAV's second antiwar mobilization. This gathering took place a few days after the Tet Offensive, which further rocked national confidence in the war effort. On the Vietnamese New Year of Tet, the North Vietnamese mounted a fierce coordinated attack in heavily populated areas of South Vietnam. Although U.S. forces were able to put down the surprise strikes, their severity, which came at a time when many Americans were

being promised an end to the war (a "light at the end of the tunnel," as the commander of U.S. forces, General William Westmoreland, promised), aggravated antiwar sentiment within the United States. Even the trusted CBS Evening News Anchor Walter Cronkite broke the famous wall of objectivity during his broadcast to say to viewers, "It seems now more certain than ever that the bloody experience of Vietnam is to end in a stalemate." Like many activists who continued to hope that public pressure could change decision-making in Washington, Tet radicalized Heschel further as he too was losing all hope that elected officials would bring an end to the war.

On the eve of the protests, CALCAV published *In the Name of America*, which superimposed news accounts of wartime atrocities next to the text of international laws. The goal was to highlight how the United States systematically violated basic international rights agreements. The booklet, which sold about thirty thousand copies and was distributed to every U.S. senator, claimed that international laws were "only [a] bare minimum of moral obligations that nations and individuals must accept even in time of war" yet "the awful truth is that on occasion after occasion we have failed in Vietnam to observe even these minimal standards of moral constraint."[108]

The second CALCAV mobilization in Washington reflected a heightened sense of national crisis. CALCAV had grown into one of the largest antiwar groups in the country. There were almost twenty thousand members and ninety-six chapters. Upon arriving in Washington, Heschel made his first stop the Religious Action Center of the Union of American Hebrew Congregations. Standing before a half-filled room of antiwar protesters, he lamented the fact that America had been a country of hope but was turning into a land of shame. Looking around at the empty seats in the room, he could not understand why there were so few Jews participating in the antiwar movement given that *rachmonus* (compassion) was a fundamental Jewish

value.[109] Of course, as he had already learned, not every Jew interpreted their tradition this way. But Heschel did. And he believed that he was on the right side of the debate. Later in the evening, there was an intense interfaith service at the Presbyterian Church. The Reverend Malcolm Boyd, an Episcopalian, opened with meditations about the war, as a younger man beside him played the guitar and said in a calm, soft voice, "Doing my sitting-up exercises—one, two, three—the sirens are screaming—four, five, six—will the bombs come closer?—seven, eight, nine." Boyd spoke about how Vietcong prisoners were being tortured and forced to drink their own urine, and he made comparisons to Auschwitz.

Then Heschel took the lectern and recited to the protesters, "The Lord roars like a lion, His word is like fire, like a hammer breaking rocks to pieces, and people go shout unmoved, undisturbed, unaware." He condemned Americans for practicing a politics that had become divorced from morality, in which power was the main concern rather than the sanctity of life. According to Heschel, "The war in Vietnam is a war against America. A pestilence stalks in the darkness, infecting our minds. The war in Vietnam is a disease, the result of a disease. A nation so rich in the appreciation of human dignity, in generosity and compassion, is destroying its own integrity in order to perform a game of power in the theater of absurdity." Citing Isaiah (21:11), Heschel said, "It is midnight in the world; and our cry turns to God, 'Watchman, what of the night? Watchman, what of the night?'" Asking if it was still possible to reverse the situation given the "gigantic forces" set into action, he assured his fellow travelers that "our protests have not been in vain. Yet our protests have certainly been far from adequate. In the face of this revolting war, no one has a right merely to shake his head or to shrug his shoulder. We must neither yield nor relent. We must not seek refuge in personal dissent. We must endeavor to reach the hearts of all Americans. . . . America

faces the question: what stands higher, human pride or human life? May we all accept the biblical answer: choose life!"[110]

On the second day of the mobilization, 6 February, CALCAV gathered at Arlington National Cemetery. Over forty buses of protesters arrived early on a crisp winter morning. The clergy was not deterred by the ruling of the Military District of Washington, which prohibited CALCAV from holding a full rally and service on the grounds that the ceremony would be too political; Fernandez believed that the decision was discriminatory and without foundation.[111] The court did, however, allow them to conduct a silent prayer vigil.

CALCAV made the most of it. Heschel walked alongside King in front of twenty-five hundred protesters in a "procession of agony."[112] Other leaders present included Rabbi Everett Gendler, a progressive rabbi at the Jewish Center in Princeton, New Jersey, who had helped connect King to civil rights leaders; Andrew Young; the Catholic bishop James Shannon; and Rabbi Maurice Eisendrath, who carried a Torah. Carrying little American flags that CALCAV had distributed, the protesters walked in somber silence until Heschel and King reached the steps in front of the Tomb of the Unknown Soldier. When the marchers settled into their places, King called out, "In this period of absolute silence, let us pray." "We prayed and waited for our leaders and never spoke," noted Edward Kaplan, the doctoral student who had been in Washington in 1966 and who kept diaries of his experience. "Nor was such a silence more powerful: we challenged the powers of the world, we engulfed all wars and took them into our personal meditation, we loved those wars, and we were embarrassed, we loved the soldiers; and we were sad, and we thought that God was in that tomb. Around us time continued and we were small."[113]

After six minutes of participants contemplating the war, Heschel broke the silence by reading out loud in Hebrew from Psalm 22 ("My Lord, My Lord, why hast Thou Forsaken me?").

This was a psalm traditionally understood to be a cry of supreme anguish that was chanted when a person appealed to a head of state. Christians considered the cry to be the final words uttered by Jesus Christ. Bishop Shannon followed Heschel by saying, "Let us go in peace. Amen."[114] They marched for half a mile. The protesters returned to the church, where King closed out the day by speaking about the moral collapse of America and the despair African Americans felt as money went to kill Vietnamese rather than help cities.

The protests drew massive media attention. In all the nation's newspapers, Heschel was pictured standing next to King in Arlington, wearing a long, black overcoat and his beanie, gripping his flag as the two men stood in front of the tomb. Although many clergy had traditionally backed away from political participation, this meeting was evidence that large numbers of them were eager to be involved.

The Yiddish press was livid about Heschel's choice of prayer. Heschel also had to defend himself from Orthodox critics who were deeply upset that he stood beside Rabbi Eisendrath as he carried a Torah in a cemetery, an act they decried as a violation of Jewish law. Heschel, who had initially opposed the plan, defended it on halakhic grounds. Others were mad on political grounds. Wolfe Kelman, still a good friend of Heschel's who had once helped introduce him to King, now cosigned a letter published in the *New York Times* with other JTS colleagues criticizing their protests about the military and warning that their words could "serve the Communist cause well."[115]

The criticism coming from the Jewish community couldn't overshadow the elation Heschel felt about being part of a burgeoning movement which was enjoying political success. The 1968 presidential primaries were under way, and, on 12 March, Eugene McCarthy, the Minnesota senator who championed the opposition to the Vietnam War, shocked the Democratic establishment with a strong second-place finish in the New

Hampshire primary, revealing how much the conflict had weakened Johnson's electoral standing. A few days later, Senator Robert Kennedy of New York, who had also said the war could not be won, joined the race as well. Public support for the conflagration kept falling. There were protests breaking out all around the globe. Almost ten thousand young Britons rallied in Trafalgar Square on 17 March and then marched to the U.S. embassy.

The relationship between religion and activism worked both ways for Heschel. It was not just that religion informed his understanding of social justice, moving him deeper into the world of protest, but that the pursuit of social justice shaped his understanding of religion. He had come to see that achieving piety, as outlined in his writing from the 1950s, was difficult if not impossible given the conditions of the world. During one protest, Heschel confessed to a reporter, "Whenever I open my prayer book I see before me images of children burning from napalm."[116] Heschel was always throwing out new ideas, no matter how unrealistic. He thought CALCAV should propose that U.S. presidents appoint a Secretary of Morality (the idea didn't get far) and that members of their organization should relinquish their salaries every other week to help fund the antiwar movement.[117] It was becoming increasingly difficult to discern the lines that separated his understanding of prayer and ritual from his work on the streets. In a 1970 article for *Conservative Judaism*, Heschel wrote, "Prayer is meaningless unless it is subversive, unless it seeks to overthrow and ruin the pyramids of callousness, hatred, opportunism, falsehoods. The liturgical movement must become a revolutionary movement, seeking to overthrow the forces that continue to destroy the promise, the hope, the vision. The world is aflame with evil and atrocity; the scandal of perpetual desecration of the world cries to high heaven."[118]

His commitment to peace was sometimes incompatible

with the desire of rabbinical students who wanted to avoid serving in the military. When peace-oriented students asked for his help to obtain conscientious objector status so as to avoid having to be part of the military chaplaincy, he pointed to letters on his desk from active soldiers seeking counsel.[119] At one point, a sizable number of students in the Class of 1968, one of the largest cohorts ever in the history of JTS, were protesting the requirement that after ordination everyone had to volunteer as a military chaplain before they could join the Rabbinical Assembly. Given the geopolitical situation, they were telling the administration they would refuse to legitimate the war by serving. Not knowing what to do, the administration turned to Heschel, whose impeccable antiwar credentials would give his words weight unlike anyone else. Packed into the Green Room, where admission interviews took place, Heschel delivered a rousing talk in which he insisted that everyone in attendance had an obligation to volunteer as long as Jewish soldiers were in the theater of conflict. He comforted them by saying that being a military chaplain did not indicate supporting the immoral war.[120]

Heschel's close relationship to King—memorialized in the famous photos from Selma and Arlington—was becoming a symbol of the Jewish–African American progressive alliance in the 1960s. Even as tensions rose between the African American activists and Jewish liberals over Israel, the deep connection between King and Heschel never dissipated. Heschel downplayed the severity of the friction between their respective communities, emphasizing instead the points of commonality. King attended the Rabbinical Assembly convention at the Concord Hotel in upstate New York for a belated celebration of Heschel's sixtieth birthday on 25 March. When King entered the auditorium, the rabbis rose and linked arms as they chanted "We Shall Overcome" in Hebrew.[121] Heschel introduced his friend by asking, "Where in America do we hear a voice like

the voice of the prophets of Israel? Martin Luther King is a sign that God has not forsaken the United States of America. His presence is the hope of America." King returned the compliment by praising his activism for civil rights, Soviet Jewry, and Vietnam and by expressing support for Israel. He called it an honor "[to] be here on the occasion of the sixtieth birthday of a man that I consider one of the truly great men of our day and age . . . one of the persons who is relevant at all times, always standing with prophetic insights to guide us through these difficult days." King told the rabbis that Heschel had been an inspiration to "clergymen of all the religious faiths of our country . . . [one of the] truly great men of our day and age . . . indeed a truly great prophet."[122]

Ten days later, James Earl Ray shot and killed King as he stood on the balcony of his second-story room at the Lorraine Motel in Memphis, Tennessee. King was in Memphis for his Poor People's Campaign. African Americans expressed sorrow and fury about the slain leader. In several cities, including Washington, African Americans protested on the streets, and some became violent. Heschel was devastated by the loss of his good friend and also by the general climate of the country. The riots saddened him. "The assassination of Martin Luther King has served awesome notice on Americans," he noted. "This is no longer the struggle between black and white, between oppressed and oppressor, between rich and poor, but the more terrifying opposition of spiritual love and hate. The death of Dr. King and the deaths that may occur as a result of this event cannot be seen as destruction of human life but as an omen of the extinction of the human soul."[123]

Coretta Scott King invited Heschel to participate in the funeral procession. He flew down to Atlanta with Sylvia and his friend Rabbi Seymour Siegel. They attended both services, the first at Ebenezer Baptist Church and the second at Morehouse College. At Morehouse, Heschel read a passage from the Old

Testament: "He was despised and rejected by men; A man of sorrows, and acquainted with grief; and as one from whom men hid their faces. He was despised, and we esteemed him not."[124] Four days after King's death, CALCAV organized a three-day fast for peace in his honor.[125] Calling these days a national emergency for all faiths, CALCAV announced, "We hope that each individual will manifest this concern in a manner in keeping with the disciplines of faith. We have witnessed the moral erosion in this country and abroad as a result of the war in Vietnam. We deplore the racial crisis among our people and the moral degradation which led to the death of Martin Luther King and we mourn the passing of this great soul."[126] Heschel also honored his friend by serving as the vice-chairman of Operation Connection, an interfaith group of Protestant, Catholic, and Jewish leaders that was part of the Poor People's Campaign. King's final campaign before his death, it had focused on ending economic inequality for all races.[127] Operation Connection sought to raise $10 million for housing, health, job training, and poverty programs.

On 31 March 1968, days before King's assassination, President Johnson had shocked the nation by announcing that he would not run for reelection, a decision that pleased antiwar activists, who preferred McCarthy or Kennedy. "It represents a victory of America. Period," Heschel declared.[128] But McCarthy could not keep up with the party's appointed replacement, Vice President Hubert Humphrey, who stood by the administration's positions. On 6 June, Robert Kennedy, who had been gaining momentum in the primaries, was assassinated at the Ambassador Hotel in Los Angeles, where Heschel had spoken the previous year. Sirhan Sirhan, the man who shot Kennedy, was a Palestinian from Jordan who disagreed with the senator's strong support for Israel. America, it appeared, was unraveling at the seams.

The divisions within the Democratic Party were on full dis-

play at the 1968 convention in Chicago. When violence spilled out onto the streets as police clashed with antiwar activists, the party seemed to be collapsing under the weight of bitter infighting between antiwar forces and Democratic leaders. Humphrey said he could smell the smoke from the tear gas rising up past his hotel window. The year ended with Humphrey losing to former vice president Richard Nixon. The Republican nominee ran on a vague platform that vowed to bring an end to the Vietnam War, to impose law and order in the cities, and to contain federal spending. As much as they had come to despise Johnson and Humphrey, many on the Left saw Nixon as a vicious, untrustworthy, red-baiting politician. Heschel had been one of the cosigners of a CALCAV statement supporting Humphrey and denouncing Nixon as an "intransigent believer in the cold war in both Europe and Asia."[129] Heschel felt a certain level of despondency with what he saw, pondering the outcome. "We stand at the brink of the abyss. A nuclear holocaust is a possibility," he wrote in his notes. "The surrender of freedom to demagogues is a likelihood. The possibility of total disaster and the insecurity of freedom are a situation which calls for radical decisions. What is the truth man faces in examining his life within society? Is it against our own nature to live in peace with one another?"[130]

The antiwar movement was massive by the time President Nixon started his term. Heschel was one player among thousands of activists, religious and otherwise, who kept taking to the streets as the government refused to change its ways. Tactical moderation lost its appeal, which was evident in early February, soon after Nixon's inauguration, at the third national CALCAV mobilization. The shift in tone among the clergy was evident as CALCAV now emphasized its support for amnesty to draft resisters as much as they called for ending the war. When asked about university students who shut down administration buildings and disrupted campuses, Heschel said, "They are pro-

testing the hypocrisy and mendacity of our government."[131] "We feel that no one should be penalized simply because his eyes were opened after entering the military service," he said.[132]

There was no longer much daylight separating Heschel from the rest of the movement. By the time Nixon took office, there was broad opposition to the military operations being carried out in Vietnam. There were rallies against Nixon on the weekend he took the oath of office. Demonstrations continued to sprout up on campuses and in cities. Antiwar activism was a familiar part of the national conversation, with images and voices from the movement appearing constantly in the news and throughout popular culture. Many families, even high-level of-ficials in Washington, had young antiwar activists in their homes. And Heschel's opposition, grounded in a theological under-standing of the situation, led him to continue speaking in fiery rhetoric that elevated the stakes of what the president would do. Yet he and his allies still believed that their background as religious leaders would bolster support for the movement as increasingly radical voices took center stage with chants like "One Side's Right, One Side's Wrong, Victory to the Viet Cong."

The CALCAV protests started at the Metropolitan A.M.E. Church. Standing on the stage with the congressional antiwar Democratic senator George McGovern, Heschel spoke about the need to forgive draft resisters: "If Americans cannot forgive those who objected to the war, then it destroys the bridge over which it must pass herself—to receive forgiveness from those who are victims of this war. 'Thou shalt not bear a grudge against the children of your people.' (Lev. 19)."[133] CALCAV now sounded much more radical than it had at its founding. The national committee released a position paper which was bolder than any of their earlier proclamations, raising questions not only about Vietnam but also about the Cold War, including in areas like Central America. They called for more spending on economic assistance to poor nations and transferring military funds to

domestic programs. Besides amnesty, CALCAV endorsed eliminating the draft and compensating Black citizens who had been harmed because of the costs they bore from the U.S. fighting.[134]

Heschel did not mince words when the clergy, joined by Coretta King, met with National Security Advisor Henry Kissinger for forty minutes. The encounter was extraordinarily frustrating. Heschel didn't discern any serious indications that the administration was planning to change course. Just as he had done in his meeting with Secretary McNamara, Heschel lashed out. This time was different: his message was more personal as he was speaking to a fellow Jew. As Kissinger complained about how hard it was to change policy given the thick bureaucracies, Heschel stopped him to ask: "How could you as a good Jew prosecute a war like this?" Kissinger didn't offer much of a response. Richard Fernandez remembered that the presidential advisor was "tongue-tied" and just "muttered something." Heschel's question, he said, "was the show-stopper."[135] Kissinger, who fled from Germany in 1938, had taken a different lesson from his firsthand encounter with Nazis. The tragedy Jews experienced made him feel committed to a foreign policy based on realism and to the balance of power as a way to defend national interests and democracy. He came away from the 1940s fearful of any politician who spoke in rigid moralistic or ideological tropes. For Heschel, the lesson was the opposite. He said that continuing to bomb Vietnam would make their country "more and more like Nazi Germany." The clergy said that the administration should grant amnesty to the hundreds of draft resisters who were in prison merely for their legitimate acts of conscience.[136] With six hundred dead and forty-one hundred wounded since Nixon's inauguration (and eight hundred Vietnamese killed), the time for courtesy toward the new administration was officially over: "We fear the time is approaching, Mr. President, when we must declare your Administration accountable for the continued suffering and death in Vietnam."[137]

Relations with Democrats were tense as well. In early June 1969, CALCAV sent a questionnaire to senators. Thomas Dodd of Connecticut, a Democrat who supported the war, responded with a letter saying that the document "gives the further impression that the members of your organization have no negative feelings about Communist tyranny and consider Communism preferable to the form of government that today exists in South Vietnam." Making it clear that CALCAV opposed any "tyranny, be it fascist or Communist," Heschel responded that a majority of his organization "feel that the acts our own government are carrying out in Vietnam are far from helpful in turning back Communism in that country." He added that the South Vietnamese government allowed for the antithesis of the political freedom the United States promised civilians trapped in the carnage. "The fact that Americans continue to die by the hundreds each week in Vietnam in support of a regime that suppresses freedom and dissent among its own people causes us great agony."[138]

Over the next few years, Heschel started to lose confidence in the entire political system. He was deeply saddened at the funeral of Jeffrey Glenn Miller, a Jewish boy from New York who was one of the students killed by the National Guard at Kent State University in May 1970 during protests against Nixon, who had been secretly sending troops into Cambodia after he said he was drawing down the operations in Southeast Asia.[139] The tragic deaths of these students ignited a new wave of antiwar protest on campuses all over the country by creating a feeling on the Left that the conflict was moving in the wrong direction. During an interview with Frank Reynolds on ABC Television on Sunday, 21 November 1971, Heschel voiced his frustration that the war raged on despite the work of the movement. "We are callous to this very day, and to this very day the American air force is bombing certain cities in Southeast Asia. Undoubtedly innocent victims suffer from it and we are indif-

ferent. The war in Vietnam," Heschel said, "had become, to me, the greatest religious issue." The process of war depended on dehumanization, and when dehumanization increased, "religion is gone."[140]

One thing that Heschel never lost was his faith in the power of protest. "Faith and dissent," Heschel argued, were Judaism's "two essential ingredients." As he explained to the National Federation of Jewish Men's Clubs, "Judaism in its very essence came into being as an act of dissent, of dissent from paganism, as an act of non-conformity with the surrounding culture." The "greatness of the prophets," Heschel added, "was in their ability to voice dissent and disagreement not only with the beliefs of their pagan neighbors, but also with the cherished values and habits of their own people."[141] He was heartened by the fact that a broader range of rabbis was joining him in this cause. Irving Greenberg, a Brooklyn-born Orthodox rabbi who was a protégé of Rabbi Soloveitchik and received a doctoral degree in history at Harvard University, had taken a stand against the nation's operations in Vietnam. While helping to build a vibrant Modern Orthodox community in Riverdale, NY, Greenberg, who had been active in the campaign for Soviet Jewry, emerged as a vocal opponent of the war. On 7 May 1970, the thirty-six-year-old rabbi appeared alongside John Bennett and Bishop John Dougherty, the president of Seton Hall University, before the Senate Foreign Relations Committee. Substituting for Heschel, who was dealing with health issues, Greenberg warned the committee that when it came to political leadership "there is such a great gap between what ought to be and what actually is." The media images from the war, he said, were a "moral disaster."[142]

But Heschel was an "optimist against my better judgement," as he once said. The rabbi never stopped urging others to be active in civic life. A young undergraduate at the University of Pennsylvania, Arnold Eisen, visited Heschel in New

York for an interview with the theologian whose work had been influential as he wrestled with the limits of organized religion. Eisen, who as a high school student had felt that *God in Search of Man* perfectly captured the boredom of his synagogue, had covered Heschel's talk on campus and wanted to follow up with more questions. Exuding the skepticism of a nineteen-year-old, Eisen asked Heschel what made him think that his religiously inspired activism was making any difference given the never-ending turmoil at home and in Vietnam. Heschel, sitting in the middle of the teetering stacks of books that blanketed the entire room, responded by saying that the Jewish tradition not only gave him the right to speak out but also the obligation to do so.[143]

By this point, Heschel had become something of a celebrity. When he traveled to Rome in 1971, Heschel received an audience with Pope Paul VI on 17 March. He and Sylvia were treated like dignitaries. The pope, according to Heschel's notes, greeted them smiling "joyously, with a radiant face." He started the discussion by telling Heschel that he was reading his works, which were "spiritual and very beautiful, and that Catholics should read my books." The pope praised Heschel for the impact his work was having in "help[ing] young people understand religion."[144] At the JTS Heschel developed a devout following among a growing number of rabbinical students who were finally flocking to his courses, including one on Hasidism, which he had not been given permission to teach until the late 1960s. These future synagogue leaders were seeking from Heschel the kind of unique spiritual inspiration they saw him provide on the public stage.

Heschel no longer felt any restraint and fully immersed himself in partisan politics. During Nixon's reelection campaign in 1972, Heschel endorsed Senator George McGovern.[145] He wrote a letter to the *New York Times* claiming that the Jewish tradition inevitably pointed to a McGovern presidency:

"If the prophets Isaiah and Amos were to appear in our midst, would they accept the corruption in high places, the indifferent way in which the sick, the poor and the old are treated? Would they condone the indifference to gun control legislation that has allowed some of the finest of our national leaders to be shot dead? Would they not be standing amidst those who protest against the violence of the war in Vietnam, the decay in our cities, the hypocrisy and falsehood that surround our present administration, even at the highest level?"[146] Heschel cosigned a letter from businessmen, law school faculty, and religious leaders addressed to President Nixon that appeared in the *New York Times* on 29 October, two Sundays before the election, proclaiming, "We are increasingly disturbed that you have not yet answered recent allegations of illegal and unethical activities involving your Re-election Committee, high White House officials and former cabinet officials." Claiming that the issue went beyond party politics, the letter stated, "The charges of political espionage and sabotage—of a nature and degree unprecedented in our history—have been reported in detail by several of the nation's most responsible publications. Such charges go to the heart of the democratic process."[147]

Heschel also sparred with Jewish leaders who were becoming concerned about relations with African Americans. In 1968, when anti-Semitic comments were made during a clash between the largely African American Ocean-Hill Brownsville school board in Brooklyn and the heavily Jewish United Federation of Teachers in New York (similar kinds of clashes were taking place in other communities), Heschel stood firm behind the alliance to which he and King were so committed. Speaking at Temple Neve Shalom in Metuchen, NJ, Heschel warned against "overreacting to recent anti-Semitic statements." As he sipped tea and smoked a cigar in a study near the auditorium where a large crowd awaited him, Heschel explained to a reporter, "We must see anti-Semitism in perspective and realize that a great

many of the anti-Semitic comments that have been made in the past few weeks have been made only by a few. Anti-Semitism is not a problem that will destroy America."[148] When leaders of the Black Power movement, a radical faction of the civil rights movement that emphasized self-determination, racial pride, and self-defense, expressed fierce criticism of Israel and turned away from interracial alliances in the early 1970s on principle, Heschel told the Anti-Defamation League that Jews could not withdraw from the pursuit of racial justice. More than any other group, Heschel said, Jews who had been so "despised" needed to be sympathetic to the pain behind the anger. While denouncing the Black Power agenda as a "desecration of the Negro cause," Heschel implored his colleagues to understand that "blacks are speaking out of their agony and despair."[149] He was not alone. For a time, many Jewish leaders had expressed support for the ideas of the Black Power movement, acknowledging that the experiences of Jews and African Americans were fundamentally different and endorsing the basic principles of figures such as Stokely Carmichael.[150]

The excitement more students at JTS were feeling about Heschel as a figurehead in the Jewish community was captured when *Time* published a cover story titled "What It Means to Be Jewish" in 1972. The authors looked at the different varieties of Judaism that had taken hold. Heschel was described as the "godfather and poet" of the school of thought that argued faith was essential to a healthy community. "For Heschel . . . Judaism is 'the track of God in the wilderness of oblivion.'" They discussed the "mystical piety" that animated his work, inherited from the Hasidic culture, that was unexpectedly proving to be attractive to a new generation of younger Jews who desired a deeper experience than what they felt to be the hollowed out core of the middle-class, suburban synagogue.[151]

After years of activism and decades of protest, Heschel never abandoned his scholarship as a theologian. As he had

done in *The Earth Is the Lord's*, he strove to expose Jewish readers to the Hasidic spiritual traditions from Eastern Europe in the early twentieth century as a way to reconnect with their origins. "Since I came to America," he had explained to a Yiddish newspaper a few years earlier, "I keep speaking about Eastern European Jewry, and not forgetting the source, the crown of Jewry, is the primary task for American Jewry. With certain exceptions, American Jews have made great efforts to forget their roots. . . . This is the main tragedy of our generation. How can we expect the tree to bloom without roots?"[152] Returning to his writing about rabbinic traditions, but now in the context of a decade spent struggling for social justice in the lived world, Heschel completed two book projects—one written in English, *A Passion for Truth*, and another in Yiddish, *Kotsk: In gerangl far emesdikayt* (Kotzk: A Struggle for Integrity), about the Kotzker Rebbe Menachem Mendl Morgenstern. Both were published the year he died. In these works, he gave readers the deepest autobiographical portrait of his background in Warsaw and the struggles he had faced.

A Passion for Truth explored the dual influence of the Baal Shem Tov and Kotzker on his thinking. He compared Kotzker to his contemporary, the philosopher Kierkegaard, who was of Christian origins, as both were "outsiders, anguished by the moral and spiritual predicament of societies satisfied with their own stability." Faith required an individual to continually search for truth rather than simply adhering to doctrine or believing in God. The difference between the two of them, Heschel wrote, was that "for Kierkegaard the primary fact attendant upon man's existence was his disengagement from God and his consciousness of it. The Kotzker, on the other hand, considered the disengagement a contingency rather than a necessity, rooted in the absolute difference between man and God."[153]

Although most observers believed the two men to be opposites, Heschel perceived commonality by focusing less on

formal theological doctrine than on "depth-theology," the "moments, battles, situations rather than doctrines or belief; confrontations of the conscience with God rather than summaries of theology; involvements and appropriations rather than rituals. . . . In short, this study will deal with self-reflection rather than speculation." According to Heschel, Kotzker insisted that "truth is inwardness, inwardness is authenticity, and authenticity is attained through intense, passionate inner action. Only integrity can save man and his faith."[154] Heschel believed that Kotzker was more vital than ever. Mainstream Jewish theology in the twentieth century had become too focused on dogma, which he categorized as the content of believing as opposed to the act of believing. He saw immense value in Kotzker's insistence on self-sacrifice. "Jewry today," Heschel wrote, "continues to be satisfied with banal and bloodless customs and ceremonies . . . many popular and glittering expositions of Judaism are easily unmasked as façade, lacking in substance."[155]

With his focus on depth-theology, Heschel attempted to blend the philosophies of the two men, seeking to reconcile the internal, lifelong tensions that he felt between exultation and despair—stemming back to his own learning in Warsaw from the Baal Shem Tov and Kotzker. As he reflected: "Life in our time has been a nightmare for many of us, tranquility an interlude, happiness a fake. Who could breathe at a time when man was engaged in murdering the holy witness to God six million times?" Heschel continued: "And yet God does not need those who praise Him when in a state of euphoria. He needs those who are in love with Him when in distress, both He and ourselves. This is the task: in the darkest night to be certain of the dawn, certain of the power to turn a curse into a blessing, agony into song. To know the monster's rage and, in spite of it, proclaim to its face (even a monster will be transfigured into an angel); to go through Hell and to continue to trust the goodness of God—this is the challenge and the way."[156]

Heschel admired Kotzker's fear of human cruelty and his "obsessive preoccupation" with falsehood. Although Kotzker had not been alive during the 1940s, Heschel argued that he would not have been surprised by the Nazis: "Indeed, when human beings establish a *modus vivendi* on the basis of mendacity, the world can turn into a nightmare. . . . For the Holocaust did not take place suddenly. It was in the making for several generations. It had its origin in a lie: that the Jew was responsible for all social ills, for all personal frustrations. Decimate the Jews and all problems would be solved."[157]

Throughout the work, it was clear that Heschel saw clear lines between himself and Kotzker. It was often impossible to discern the difference between the two men. "The Kotzker did not negate the validity of logical or rational thought," he wrote, reflecting on the kind of debates that consumed him at JTS. "He insisted upon diligent study of the Talmud and was himself an admired master of dialectics. He cherished the kind of reasoning cultivated by Talmud study as indispensable to spiritual catharsis."[158] According to Heschel, who had angered so many colleagues over the course of his career with his ongoing calls for social justice and spirituality, "Antisocial, shocking, an enemy to all established convention and propriety, the Kotzker continually and relentlessly attacked the soft spots in man's self-image, pointing up the difference between candor and pretense, authenticity and sham."[159]

Heschel, who had a nearly fatal heart attack and hepatitis in 1969, was suffering physically in 1972. He was working at a frenetic schedule. The medicines that his physician had put him on were taking a heavy toll.[160] When a colleague at JTS, Yohanan Muffs, urged him to enjoy time off and see films, Heschel agreed only to read Mario Puzo's novel *The Godfather*, but would not spare the time to see the hit movie in the theater.[161] He still felt that Broadway shows, though he occasionally went with his family, were a waste of time. In the third week of Decem-

ber, Heschel called Elie Wiesel and asked if he could come see him at JTS. Sensing anguish in his voice, Wiesel immediately left a conference, jumped into a taxi, and went to meet the rabbi. When he arrived at his office at the seminary, "Heschel opened his door and, without saying a word, leaned his head on my shoulder and began to sob like a child. Rarely have I seen an adult cry like that." Before he left, Wiesel noticed that Heschel's desk, ordinarily a mess, had been cleaned.[162]

Heschel's end was drawing near. A few days before the Christmas holiday, he joined in a conference call with other religious leaders about how they should respond to the carpet bombing of Vietnam, a massive and brutal bombing attack—the Christmas Bombings, as they would be called—to force the North Vietnamese into submission. According to one rabbinic colleague who met with him after the call, Heschel was "distressed, frustrated, immensely sad."[163] On the morning of 20 December, Heschel went to a rally to welcome Reverend Philip Berrigan on his release from a thirty-nine-month sentence in a Danbury, Connecticut, prison for having destroyed draft records. One of the first people to speak when Berrigan exited, the rabbi grabbed the freed prisoner, who was much taller than he was, by the lapels and looked at him lovingly straight in the eyes.[164] "God bless you and give you peace and peace in Vietnam," Heschel said to his friend.[165] He invited the two Berrigan brothers to come have tea at his apartment the following Saturday afternoon.[166]

The teatime never came to pass. On Friday night, 22 December, a frigid winter evening, the Heschel family celebrated the Sabbath in their New York apartment. Susannah was back for winter break after her first semester at Trinity College. A number of guests came over. After they finished the dinner, the guests went home. The family went to sleep, but Heschel never woke up. During the night, he suffered a fatal heart attack.

More than five hundred people, including Mayor John

Lindsay, packed into the memorial service at the Park West Memorial Chapel on 79th Street. In the little room where the coffin was located, a group of Hasidic rabbis chanted the Psalms.[167] Susannah, in what one reporter characterized as a "trembling voice," recited from the Book of Chronicles: "And thou, Solomon, My son, know thou the God of thy father, and serve Him with a whole heart and willing mind."[168] Wiesel read a Yiddish poem that Heschel had written in the 1930s, entitled "God Follows Me Everywhere." Kelman called his friend a "voice who spoke for the downtrodden and who felt their pain" before reading directly from Heschel's own words. He ended his talk with a line from *Man Is Not Alone:* "For the pious man it is a privilege to die."[169]

7

Legacy

On Sunday afternoon, 4 February 1973, shortly after his death, Americans caught one last glimpse of Heschel. Just a few days after the U.S. entered into the Paris Peace Accords, which brought a cease fire in Vietnam and finally ended America's direct involvement in the conflict, NBC Television broadcast an episode of *The Eternal Light* featuring a posthumous conversation between him and Carl Stern, a news correspondent. It was a fitting way to mourn the rabbi, on a television show that Louis Finkelstein had launched to promote Judaism. Taped ten days before Heschel's death, Stern had asked a wide-ranging series of questions about how the rabbi reconciled his optimistic religious beliefs with the dark times. Stern explored how one could keep faith amidst so much tragedy like King's assassination. Heschel returned to his familiar answer: People don't pray to be saved but pray so that they would be "worthy of being saved." Taking a broad perspective of Heschel's life as a scholar and activist, Stern

wanted to know how his guest rectified the persistence of injustice and violence with everything that he had worked for and believed in. Heschel admitted, "We are not in the midst of an automatic progressive development of humanity, there are ups and downs. At this very moment, there is a down. . . . There is a renewal of prejudice, which is a poison." When Stern pointed to the critics who argued that religion and politics should be kept separate, Heschel returned to the Hebrew Prophets, who, had they been alive in 1972, would surely have been imprisoned. "And frankly," Heschel said, somewhat in jest, "I would say that God seems to be a non-religious person. . . . He always mixes in politics with his social issues." In an era defined by self-interest, the purpose of religion was not to seek God's salvation but to offer human beings a source of moral purpose. Living a pious existence guided individuals toward achieving a better life. "Needs are unreliable as a standard," he warned. Should man follow the false advertised needs of commerce, striving to own color televisions and a summer home? he asked. "Religion," Heschel said to Stern as he raised his right index finger in the air with dramatic flair, "says no! Man's distinction is to live by ends and for ends and goals, and not only satisfy needs." The interview concluded with Heschel delivering a poignant message to young people: "Let them remember that there is a meaning beyond absurdity. Let them be sure that every little deed counts. That every word has power, and that we can, everyone, do our share to redeem the world in spite of all absurdities and all frustrations and all disappointments. And above all, remember that the meaning of life is to build life as if it were a work of art. You are not a machine. And you are young. Start working on this great work of art called your own existence."[1]

Redeem the world: this was a concept that shaped Heschel's life. From his childhood in Warsaw hearing stories of the Baal Shem Tov to his professional maturation in New York writing about God and Man, Heschel developed an understanding of the universe in which piety enabled individuals to hear God's

voice and for God to find them. Genuine piety should guide an individual, Heschel came to believe by the 1960s, toward devoting themselves to the grassroots struggle for a just world. "A Jew is asked to take a leap of action rather than a leap of thought," he famously stated. "He is asked to do more than he understands in order to understand more than he does." When the "Militant Mystic," as *Time* magazine called him, felt the "constraints of injustice, he was not to be found in Manhattan's Jewish Theological Seminary where he taught, but on the front lines where he marched."[2] The *Washington Post* eulogized Heschel as "an influential figure in American religious life" who believed in a religion "that permeated man's entire life and in a theology that formed the basis for forthright stands on such issues of his time as racism, the Middle East, and the Vietnam war."[3] Shaped by the hardship of Eastern European Jewry in the early twentieth century as well as the devastation of the Holocaust, Heschel never lost faith in the power of a religious life to provide moral order within a dangerous world. Long after his death, Heschel came to symbolize a generation of Jews who in the aftermath of Nazi Germany understood from their religiosity the urgent imperative of improving the world.

In his lifetime, Heschel helped to carve out space for progressive religious voices on the national and international stage even as conservative forces tried to claim the church and synagogue for themselves. Clergy and intellectuals, as well as religious organizations and church associations, were integral to the leftward movements that swept through the country. Though a majority of activists were secular or atheistic, as they had been in much of the twentieth century, there was a notable group of rabbis and ministers taking to the streets who were deeply embedded in their theological traditions. At a memorial service for Heschel at the prestigious Park Avenue Synagogue in New York, Coretta Scott King called her husband's friend "one of the great men of our times." "In a day," she added, "when we

have a would-be emperor and king [Nixon] we will miss the voice of Rabbi Heschel just as we have missed the voice of Dr. Martin Luther King."[4] It was not simply that Heschel joined King on the front lines at Selma in March 1965, but that he fought against oppression wherever he saw it. As one eulogist offered, "He very publicly marched to Selma, very publicly protested the Vietnam War, very publicly protested the condition of Jews in Russia." His words and deeds had touched people all over the world, including the future president of the United States Jimmy Carter.[5]

Heschel spent an entire career laying claim through his writing and activism that being a pious Jew meant to adhere to tradition, to open oneself to God, and to devote one's entire being to pursuing social justice in the here and now. While many Jews didn't accept the last leg of this trifecta, which became as relevant to him as the other elements of his theology, Heschel's contributions established an archetype for those who did see religion—Judaism and other faiths—in this light.

Just as Heschel passed, so too did the world where progressive piety had come to gain a serious foothold in American political culture. Heschel gradually seemed like a relic from a bygone era. By the time Ronald Reagan, a conservative Republican, was elected president in 1980, the Moral Majority had come to signify the influence of religion in American politics. The niche that progressive clergy had been carving out during the divisive battles over civil rights and Vietnam in the 1960s quickly narrowed. One side of the religious–political relationship came to dominate the public square. The founder of the Moral Majority, the televangelist Jerry Falwell, and other preachers mobilized their congregations from the pews, on radio, and on television, arguing that the logic of faith inevitably pointed toward a right-wing agenda of tax cuts, minimal government, restriction of reproductive rights, and cultural conservatism. Falwell, who in 1964 had criticized ministers involved in the civil rights

movement for being too political, made a 180-degree turn six-
teen years later. "As a preacher of the Gospel, I not only believe
in prayer and preaching, I also believe in good citizenship. If a
labor union in America has the right to organize and improve
its working conditions, then I believe that the churches and the
pastors, the priests, and the rabbis of America have a responsi-
bility, not just the right, to see to it that the moral climate and
conscience of Americans is such that this nation can be healed
inwardly." His targets were "the Equal Rights Amendment, the
feminist revolution and the homosexual revolution." Conser-
vative religious voters—Evangelicals, Catholics, Protestants,
and others—stood as a vital block in the new Republican coali-
tion and were devoted to the party even when President Rea-
gan and other elected officials disappointed them. With each
election, conservative pastors and congregants were certain to
cast their ballots for the Grand Old Party. The neoconservative
Jewish intellectuals Norman Podhoretz and Irving Kristol fo-
cused on the ways that government programs produced unin-
tended consequences and how the social movements of the 1960s
had allegedly become far too extremist. They complained about
what they believed to be a growing number of anti-Semitic
voices on the Left. Tensions over Israeli policy toward the West
Bank, Gaza, and East Jerusalem after the 1967 and 1973 wars led
numerous Jews, some of whom were otherwise liberal, to break
with allied organizations that they believed were unjustifiably
hostile toward Israel. Neoconservatives championed a muscu-
lar foreign policy agenda that many Democratic leaders were
unwilling to embrace in the aftermath of Vietnam.

Had he lived, Heschel would have found himself on the
margins of this rightward-leaning country. To be sure, a few pro-
gressive religious clergy were relevant. They joined the fight
against U.S. policies in Central America and the nuclear freeze
movement. But these leaders, though present and active, didn't
receive nearly the same amount of attention in the press as

Heschel nor could they claim comparable political power. Their influence was nothing like the window that had opened up in the Age of Aquarius, when someone like Heschel found himself meeting with presidents and legislators as well as receiving front-page newspaper coverage. According to Rabbi Jill Jacobs, the executive director of T'ruah, a progressive rabbinic association committed to human rights, "Public religious space has largely been claimed by the Christian right. Those who speak from a religious standpoint are assumed to care most about banning abortion and limiting the rights of gays and lesbians. . . . [M]any progressives worry that speaking from our own religious tradition will lead to a debate about which religion has the better claim to truth, or will unwittingly legitimatize others who claim to know God's political preferences."[6]

None of this meant that progressive Judaism disappeared. The Black Power movement, as one historian discovered, generated interest among Jews in their own efforts to nurture identity—from creating summer camps to supporting Israel—and organize Jewish-based activism. These shared values kept them in a common alliance with African Americans who valued group-based identity politics.[7] In the realm of partisan politics, a majority of American Jews continued to vote Democratic. The best that any Republican presidential candidates were able to do with the Jewish vote took place with Reagan in 1980, who secured 39 percent of the vote against President Jimmy Carter, and Vice President George H. W. Bush in 1988, who received 35 percent in defeating Governor Michael Dukakis of Massachusetts. Jewish elected officials remained highly visible in the upper echelons of the Democratic Party. After President Donald Trump aggressively courted the Jewish vote by enacting policies desired by Prime Minister Benjamin Netanyahu of Israel, over three-quarters of American Jews voted for his opponent in 2020, Joe Biden. There is a disproportionate number

of Jewish liberal activists, publishers, pundits, organizational leaders, and politically engaged celebrities.

Within progressive bastions that stood their ground to the Right, Heschel was a hugely influential figure. His roles in the civil rights and antiwar movements grew in relevance as progressive Jews and non-Jews searched for a history that could offer a counterpoint to the rise and triumph of the Religious Right.[8] Heschel's story was incorporated into contemporary narratives that American Jews, who now lived in great material comfort, encountered all the time. The heroic tale of his march in Selma, along with the famous photograph of it in which he appears, became staples in conversations about the Jewish–African American alliance that had thrived in the mid-1960s.

It did not come as a surprise when Rabbi Michael Lerner, who founded the progressive magazine *Tikkun* in 1986, regarded Heschel as being at the core of his project. Lerner first met Heschel when he was a scholar-in-residence at his synagogue and was then inspired upon reading *God in Search of Man* and *The Sabbath*.[9] He studied with him at JTS.[10] The inside cover of the first issue of *Tikkun* started with a quote from Heschel: "Modern thinking has often lost its way by separating the problem of truth from the problem of living, cognition from the total human situation. . . . Reflection alone will not procure self-understanding. The human situation is disclosed in the thick of living. By whatever we do, by every act we carry out, we either advance or obstruct the drama of redemption; we either reduce or enhance the power of evil." Lerner wrote in his introduction, "Keeping the Prophetic tradition alive, as our spiritual mentor Abraham Joshua Heschel pointed out in his book *The Prophets*, means immersion in the details of daily life."[11]

One of the first people to build an actual memorial to Heschel was a civil rights and antiwar activist named Peter Geffen, the son of a Conservative rabbi. "Here we were burn-

ing draft cards," Geffen recalled of the 1960s. "We were burning American flags. We were angry at the country of our birth."[12] A Jewish educator, Geffen worked in various organizations that promoted a peaceful resolution to the Israeli–Palestinian conflict and with groups who were seeking to create alternative, spiritual forms of prayer. Inspired by his work on the streets, Geffen envisioned a new model of Jewish education that grew out of a political and ethical commitment to social justice. Heschel had been his role model, Geffen recalled, because he was "at the same time, a deeply committed Jew in practice and in knowledge, and on the other hand he was a social activist, he was in the streets."[13] In his twenties, profoundly influenced by Heschel's writing about Jewish education, Geffen translated these ideas into the Park Avenue Synagogue's high school in New York, where he worked as the director. Geffen believed that Judaism ultimately should be a source of moral guidance for all of society, not just the Jews, to stamp out injustice. "What is expected of me? What is demanded of me?" Heschel had asked in ways that inspired Geffen's approach to Jewish education.

Eventually, Geffen established a school to honor Heschel. He aimed to transpose the ideas from the synagogue to create a new kind of Jewish day school, one that limited the "inherent insularity" of the experience of most Jewish education. He sought to blend the "universal values and humanist concerns" within an imaginative approach to Jewish studies.[14] Meeting with major philanthropists in their living rooms in the early 1980s, Geffen outlined "an integrated curriculum based on principles of pluralism and diversity."[15] In 1983, he founded the Abraham Joshua Heschel School on the Upper West Side, combining traditional Jewish courses with progressive educational content and structure.

Heschel's legacy was also defined through a body of scholarship that took seriously his work as a theologian and his work as a political activist. Susannah, a major scholar of Jewish stud-

ies at Dartmouth College in her own right, published articles in the Jewish press and edited a volume of her father's essays. She spoke of his work at universities and synagogues, of the import of his writing about humans' relationship to God and his role as an activist, especially his relationship to King. After Heschel died, one of his most beloved students, Samuel Dresner, published a collection of essays in Heschel's honor. "I have said that Heschel was a *nasi*, a prince of his people," Dresner wrote, "and *shalem*, a whole person. He was, finally, a *zaddik*. . . . To read Heschel is to peer into the heart of that rarest of human phenomena, the holy man."[16] Edward Kaplan, a professor at Brandeis University who had followed Heschel at the peak of the antiwar movement, released a two-volume biography about him. The second book, centering on his life in America, was titled *Spiritual Radical*.[17] Rabbi Shai Held wrote, *Abraham Joshua Heschel: The Call of Transcendence*, which laid out the case for the centrality of Heschel's theological and philosophical contributions. Dismissing criticism that he was a hyperbolic poet, Held praised Heschel for writing in a manner meant to evoke spiritual awareness in readers and for developing an argument about self-transcendence that served as a through-line connecting most of his scholarship. All the while, Held was critical of elements of his work, such as his downplaying views on religious doubt and his sidestepping of the ways in which religion could conflict with ethical values.[18]

The photograph of Heschel and King in Selma became a familiar image in the Jewish landscape. It could be found in the halls of synagogues and on the walls of summer camp buildings, reprinted in magazines and in books, an ongoing reminder of the interracial alliance that bound Jews and African Americans together in a fight for social justice. "The period of genuine empathy and principled alliances between Jews and blacks constitutes a major pillar of American progressive politics in this century," the philosopher Cornel West wrote in the *New*

York Times.[19] For West, Heschel and King were the epitome of that bond. West argued that the rabbi's 1963 speech in Chicago on race and religion was the toughest reprimand of racism by a white man since William Lloyd Garrison.[20] When Reverend Jesse Jackson, head of the Rainbow/PUSH Coalition, spoke at the 1984 Democratic Convention, he invoked King and the rabbi: "We are bound by Dr. Martin Luther King Jr. and Rabbi Abraham Heschel, crying out from their graves for us to reach common ground." In 2008, the writer Richard Michelson and the illustrator Raul Colon published *As Good as Anybody*, a children's book about King and Heschel. With an illustration of the Selma march on the cover, the book offered children biographies of King and Heschel, emphasizing the ways in which each grew up in modest circumstances, confronted discrimination, and joined hands to march for voting rights. "In the next world, Abraham and Martin have finally found freedom," the book ended by saying. "In this world, their family, friends, and followers are still marching."[21]

Not surprisingly, a fair amount of mythmaking and exaggeration took place among his admirers. Heschel was not actually present on Bloody Sunday on 7 March 1965, the day that the Alabama authorities fiercely attacked protesters like John Lewis. Nor did Heschel experience the same kind of terrifying violence as thousands who participated in protests that ended in attacks. Others played much bigger roles in the nuts and bolts of organizing, the lifeblood of activism.

What was so important about Heschel was not that he heroically risked his life but that he became an emblem for a kind of moral heroism that inspired, and continued to inspire, others long after his moment had passed. He serves as a reminder of the often-forgotten role that deep religious conviction held within progressive movements that bent the arc of the universe toward justice.

Heschel's lasting relevance also stems from his early warn-

ings about the difficulties Conservative Judaism would encounter if they did not offer individuals meaningful engagement. In 2013, the Pew Research Center reported the results of a major study which found that a growing number of the 6.8 million Jews in America would not raise their children as Jews and were not connected to Jewish institutions. The rates of intermarriage increased from 17 percent before 1970 to about 46 percent in 1990 to 58 percent in 2013. Thirty-two percent of U.S. Jewish millennials reported that they had no religion. Forty-two percent reported that a good sense of humor was Jewish compared to only 19 percent who said their identity came from adhering to Jewish law. Less than 40 percent of those surveyed belonged to a synagogue. Fewer Jews kept kosher homes or attended Sabbath services.[22]

As rabbis struggled to find words to share with congregants to dissuade them from drifting away, they frequently turned to Heschel's poetic prose about the Jewish tradition and his answers to the debates he had been wrestling with since Warsaw straight through to JTS. His writing contained inspirational messages on prayer and observance that felt desperately needed as greater numbers of Jews weren't sure why they should keep coming to the institutions that earlier generations had built. "We have built organizations, but how Jewish is their membership?" Heschel had asked. "Our synagogues are beautiful, but the homes are a wilderness. We have developed forms of living socially as Jews. Jews attend Jewish meetings, belong to Jewish organizations, contribute to communal and national funds. But when left alone, or retired in our homes—they are poor in religious spirit. . . . The true goal includes becoming a Jew as well as belonging to a synagogue. . . . Every individual is a pillar on which the future of Judaism rests. There is no vicarious Judaism; no institution can discharge the responsibilities of the individual."[23]

In death, Heschel's words and the record of how he lived

by them became a spiritual source of renewal for Jews yearning to preserve their tradition. Perhaps most fittingly, Heschel's presence could be felt at Sabbath and holiday religious services across the country. Rabbis regularly quoted Heschel in their sermons, using his words to capture the essence of what it means to believe in God and live a devout life. Heschel's style of writing, which consisted of putting together short thoughts that he scribbled on pieces of paper, lent themselves toward pithy inspirational ideas that could be incorporated into the weekly services—combined with references to his compelling work with the iconic Reverend King. Heschel's willingness to speak openly and directly about issues like spirituality and God, in a way that many of the other giants from JTS did not, made him appealing.[24]

When the Conservative movement published a new High Holiday prayer book in 2010, *Mahzor Lev Shalem*, and a new weekly Sabbath siddur in 2016, *Siddur Lev Shalem*, the texts were filled with commentary from Heschel in the margins alongside the traditional prayers. The editor was Edward Feld, a rabbi and college Hillel director who had taken classes with Heschel at the seminary. Feld marveled at Heschel's abilities as a phenomenologist. Whenever Feld needed a passage for the fourth column of the text, which provided commentary and interpretation of the prayers, he looked to Heschel.[25] As JTS Chancellor Arnold Eisen proclaimed in the foreword, "Like Conservative Judaism as a whole—[Heschel] takes tradition forward in a way at once faithful, learned, loving and bold. . . . [It] invites us to 'dream the dream of God,' as Abraham Joshua Heschel put it, in words that join our hearts and minds to those of our ancestors."

According to the associate editor, Jan Uhrbach, the new text was written with the purpose of addressing the "crisis in prayer" that Heschel warned about in 1954 and to offer Jews "a vocabulary of Jewish concepts and different entry points on how to think about prayer."[26] Also relevant, the prayers were inclusive for single parents, same-sex couples, and religiously mixed families.

At the JTS, feelings about Heschel improved significantly. To be sure, tensions persisted. Many rabbis continued to dismiss his scholarship and felt that his reputation overshadowed his contributions. His stinging critique of their work in suburban communities never faded.[27] Nonetheless, in 1998 the seminary convened a major two-day conference to celebrate Heschel's scholarly work. "He is the most important Jewish thinker of the modern period," said the chancellor of the JTS, Rabbi Ismar Schorsch.[28] In 2007, Schorsch was succeeded by Arnold Eisen, a Stanford professor who had seen Heschel as a role model since they met in 1971 and who frequently cited his work: "He changed my life by giving me the example of a man who on the one hand marches with Martin Luther King, protests the war on Vietnam, marches for Soviet Jewry, and meets with the pope, but on the other hand is deeply immersed in tradition and speaks out of that tradition."[29] As more rabbis were entering the profession driven by a desire to rekindle spirituality in the Jewish community or to promote social justice, few figures from the past could equal Heschel as role models.[30]

And Heschel's appeal went beyond Conservative Judaism. Ten years after Heschel died, there were celebrations all over the country to commemorate his written work.[31] On the twenty-fifth anniversary of his death in 1998, the Reform movement announced that *The Sabbath* should be suggested reading for the more than one million people who belonged to congregations. They too hoped the book would offer a way to teach their members about core rituals that seemed to be foreign to them.[32]

His popularity, however, did not extend into the world of Orthodox Judaism. Tense feelings toward Heschel lingered, stemming from his willingness to discuss church doctrine with the Vatican in the early 1960s, which Soloveitchik had strongly condemned. Heschel was much more interested in the Jewish commandments from the Bible than in a rigid adherence to

Jewish law. Nor did many rabbinical students at Yeshiva University read Heschel's work or treat him as a major thinker. "Partly it's a matter of him not sharing all the Orthodox commitments," explained a faculty member, the philosopher Sholom Carmy. "One goes to look at people within your camp before you look without."[33] His writing was not a familiar reference point in Orthodox services. Despite Heschel's criticism that the Orthodox were becoming too rigidly focused on Jewish law, most leaders refused to turn in a different direction. Rebbes maintained an extraordinarily strong hand over their communities, allowing minimal room for individuals to discover their own ways of authentic prayer.

His relative absence in these communities, who practiced most closely the kind of ritual observance that Heschel was used to, reflected a sharp bifurcation that opened up between the Orthodox and the rest of the Jewish community decades after his passing. "In facing the loss of the *sho'ah*," Arthur Green reflected, Heschel "felt a great need to stand as a representative voice of the entire tradition, often speaking in the language of biblical imperatives."[34] Whereas in Heschel's day there were consensual political values that held together most in the three major denominations, along with a certain level of fluidity among Jews of the traditional variety, in later days the lines that separated Jew versus Jew hardened, as the journalist Samuel Freedman argued.[35] JTS, for example, lost most of the blended character that founders such as Cyrus Adler and Louis Finkelstein had envisioned back in the 1940s. Orthodox scholars moved into institutions like Yeshiva University. In the early 2000s, moreover, a majority of Orthodox Jews veered sharply to the right politically. Even the "modern" variety became the most politically conservative community in American Judaism—moving far from the values that animated Heschel in the last decade of his life. By and large they voted for Republicans in national elections, and they didn't incorporate the social rights

traditions into their treatment of women and children. Heschel's canonical presence in Reform and Conservative congregations, contrasted with his invisibility among the Orthodox, was in itself one of the most powerful indications of fracture among American Jews.

Nonetheless, the Hasidic rabbi who had left Berlin for the United States just as the slaughter of innocents had started, who had once been marginalized within JTS and ostracized by some students as a wild-eyed mystic, has in the twenty-first century come to be remembered as one of the most prominent voices in Jewish religious observance as well as a model of religious social engagement. When over eight hundred rabbis and cantors released a statement expressing their support for peaceful protest against racism during the demonstrations in 2020, they began by invoking Heschel: "As Rabbi Abraham Joshua Heschel said, to march is to pray with our feet."[36]

Rabbis weren't the only ones invoking Heschel. Following the tumultuous 2020 election, the fate of the U.S. Senate came down to two special elections in Georgia. If the Democrats running for both of those seats won, the party would regain control of the upper chamber and provide President Joe Biden an opportunity to move legislation. In mid-December, one of the Democratic candidates, the progressive Reverend Raphael Warnock, released an ad about the fact that he, an African American minister, and the other Democrat running, a Jewish American named Jon Ossoff, had "shared values, shared commitment." Looking back at the 1960s to contextualize the moment, the reverend said to the camera, "I think about Martin Luther King Jr. and Abraham Joshua Heschel. Heschel said 'when I marched with Dr. King, I felt like my legs were praying.' And in this moment, what we need is praying legs, praying feet to redeem the soul of America."[37]

Heschel's insistence on the ways that religious piety and social justice intertwined enriched the meaning of American

Judaism during his lifetime. He and like-minded Jewish American leaders propagated an understanding of their religion that inspired a greater commitment toward fighting for a world that respected human rights and social equality. He teased out key elements of the theology that were too often being ignored as middle-class Jewish Americans settled into the material comforts of assimilated Cold War America. His writing offered them a spiritually infused interpretation of their religion and religious practice, different from the ritualistic and socially oriented version that dominated most suburban synagogues. All of his work, from *The Sabbath* to *The Prophets*, was grounded in his vision of an intimate relationship between God and humans. He put forth a deep, poetic interpretation of why congregants should spend their time praying and adhering to tradition. For progressive political movements outside of the Jewish community, Heschel and his generation of preachers offered a spiritual foundation for social justice struggles that were often fought on secular grounds. In a country where religious institutions still held a respected place in mainstream communities, these voices helped grassroots activism appeal to a wider range of the populace even on the most controversial of matters.

Like the Hebrew Prophets, Heschel tried to answer the spiritual crisis facing the modern world. He saw politics in moral terms. The emptiness of our souls was directly connected to the violence all around us. Jews needed to open themselves up to the radical amazement of accepting the reality of the divine and living a life where every action was informed by religious values. That will remain his clarion call to action until the "terrible wrongs," as Heschel called them, are wiped away when crass materialism, social injustice, and unnecessary military force stop claiming the powerful hold they still have on our society.

Abbreviations for Archival Collections

Rabbi Abraham Joshua Heschel Papers, Duke University (AJHP)
Edward Kaplan Papers, Jewish Theological Seminary (EKP)
Marc Tanenbaum Papers, Center for Jewish History (MTP)
Samuel Dresner Papers, Jewish Theological Seminary (SDP)
The Jacob Rader Marcus Center of the American Jewish Archives,
 Hebrew Union College (AJA)

Acknowledgments

1. Email, Arnold Eisen to Friends, 3 June 2020.

Prologue

1. Peter S. Temes, *The Future of the Jewish People in Five Photographs* (Lincoln: University of Nebraska Press, 2012), 84–86.

2. Elaine Tyler May, *Homeward Bound: American Families in the Cold War Era*, rev. ed. (New York: Basic Books, 1988), 29.

3. Kevin Kruse, *One Nation Under God: How Corporate America Invented Christian America* (New York: Basic Books, 2015).

4. For a few fascinating recent works on religious liberalism in the postwar period, see Jack Jenkins, *American Prophets: The Religious Roots of Progressive Politics and the Ongoing Fight for the Soul of the Country* (New York: Harper, 2020); L. Benjamin Rolsky, *The Rise and Fall of the Religious Left: Politics, Television and Popular Culture in the 1970s and Beyond* (New York: Columbia University Press, 2019); Vanessa Cook, *Spiritual Socialists: Religion and the American Left* (Philadelphia: University of Pennsylvania Press, 2019); David L. Chappell, *A Stone of Hope: Prophetic Religion and the Death of Jim Crow* (Chapel Hill: University of North Carolina Press, 2004); Gary Dorrien, *Breaking White Supremacy: Martin Luther King Jr. and the Black Social Gospel* (New Haven: Yale University Press, 2018); Cathleen Kaveny, *A Culture of Engagement: Law, Religion and Morality* (Washington: Georgetown University Press, 2016); Andrew Preston, Bruce J. Schulman, and Julian E. Zelizer, eds., *Faithful Republic: Religion and Politics in Modern America* (Philadelphia: University of Pennsylvania Press, 2015); Elesha J. Coffman, *The Christian Century and the Rise of the Protestant Mainline* (New York: Oxford University Press, 2013); Matthew Hedstrom, *The Rise of Liberal Religion: Book Culture and American Spirituality in the Twentieth Century* (New York: Oxford University Press, 2013); Leigh Eric Schmidt and Sally M. Promey, eds., *American Religious Liberalism* (Bloomington: Indiana University Press, 2012); Marc Dollinger, *Quest for Inclusion: Jews and Liberalism in Modern America* (Princeton: Princeton University Press, 2000); Doug C. Rossinow, *The Politics of Authenticity: Liberalism, Christianity and the New Left in America* (New York: Columbia University Press, 1998).

5. Philip Mendes, *Jews and the Left: The Rise and Fall of a Political Alliance* (New York: Palgrave, 2014).

6. Ira Katznelson, *Fear Itself: The New Deal and the Origins of Our Time* (New York: Liveright, 2013), 48–49; Edward K. Kaplan,

Abraham Joshua Heschel: Mind, Heart, and Soul (Lincoln: University of Nebraska Press, 2019), 280.

7. Daniel T. Rodgers, *Atlantic Crossings: Social Politics in the Progressive Age* (Cambridge: Harvard University Press, 1998).

8. Abraham Joshua Heschel, "What We Might Do Together," *Religious Education* 62, no. 2 (1967): 139.

9. Kruse, *One Nation Under God*; Darren Dochuk, *From Bible Belt to Sun Belt: Plain-Folk Religion, Grassroots Politics and the Rise of Evangelical Conservatism* (New York: Norton, 2010).

10. Kruse, *One Nation Under God*, 236.

11. Barry Gewen, *The Inevitability of Tragedy: Henry Kissinger and His World* (New York: Norton, 2020); Jeremi Suri, *Henry Kissinger and the American Century* (Cambridge: Harvard University Press, 2007).

12. Nancy Sinkoff, *From Left to Right: Lucy S. Dawidowicz, the New York Intellectuals, and the Politics of Jewish History* (Detroit: Wayne State University Press, 2020).

13. Abraham Joshua Heschel, "The Individual Jew and His Obligations," in *The Insecurity of Freedom: Essays on Human Existence* (New York: Farrar, Straus and Giroux, 1967), 197.

Chapter 1. Warsaw

1. Rebecca Kobrin, *Jewish Bialystok and Its Diaspora* (Bloomington: Indiana University Press, 2010).

2. Cornelia Aust, "Merchants, Army Suppliers, Bankers: Transnational Connections and the Rise of Warsaw's Mercantile Elite," in *Warsaw: The Jewish Metropolis, Essays in Honor of the 75th Birthday of Professor Antony Polonsky*, ed. Glenn Dynner and François Guesnet (Leiden: Brill, 2015), 42–43.

3. Antony Polonsky, *The Jews in Poland and Russia*, vol. 2, *1881 to 1914* (Oxford: Littman Library of Jewish Civilization, 2010), 172.

4. Leora Batnitzky, *How Judaism Became a Religion: An Introduction to Modern Jewish Thought* (Princeton: Princeton University Press, 2011); see Ezra Mendelsohn, ed., *Essential Papers on Jews and the Left* (New York: New York University Press, 1997), 349–52.

5. Antony Polonsky, *The Jews in Poland and Russia*, vol. 3, *1914–2008* (Oxford: Littman Library of Jewish Civilization, 2012), 185–92.

6. Glenn Dynner, *Men of Silk: The Hasidic Conquest of Polish Jewish Society* (New York: Oxford University Press, 2006); Glenn Dynner, "The Garment of Torah: Clothing Decrees and the Warsaw Career of the First Gerer *Rebbe*," in *Warsaw*, 93–94; Glenn Dynner, *Yankel's Tavern: Jews, Liquor and Life in the Kingdom of Poland* (New York: Oxford University Press, 2014).

7. Arthur Green and Ariel Evan Mayse, eds., *A New Hasidism: Roots* (Philadelphia: Jewish Publication Society, 2019), xvii–xxi.

8. David Biale, David Assaf, Benjamin Brown, Uriel Gellman, Samuel Heilman, Moshe Rosman, Gadi Sagiv, Marcin Wodziński, *Hasidism: A New History* (Princeton: Princeton University Press, 2018), 1–2.

9. Dynner, *Men of Silk*, 5, 115.

10. Biale et al., *Hasidism*, 169.

11. Polonsky, *The Jews in Poland and Russia*, 2:276.

12. Ibid., 2:173.

13. Selections from Yehkiel Hofer, *A Hoyf af Muranow*, trans. Jonathan Boysarin, SDP, Box 4, File: Warsaw.

14. Edward K. Kaplan and Samuel H. Dresner, *Abraham Joshua Heschel: Prophetic Witness* (New Haven: Yale University Press, 1998), 9–11.

15. Ibid., 12.

16. Ibid., 29–30.

17. Abraham Joshua Heschel, "Hasidism as a New Approach to Torah," in *Moral Grandeur and Spiritual Audacity*, ed. Susannah Heschel (New York: Farrar, Straus and Giroux, 1996), 38.

18. Samuel H. Dresner, "Heschel the Man," in *Abraham Joshua Heschel: Exploring His Life and Thought*, ed. John C. Merkle (New York: Macmillan, 1985), 13.

19. Arthur Green, *The Heart of the Matter: Studies in Jewish Mysticism and Theology* (Philadelphia: Jewish Publication Society, 2015), 334.

20. Susannah Heschel, "Introduction," in Abraham Joshua Heschel, *Man's Quest for God: Studies in Prayer and Symbolism*, rev. ed. (Santa Fe: Aurora Press, 1996), 2.

21. Abraham Joshua Heschel, *A Passion for Truth*, Sixth Printing (Woodstock, VT: Jewish Lights, 2013), 4–5.

22. Steven J. Zipperstein, *Imagining Russian Jewry: Memory, History, Identity* (Seattle: University of Washington Press, 1999), 42–45.

23. Kaplan and Dresner, *Abraham Joshua Heschel*, 24–25.

24. Samuel Kassow, "Introduction," in *The Shtetl: New Evaluations*, ed. Steven T. Katz (New York: New York University Press, 2007), 9.

25. Susannah Heschel, "Introduction," in *Moral Grandeur and Spiritual Audacity*, ix.

26. Steven Zipperstein, *Pogrom: Kishinev and the Tilt of History* (New York: Liveright, 2018).

27. Scott Ury, *Barricades and Banners: The Revolution of 1905 and the Transformation of Warsaw Jewry* (Palo Alto: Stanford University Press, 2012), 214–72.

28. Abraham Joshua Heschel, "Preface," Unpublished Manuscript, AJHP, Box 61, File: Dr. Heschel Undated.

29. Selections from Yehiel Hofer, *A Hoyf of Muranow*, trans. Jonathan Boyarin, SDP, Box 4, File: Warsaw.

30. Transcript, "Directions," ABC Television, 1964, AJHP, Box 84, File: TV, 1964. For a fascinating look at the roots of this community, see Gershon David Hundert, *Jews in Poland–Lithuania in the Eighteenth Century: A Genealogy of Modernity* (Berkeley: University of California Press, 2004).

31. David Assaf, ed., *Journey to a Nineteenth-Century Shtetl: The Memoirs of Yekhezkel Kotik* (Detroit: Wayne State University Press, 2002), 138. See also Bernard Goldstein, *Twenty Years with the Jewish Labor Bund* (West Lafayette: Purdue University Press, 2016), 149.

32. Transcript, "Directions."

33. Kaplan and Dresner, *Abraham Joshua Heschel*, 34–36.

34. Marke Cejka and Roman Kofan, *Rabbis of Our Time: Au-*

thorities of Judaism in the Religious and Political Ferment of Modern Times (London: Routledge, 2016), 58.

35. Alexander Even-Chen and Ephraim Meir, *Between Heschel and Buber: A Comparative Study* (Boston: Academic Studies Press, 2012), 208–12.

36. Ezra Mendelsohn, *The Jews of East Central Europe: Between the World Wars* (Bloomington: Indiana University Press, 1983), 35.

37. Polonsky, *The Jews in Poland and Russia*, 3:31.

38. Götz Aly, *Europe Against the Jews, 1880–1945* (New York: Metropolitan Books, 2020), 15–37.

39. Mendelsohn, *The Jews of East Central Europe*, 40.

40. Cited in Konrad Zielinski, "The Shtetl in Poland, 1914–1918," in *The Shtetl*, 112.

41. Susannah Heschel, "Following in My Father's Footsteps," *Vox*, 4 April 2005.

42. Ezra Mendelsohn, *On Modern Jewish Politics* (New York: Oxford University Press, 1993).

43. Kaplan and Dresner, *Abraham Joshua Heschel*, 46–47.

44. Ibid., 44–45.

45. Nathan Cohen, "Distributing Knowledge: Warsaw as Center of Jewish Publishing, 1850–1914," in *Warsaw*, 180–206; Kenneth B. Moss, *Jewish Renaissance in the Russian Revolution* (Cambridge: Harvard University Press, 2009), 106–7.

46. Ury, *Barricades and Banners*, 162.

47. Ibid., 154.

48. David Aberbach, "Hebrew Literature and Jewish Nationalism in the Tsarist Empire, 1881–1917," in *The Emergence of Modern Jewish Politics: Bundism and Zionism in Eastern Europe*, ed. Zvi Gitelman (Pittsburgh: University of Pittsburgh Press, 2003), 132–50.

49. Interview with Bernard Perlow, 17 February 1981, EKP, Box 9, File: Family.

50. Scott Ury, "In Kotik's Corner: Urban Culture, Bourgeois Politics, and the Struggle for Jewish Civility in Turn of the Century Eastern Europe," in *Warsaw*, 214–15.

51. Assaf, ed., *Journey to a Nineteenth-Century Shtetl*, 31. On the importance of the coffeehouse culture to Jewish culture in Warsaw,

see Shachar M. Pinsker, *A Rich Brew: How Cafés Created Modern Jewish Culture* (New York: New York University Press, 2018), 55–97.

52. Kaplan and Dresner, *Abraham Joshua Heschel*, 68–69.

53. Ibid., 52–55.

54. For more on the changing nature of the Hasidic community, see Biale et al., *Hasidism;* Green and Mayse, *A New Hasidism*, xxi; Yehudah Mirsky, "The Rhapsodist," *New Republic*, 19 April 1999, 36–42A; Mendel Piekarz, *Ideological Trends of Hasidism in Poland during the Interwar Period and the Holocaust* (Jerusalem: Bialik Institute, 1990); Morris M. Faierstein, "Hasidism: The Last Decade in Research," *Modern Judaism* 11, no. 1 (February 1991): 111–24.

55. Kaplan and Dresner, *Abraham Joshua Heschel*, 64–65.

56. Ibid., 64–65.

57. Aly, *Europe Against the Jews, 1880–1945*, chapter 1.

58. Arthur Green, "Abraham Joshua Heschel: Recasting Hasidism for Moderns," *Tikkun* 14, no. 1 (1999): 63.

59. Kaplan and Dresner, *Abraham Joshua Heschel*, 68–69.

60. Ibid., 69.

61. Interview with Jacob Perlow, February 1979, EKP, Box 9, File: Family.

62. Michael Marmur, *Abraham Joshua Heschel and the Sources of Wonder* (Toronto: University of Toronto Press, 2016), 227.

63. Kaplan and Dresner, *Abraham Joshua Heschel*, 68–69.

64. Samuel Dresner, *Heschel, Hasidism, and Halakha* (New York: Fordham University Press, 2001), 62.

65. Steven Z. Zipperstein, *The Jews of Odessa: A Cultural History, 1794–1881* (Palo Alto: Stanford University Press, 1986), 12.

66. Kalman Weiser, "The Capital of 'Yiddishland'?" in *Warsaw*, 305–9.

67. Cecile Esther Kuznitz, *YIVO and the Making of Modern Jewish Culture: Scholarship for the Yiddish Nation* (New York: Cambridge University Press, 2014).

68. Dresner, *Heschel, Hasidism, and Halakha*, 8; Edward K. Kaplan, *Abraham Joshua Heschel: Mind, Heart, Soul* (Philadelphia: Jewish Publication Society and Lincoln: University of Nebraska

Press, 2019), 23. On the growing desire among traditional Jews to avoid the rabbinic ordinance of cutting a man's facial hair, see Jeffrey S. Gurock, *Orthodox Jews in America* (Bloomington: Indiana University Press, 2009), 167–68.

69. Kaplan and Dresner, *Abraham Joshua Heschel*, 84–85.

70. Jon Levenson, "The Contradictions of A. J. Heschel," *Commentary*, 1 July 1998, 35.

71. Kaplan and Dresner, *Abraham Joshua Heschel*, 96.

72. Abraham Joshua Heschel, "Millions of Eyes, Clogged," in *The Ineffable Name of God* (New York: Continuum, 2007), 35. See also, "Repentance," 201.

Chapter 2. Berlin

1. Eric D. Weitz, *Weimar Germany: Promise and Tragedy* (Princeton: Princeton University Press, 2007).

2. Heschel, "Toward an Understanding of Halacha," in *Moral Grandeur and Spiritual Audacity*, ed. Susannah Heschel (New York: Farrar, Straus and Giroux, 1996), 130.

3. Susannah Heschel, "Foreword," in *In This Hour: Heschel's Writings in Nazi Germany and London Exile*, ed. Helen Plotkin (Philadelphia: Jewish Publication Society, 2019), xi–xii.

4. Detlev J. K. Peukert, *The Weimar Republic* (New York: Hill & Wang, 1987).

5. Peter Pulzer, *The Rise of Anti-Semitism in Germany and Austria* (New York: Wiley, 1964).

6. Gershom Scholem, *From Berlin to Jerusalem: Memories of My Youth* (Philadelphia: Paul Dry Books, 2012).

7. Peukert, *The Weimar Republic*.

8. Steven E. Aschheim, *Brothers and Strangers: The East European Jew in German and German Jewish Consciousness, 1800–1923* (Madison: University of Wisconsin Press, 1982), 58–60.

9. Alexander Even-Chen, "Abraham Joshua Heschel's Pre- and Post-Holocaust Approach," *Modern Judaism* 34, no. 2 (May 2014): 146.

10. Michael Brenner, *The Renaissance of Jewish Culture in Weimar Germany* (New Haven: Yale University Press, 1996), 52–54.

11. Michael A. Meyer, *Response to Modernity: A History of the Reform Movement of Judaism* (Detroit: Wayne State University Press, 1988).

12. Helen Plotkin, "Introduction," in *In This Hour*, xix.

13. Cited in Michael Marmur, "In Search of Heschel," in *Abraham Joshua Heschel Today: Voices from Warsaw and Jerusalem*, ed. Harold Kasimow (Eugene, OR: Wipf & Stock, 2020), 9–10.

14. *In This Hour*, xx.

15. Brenner, *The Renaissance of Jewish Culture in Weimar Germany*, 110.

16. Nicholas Murray, *Kafka* (New Haven: Yale University Press, 2004), 367.

17. Edward K. Kaplan, "Jewish Renewal in Pre-Nazi Germany: Abraham Heschel Interprets William James," *CrossCurrents* 53, no. 3 (2003): 438–39.

18. Arthur Green, "Abraham Joshua Heschel: Recasting Hasidism for Moderns," *Modern Judaism* 29, no. 1 (February 2009): 69.

19. Heschel, "The Biblical View of Reality," in *Moral Grandeur and Spiritual Audacity*, 364.

20. Brenner, *The Renaissance of Jewish Culture in Weimar Germany*, 142–45.

21. Aschheim, *Brothers and Strangers*, 144–50.

22. On the reception that Eastern European Jews received in Germany during this period, see Jack Wertheimer, *Unwelcome Strangers: Eastern European Jews in Imperial Germany* (New York: Oxford University Press, 1987).

23. David Biale et al., *Hasidism: A New History* (Princeton: Princeton University Press, 2018), 556–72.

24. Aschheim, *Brothers and Strangers*.

25. Paul Mendes-Flohr, *Martin Buber: A Life of Faith and Dissent* (New Haven: Yale University Press, 2019), 66.

26. Leora Batnitzky, *How Judaism Became a Religion: An Introduction to Modern Jewish Thought* (Princeton: Princeton University Press, 2011), 74–81.

27. Biale et al., *Hasidism*, 564–65.

28. Aschheim, *Brothers and Strangers*, 135.

29. Ibid., 114–15, 134–35.

30. Cited in Chaim Potok, "Foreword," in Martin Buber, *Tales of the Hasidim* (New York: Schocken Books, 1991), viii.

31. Joseph Harp Britton, *Abraham Heschel and the Phenomenon of Piety* (London: Bloomsbury, 2013), 84.

32. Heschel, "Toward an Understanding of Halacha," in *Moral Grandeur and Spiritual Audacity*, 127–29.

33. Ibid., 129.

34. Kaplan and Dresner, *Abraham Joshua Heschel*, 143, 151.

35. Albert J. Raboteau, *American Prophets: Seven Religious Radicals and Their Struggle for Social and Political Justice* (Princeton: Princeton University Press, 2016), 4.

36. Edward Kaplan, "Introduction," in Abraham Joshua Heschel, *The Ineffable Name of God* (New York: Continuum, 2007), 14.

37. Susannah Heschel, "Introduction," in *Moral Grandeur and Spiritual Audacity*, xiv.

38. "Repentance" and "Forgiveness," in Heschel, *The Ineffable Name of God*, 177, 201.

39. Kaplan and Dresner, *Abraham Joshua Heschel*, 221.

40. "The Auto-da-Fé of the Mind," 1933, in Joseph Roth, *What I Saw* (New York: Norton, 1996), 207.

41. Abraham Joshua Heschel, "On the Day of Hate," in *Moral Grandeur and Spiritual Audacity*, 71–72.

42. Abraham Joshua Heschel, *Maimonides*, rev. ed., trans. Joachim Neugroschel (New York: Fall River Press, 2012), 222–23.

43. John C. Merkle, *Approaching God: The Way of Abraham Joshua Heschel* (Collegeville, MN: Liturgical Press, 2009), 6.

44. Britton, *Abraham Heschel and the Phenomenon of Piety*, 94.

45. Brenner, *The Renaissance of Jewish Culture in Weimar Germany*, 86, 214.

46. Susannah Heschel, "Introduction," in *Moral Grandeur and Spiritual Audacity*, xv–xvi.

47. Rosie Hertz, oral history interview, N.D., EKP, Box 25, Binder.

48. Kaplan and Dresner, *Abraham Joshua Heschel*, 246–48; Kaplan, *Abraham Joshua Heschel: Mind, Heart, Soul* (Philadelphia: Jewish Publication Society and Lincoln: University of Nebraska Press, 2019), 84–85.

49. Susannah Heschel, "Introduction," *Man's Quest for God: Studies in Prayer and Symbolism* (Santa Fe: Aurora Press, 1998).

50. Heschel, "On the End of Time," in *In This Hour*, 129.

51. Plotkin, "Introduction," in *In This Hour*, xxi.

52. Michael A. Chester, *Divine Pathos and Human Being: The Theology of Abraham Joshua Heschel* (London: Vallentine Mitchell, 2005), 8.

53. Heschel, "Introduction," in *Moral Grandeur and Spiritual Audacity*, xiv.

54. Abraham Heschel to Martin Buber, September 1938, trans. Samuel Dresner, SDP, Box 1, File: Buber.

55. Kaplan and Dresner, *Abraham Joshua Heschel*, 266.

56. Alexander Even-Chen and Ephraim Meir, *Between Heschel and Buber: A Comparative Study* (Boston: Academic Studies Press, 2012), 16.

57. Abraham Joshua Heschel to Martin Buber, 9 November 1938, SDP, Box 1, File: Buber.

58. Jonathan D. Sarna and Nancy H. Klein, *The Jews of Cincinnati* (Cincinnati: Center for the American Jewish Experience, 1989), 128; Samuel S. Cohon, "The History of the Hebrew Union College," *Publications of the American Jewish Historical Society* 4, no. 1 (1950): 46–48.

59. Meyer, *Response to Modernity*, 309–14.

60. Sarna and Klein, *The Jews of Cincinnati*, 145–46; Michael A. Meyer, "The Refugee Scholars Project of the Hebrew Union College," in *A Bicentennial Festschrift for Jacob Rader Marcus*, ed. Bertram W. Korn (Waltham, MA: American Jewish Historical Society, 1976), 359–63.

61. Jeffrey S. Gurock, "American Judaism Between the Two World Wars," in *The Columbia History of Jews and Judaism in America*, ed. Marc Lee Raphael (New York: Columbia University Press, 2008), 101.

62. Julian Morgenstern to Abraham Joshua Heschel, 6 April 1939, AJA, Julian Morgenstern Papers, MS-30, Box 5, Folder 23.

63. Abraham Joshua Heschel to Julian Morgenstern, 30 April 1939, AJA, Julian Morgenstern Papers, MS 30, Box 5, Folder 23.

64. Chester, *Divine Pathos and Human Being*, 8–9.

65. Ibid., 10.

66. Heschel, "The Idea of Jewish Education," in *In This Hour*, 8, 13–14.

67. Heschel, "On Return," 1939, in *In This Hour*, 166–67.

68. Kaplan and Dresner, *Abraham Joshua Heschel*, 264.

69. Abraham Joshua Heschel to Julian Morgenstern, 31 January 1940, AJA, Julian Morgenstern Papers, MS-30, Box 5, Folder 23.

70. *In This Hour*, 4.

71. "*Lancastria* Here, Battered by Sea," *New York Times*, 22 March 1940.

72. Abraham Joshua Heschel to Julian Morgenstern, 21 March 1940, AJA, Julian Morgenstern Papers, MS-30, Box 5, Folder 23.

Chapter 3. Cincinnati

1. "Stanley Denies War Is 'Phoney'; Bids Us Let Belligerents Run It," *New York Times*, 21 March 1940.

2. Hasia Diner, "Like the Antelope and the Badger: The Founding and Early Years of the Jewish Theological Seminary, 1886–1902," in *Tradition Renewed: A History of the Jewish Theological Seminary of America*, vol. 1, ed. Jack Wertheimer (New York: Jewish Theological Seminary, 1997), 7.

3. Ira Robinson, "Cyrus Adler: President of the Jewish Theological Seminary, 1915–1960," in *Tradition Renewed*, 138–39.

4. Abraham Heschel to Julian Morgenstern, 21 March 1940, and Morgenstern to Heschel, 25 March 1940, AJA, Julian Morgenstern Papers, MS-30, Box 5, Folder 23.

5. Michael B. Greenbaum, *Louis Finkelstein and the Conservative Movement: Conflict and Growth* (Binghamton, NY: Global Publications, 2001), 53–63.

6. Louis Finkelstein, "Three Meetings with Abraham Heschel," *America*, 10 March 1973, 203.

7. Howard M. Sachar, *A History of the Jews in America* (New York: Knopf, 1992), 455.

8. Leonard Dinnerstein, *Anti-Semitism in America* (New York: Oxford University Press, 1994), 131.

9. Amy Hill Shevitz, *Jewish Communities on the Ohio River: A History* (Lexington: University of Kentucky Press, 2007), 134.

10. Hasia R. Diner, *The Jews of the United States, 1654–2000* (Berkeley: University of California Press, 2004), 71–111.

11. Rebecca Kobrin, *Jewish Bialystok and Its Diaspora* (Bloomington: Indiana University Press, 2010).

12. Diner, *The Jews of the United States*, 113.

13. Lizabeth Cohen, *Making a New Deal: Industrial Workers in Chicago, 1919–1939* (New York: Cambridge University Press, 1990).

14. Avi Y. Decter, *Interpreting American Jewish History at Museums and Historic Sites* (New York: Rowman & Littlefield, 2017), 71.

15. Diner, *The Jews of the United States*, 120; Michael A. Meyer, *Response to Modernity: A History of the Reform Movement in Judaism* (Detroit: Wayne State University Press, 1988), 250–63.

16. Jeffrey S. Gurock, *Orthodox Jews in America* (Bloomington: Indiana University Press, 2009), 148–84.

17. Shevitz, *Jewish Communities on the Ohio River*, 87.

18. Jonathan D. Sarna, *American Judaism: A History* (New Haven: Yale University Press, 2004), 144–45.

19. Ibid., 149.

20. Edward K. Kaplan, *Spiritual Radical: Abraham Joshua Heschel in America, 1940–1972* (New Haven: Yale University Press, 2007), 7–13.

21. Benny Kraut, *German-Jewish Orthodoxy in an Immigrant Synagogue: Cincinnati's New Hope Congregation and the Ambiguities of Ethnic Religion* (New York: Markus Weiner, 1988), 44–45.

22. John S. Fine and Fredric J. Krome, *Jews of Cincinnati* (Charleston, SC: Arcadia, 2007), 36.

23. Rabbi Albert Plotkin, interview with Samuel Dresner, 6 December 1990, SDP, Box 3, File: Plotkin, Albert.

24. Herbert Drooze to Daniel Breslauer, 15 August 1972, AJHP, Box 18, File: Breslauer 1972.

25. Dana Evan Kaplan, *American Reform Judaism: An Introduction* (New Brunswick: Rutgers University Press, 2003), 18–19.

26. Kaplan, *Spiritual Radical*, 7.

27. Drooze to Breslauer, 15 August 1972.

28. Edward K. Kaplan, *Abraham Joshua Heschel: Mind, Heart and Soul* (Lincoln: University of Nebraska Press, 2019), 117.

29. Meyer, *Response to Modernity*, 327.

30. Sarna, *American Judaism*, 159–60, 174–75.

31. Meyer, *Response to Modernity*, 296.

32. Sarna, *American Judaism*, 174–75; Meyer, *Response to Modernity*, 322.

33. Kaplan, *Spiritual Radical*, 21–23.

34. Dresner, *Heschel, Hasidism, and Halakha*, 24.

35. Michael A. Chester, *Divine Pathos and Human Being: The Theology of Abraham Joshua Heschel* (London: Vallentine Mitchell, 2005), 78–88; Susannah Heschel, "Reading Abraham Joshua Heschel Today," in *Thunder in the Soul: To Be Known by God: Abraham Joshua Heschel*, ed. Robert Erlewine (Walden, NY: Plough Publishing House, 2021), xxviii.

36. Jacob Rader Marcus, interview, 9 November 1987, EKP, Box 27, Binder.

37. Samuel Dresner, "Cincinnati," EKP, Box 20, File: Cincinnati.

38. Michael Marmur, *Abraham Joshua Heschel and the Sources of Wonder* (Toronto: University of Toronto Press, 2016), 176–77; Kaplan, *Spiritual Radical*, 22–24.

39. Notes, "Cincinnati—Cronbach," Undated, SDP, Box 1, File: Cincinnati. Years later, Cronbach would be the only Jewish rabbi who had the courage to fly himself to the funeral of Julius and Ethel Rosenberg, who were executed in 1953 after having been convicted of spying.

40. Kaplan, *Spiritual Radical*, 37–42; Chester, *Divine Pathos and Human Being*, 184.

41. Rabbi Joseph Gumbiner to Colleague, 9 August 1979, SDP, Box 1, File: Blacks.

42. Edward Kaplan, "Coming to America: Abraham Joshua Heschel," *Modern Judaism* 27, no. 2 (May 2007): 135.

43. Samuel Dresner, audiotape interview, N.D., EKP, Audiotape Collection.

44. Drooze to Breslauer, 15 August 1972.

45. Shulamit Eden, oral history interview, 11 November 1987, EKP, Box 25, Binder.

46. Jonathan D. Sarna and Nancy H. Klein, *The Jews of Cincinnati* (Cincinnati: Center for the Study of the American Jewish Experience, 1989), 119.

47. Chester, *Divine Pathos and Human Being*, 13.

48. Kaplan, *Spiritual Radical*, 15–16, 57.

49. Susannah Heschel, "Introduction," in *Moral Grandeur and Spiritual Audacity*, xix.

50. Abraham Heschel to Martin Buber, 1 March 1942, translated copy, EKP, Box 24, File: Buber Letters.

51. Henry L. Feingold, *Zion in America: The Jewish Experience from Colonial Times to the Present* (New York: Twayne, 1974), 294.

52. Rafael Medoff, *The Jews Should Keep Quiet: Franklin D. Roosevelt, Rabbi Stephen S. Wise and the Holocaust* (Lincoln: University of Nebraska Press and Philadelphia: Jewish Publication Society, 2019), 97–138; Howard M. Sachar, *A History of the Jews in America* (New York: Knopf, 1992), 475; Kaplan, *Spiritual Radical*, 43.

53. Abraham Joshua Heschel, "An Analysis of Piety," in *Moral Grandeur and Spiritual Audacity*, 305–8.

54. "Meeting Hears Roosevelt Note," *Los Angeles Times*, 22 July 1942; "Nazi Punishment Seen by Roosevelt," *New York Times*, 22 July 1942; "Nazi Massacres of Europe's Jews to Be Protested at New York Meeting Today," *Jewish Telegraph Agency*, 21 July 1942; Duane Tananbaum, *Herbert H. Lehman: A Political Biography* (Albany: State University of New York Press, 2016), 54.

55. Cited in Dresner, *Heschel, Hasidism, and Halakha*, 24.

56. Alexander Even-Chen, "God's Omnipotence and Presence in Abraham Joshua Heschel's Philosophy," in *Abraham Joshua Heschel Today: Voices from Warsaw and Jerusalem* (Eugene, OR: Wipf & Stock, 2020), 42.

57. Abraham Joshua Heschel, "The Meaning of This War," *Hebrew Union College Bulletin* 2, no. 3 (March 1943): 1–2, 18.

58. Lillian Faderman, *Harvey Milk: His Lives and Death* (New Haven: Yale University Press, 2018), 16–17.

59. Drooze to Breslauer, 15 August 1972.

60. Samuel Dresner, "Heschel the Man," in *Abraham Joshua Heschel: Exploring His Life and Thought*, ed. John C. Merkle (New York: Macmillan, 1985), 3–27.

61. Kaplan, *Abraham Joshua Heschel*, 108–9.

62. Chester, *Divine Pathos and Human Being*, 12.

63. Gurock, *Orthodox Jews in America*, 159–60, 172–74.

64. Sarna and Klein, *The Jews of Cincinnati*, 124–25; Frederic Krome, *The Jewish Hospital and Cincinnati Jews in Medicine* (Charleston, SC: History Press, 2015), 92–95.

65. Gurock, *Orthodox Jews in America*, 219.

66. Aaron Rakeffet-Rothkoff, *The Silver Era: Rabbi Eliezer Silver and His Generation* (Jerusalem: Feldheim Publishers; New York: Yeshiva University Press, 1981).

67. Diner, *The History of American Jews*, 218.

68. Medoff, *The Jews Should Keep Quiet*, 196–97.

69. Kaplan, *Spiritual Radical*, 52; Rafael Medoff, "The Day the Rabbis Marched," The David S. Wyman Institute for Holocaust Studies, 21 January 2005, EKP, Box 7, File: Holocaust.

70. Medoff, *The Jews Should Keep Quiet*, 116–23.

71. Martin Kavka, "The Meaning of That Hour: Prophecy, Phenomenology, and the Public Sphere in the Early Writings of Abraham Joshua Heschel," in *Religion and Violence in a Secular World: Toward a New Political Theology*, ed. Clayton Crockett (Charlottesville: University of Virginia Press, 2006), 108–34.

72. Drooze to Breslauer, 15 August 1972.

73. "The Meaning of This War (World War II)," *Liberal Judaism* 11, no. 10 (February 1944): 18–21.

74. Abraham Joshua Heschel to Julian Morgenstern, 29 August 1945, AJA, Hebrew Union College Records, MS-5, Box A-11, Folder 2.

75. Greenbaum, *Louis Finkelstein and the Conservative Move-*

ment, 53–63. On the relationship between Kaplan and Heschel, see Mel Scult, *The Radical American Judaism of Mordecai M. Kaplan* (Bloomington: Indiana University Press, 2013), 211–13.

76. Abraham Joshua Heschel to Louis Finkelstein, 29 May 1945, SDP, Box 2, File: JTS.

77. Julian Morgenstern to Abraham Joshua Heschel, 19 May 1945, AJA, Hebrew Union College Records, MS-5, Box A-11, Folder 2.

78. Though the word "Holocaust" did not find its way into popular usage until the 1960s, I will use the term throughout as a matter of clarity. For the history of the term, see Peter Novick, *The Holocaust in American Life* (Boston: Houghton Mifflin, 1999).

79. Shai Held, *Abraham Joshua Heschel: The Call of Transcendence* (Bloomington: Indiana University Press, 2013); Edward Kaplan, *Holiness in Words: Abraham Joshua Heschel's Poetics of Piety* (New York: State University of New York Press, 1996); Robert Eisen, "A. J. Heschel's Rabbinic Theology as a Response to the Holocaust," *Modern Judaism* 23, no. 3 (October 2003): 211–25; Morris M. Faierstein, "Abraham Joshua Heschel and the Holocaust," *Modern Judaism* 19, no. 3 (October 1999): 255–75.

Chapter 4. New York City

1. UJA Federation of New York, *Jewish Community Study of New York: 2011 Comprehensive Report*, June 2012, 39.

2. Eli Lederhendler, "New York City, the Jews, and the Urban Experience," in *Studies in Contemporary Jewry Annual XV* (1999), 52. See also Deborah Dash Moore, Jeffrey S. Gurock, Annie Polland, Howard B. Rock, and Daniel Soyer, *Jewish New York: The Remarkable Story of a City and a People* (New York: New York University Press, 2017).

3. Cited in Lederhendler, "New York City, the Jews, and the Urban Experience," 49–52.

4. Beth S. Wenger, *New York Jews and the Great Depression: Uncertain Promise* (New Haven: Yale University Press, 1996), 94–95.

5. Max Scult, "Schechter's Seminary," in *Tradition Renewed: A History of the Jewish Theological Seminary of America*, vol. 1, ed.

Jack Wertheimer (New York: Jewish Theological Seminary of America, 1997), 58.

6. Ira Robinson, "Cyrus Adler: President of the Jewish Theological Seminary, 1915–1940," and Michael B. Greenbaum, "The Finkelstein Era," in *Tradition Renewed*, 45–232.

7. Louis Finkelstein to Faculty, 31 August 1945, AJHP, Box 22, File 2: Correspondence 1938–1947 (5 of 5).

8. Lila Corwin Berman, *Speaking of Jews: Rabbis, Intellectuals and the Creation of An American Public Identity* (Berkeley: University of California Press, 2009), 81–88.

9. Press Release, The Jewish Theological Seminary of America, 16 November 1945, AJHP, Box 22, File: 9 Miscellaneous, 1939–1950.

10. Michael B. Greenbaum, *Louis Finkelstein and the Conservative Movement: Conflict and Growth* (Binghamton, NY: Global Publications, 2001), 138.

11. Cyrus Adler, *Cyrus Adler: Selected Letters, 1883–1919; 1920–1926* (Philadelphia: Jewish Publication Society of America, 1983), 398. See also Elijah J. Schochet and Solomon Spiro, *Saul Lieberman: The Man and His Work* (New York: JTS, 2005), 17–18.

12. Edward K. Kaplan, *Spiritual Radical: Abraham Joshua Heschel in America* (New Haven: Yale University Press, 2007), 83–85.

13. Edward K. Kaplan, *Abraham Joshua Heschel: Mind, Heart, Soul* (Philadelphia: Jewish Publication Society and Lincoln: University of Nebraska Press, 2019), 150–51.

14. Kaplan, *Spiritual Radical*, 76.

15. Shai Held, *Abraham Joshua Heschel: The Call of Transcendence* (Bloomington: Indiana University Press, 2013).

16. Jon Butler, *God in Gotham: The Miracle of Religion in Modern Manhattan* (Cambridge: Harvard University Press, 2020), 154.

17. "To Be or Not to Be," *Time*, 16 March 1959, 47.

18. Reuven Kimmelman, "Rabbis Joseph B. Soloveitchik and Abraham Joshua Heschel on Jewish–Christian Relations," *Modern Judaism* 24, no. 3 (October 2004): 251–52.

19. David Hartman, "Foreword," in Abraham J. Heschel, *Between God and Man: An Interpretation of Judaism*, 2d ed., ed. Fritz Rothschild (New York: Free Press, 1997), 2–4.

20. Joseph B. Soloveitchik, *Halakhic Man* (Philadelphia: Jewish Publication Society, 1983), 19.

21. Butler, *God in Gotham*, 173–75.

22. Abraham Joshua Heschel, *The Earth Is the Lord's: The Inner World of the Jew in Eastern Europe* (repr.; Woodstock, VT: Jewish Lights, 2014), *10*, 26.

23. Ibid., 44.

24. Ibid., 36, 102.

25. Hartman, "Foreword," 1–2.

26. For a broader analysis of nostalgia about conditions in Eastern Europe, see Steven J. Zipperstein, *Imagining Russian Jewry: Memory, History, Identity* (Seattle: University of Washington Press, 1999), 16–41.

27. Marc Dollinger, *Quest for Inclusion: Jews and Liberalism in Modern America* (Princeton: Princeton University Press, 2000), 120.

28. Louis Finkelstein to Henry Schuman, 29 December 1949, AJHP, Box 147, File: Earth 1949–1951.

29. Julian Morgenstern to Abraham Heschel, 28 June 1950, AJHP, Box 147, Folder: Earth 1949–1951.

30. Maurice Friedman to Abraham Joshua Heschel, 3 September 1950, AJHP, Box 136, Folder: Criticism 1950–1952.

31. Reinhold Niebuhr to Abraham Heschel, 26 February 1953, AJHP, Box 5, File 4: Niebuhr.

32. Michael Marmur and David Ellenson, "Introduction," in Jill Jacobs, "There Shall Be No Needy," in *American Jewish Thought Since 1934: Writings on Identity, Engagement, and Belief*, ed. Marmur and Ellenson (Waltham: Brandeis University Press, 2020), xix–xx.

33. Marvin Lowenthal, "The Jewish Community: What It Means to the West," *New York Herald Tribune*, 2 July 1950.

34. Herman Kieval, "Review: The Earth Is the Lord's," *Conservative Judaism* 7, no. 3 (April 1951): 25–30.

35. Heschel's work, which doesn't directly talk about the Holocaust but is clearly an ongoing response to the horrors his family and community faced, supports Hasia R. Diner, *We Remember with Reverence and Love: American Jews and the Myth of Silence after the Holocaust, 1945–1952* (New York: New York University Press, 2009).

Diner dismantled the claim that the Jewish community ignored the Holocaust before the 1960s. The classic example of this argument comes from Peter Novick, *The Holocaust in American Life* (Boston: Houghton Mifflin, 1999).

36. Diner, *We Remember with Reverence and Love*, 91–94, 97, 130.

37. Kaplan, *Spiritual Radical*, 124.

38. Heschel, "Pikuach Neshama: To Save a Soul," 1949, in *Moral Grandeur and Spiritual Audacity*, 58–59.

39. Dov Waxman, *Trouble in the Tribe: The American Jewish Conflict over Israel* (Princeton: Princeton University Press, 2016), 33–34.

40. Howard M. Sachar, *A History of the Jews in America* (New York: Knopf, 1992), 595.

41. Jonathan D. Sarna, *American Judaism: A History* (New Haven: Yale University Press, 2004), 334.

42. "Salute to Israel to Be Given at Garden Tonight," *New York Herald Tribune*, 16 May 1948.

43. Ethel Samuels, "2,000 at Rally Sponsored by Cincinnati to Celebrate Declaration, Recognition End of Embargo on Shipment of Arms," *American Israelite*, 20 May 1948.

44. "Jews Hail U.S. Support for State of Israel," *Palestine Post*, 17 May 1948.

45. Sarna, *American Judaism*, 335.

46. Jenna Weissman Joselit, *The Wonders of America: Reinventing Jewish Culture, 1880–1950* (New York: Hill & Wang, 1994), 241.

47. "A Trumpet for All Israel," *Time*, 15 October 1951, 52.

48. Kaplan, *Spiritual Radical*, 108–10.

49. Sarna, *American Judaism*, 244; Adam Kirsch, *The Blessing and the Curse: The Jewish People and Their Books in the Twentieth Century* (New York: Norton, 2021), 224–25.

50. Mordecai M. Kaplan, *Judaism as a Civilization: Toward a Reconstruction of American-Jewish Life*, 6th ed. (Philadelphia: Jewish Publication Society, 2010), 29.

51. Mel Scult, *The Radical American Judaism of Mordecai M. Kaplan*, xiv, 225; *Communings of the Spirit: The Journals of Mordecai M. Kaplan*, vol. 3, *1942–1951*, ed. Scult (Detroit: Wayne State University Press, 2020), 116–17.

52. Scult, *The Radical American Judaism of Mordecai M. Kaplan*, 212–13.

53. Michael R. Cohen, *The Birth of Conservative Judaism: Solomon Schechter's Disciples and the Creation of An American Religious Movement* (New York: Columbia University Press, 2012), 81.

54. Butler, *God in Gotham*, 186.

55. Kaplan, *Judaism as A Civilization*, 428–29.

56. Diner, *The Jews of the United States*, 128.

57. This formulation comes from Michael Marmur and David Ellenson, "Introduction," in Jill Jacobs, "Revelation and Commandment," in *American Jewish Thought Since 1934*, 40.

58. Abraham Joshua Heschel, *The Sabbath*, 3d ed. (New York: Farrar, Straus and Giroux, 2005), 79.

59. Ibid., 13.

60. Kaplan, *Spiritual Radical*, 128.

61. Rabbi David Telsner, "Review: The Sabbath," *American Judaism*, April 1952, 17.

62. A. M. Klein, "Review: The Sabbath," *Our Voice*, May 1952.

63. Israel H. Levinthal, "A Book on Sabbath," *Brooklyn Jewish Center Review*, January 1952.

64. Joseph Kaminetsky, "Review: The Sabbath," *Jewish Parents Magazine*, December 1951, 17.

65. Rabbi Samuel Schulman to Abraham Heschel, 23 September 1952, AJHP, Box 164, File: Sabbath 1 of 2 (1951–1953).

66. Marvin Fox to Abraham Heschel, 28 March 1952, AJHP, Box 163, File: Sabbath Letters, 1951–1952.

67. Jacob Neusner, oral history interview, N.D., SDP, Box 3, File: Neusner, Jacob.

68. Mordechai Kaplan to Abraham Heschel, 24 December 1951, AJHP, Box 3, File: 8.

69. Maurice S. Friedman, *Abraham Joshua Heschel, Philosopher of Wonder: Our Thirty-Year Friendship and Dialogue* (Eugene, OR: Cascade Books, 2012), 15.

70. Abraham Joshua Heschel, *Man Is Not Alone: A Philosophy of Religion* (New York: Farrar, Straus and Giroux, 1951), 146.

71. Ibid., 151.

72. Ibid.

73. Ibid., 152.

74. Ibid., 37.

75. Ibid., 11.

76. Held, *Abraham Joshua Heschel*, 29–31.

77. "Abraham Joshua Heschel," January 18, 2008, PBS, Religion and Ethics Newsweekly.

78. Held, *Abraham Joshua Heschel*, 40.

79. Heschel, *Man Is Not Alone*, 139.

80. Ibid., 78.

81. Held, *Abraham Joshua Heschel*, 137.

82. Heschel, *Man is Not Alone*, 244.

83. Ibid., 67.

84. Ibid., 39.

85. Samuel Dresner, *Heschel, Hasidism, and Halakha* (New York: Fordham University Press, 2001), 60; Hartman, "Foreword," 2.

86. Heschel, *Man Is Not Alone*, 176.

87. Reinhold Niebuhr, "Masterly Analysis of Faith," *New York Herald Tribune*, 1 April 1951.

88. FSY, Press Release, 28 March 1951, AJHP, Box 136, File: Man, 1950–1951.

89. Louis Finkelstein to Abraham Heschel, 9 October 1950, AJHP, Box 136, File: Man, 1950–1951.

90. Mark Greif, *The Age of the Crisis of Man: Thought and Fiction in America, 1933–1973* (Princeton: Princeton University Press, 2015).

91. Alexander Altmann to Abraham J. Heschel, 2 September 1942, in "Letters from England: A Contribution to the Intellectual Biography of Alexander Altmann," ed. Ira Robinson, *Jewish Quarterly Review* 109, no. 2 (Spring 2019): 325.

92. Alexander Altmann to Abraham J. Heschel, 16 May 1952, in "Letters from England: A Contribution to the Intellectual Biography of Alexander Altmann," 329.

93. Barnett Brickner, Robert Gordis, and Leo Jung to Colleagues, 1951, University of Pennsylvania Special Collections Library, Abraham Neuman Papers, Box 54, File: 13.

94. Alan Jacobs, "The Watchmen: What Became of Christian Intellectuals?" *Harpers*, September 2016.

95. Kevin Kruse, *One Nation Under God: How Corporate America Invented Christian America* (New York: Basic Books, 2015).

96. Sarna, *American Judaism*, 281.

97. "Religion: A Trumpet for All Israel," 52.

98. Sarna, *American Judaism*, 279.

99. "To the Men and Women of the Conservative Movement" and "Synagogues Summoned to Sanctify Sabbath," *United Synagogue Review*, October 1951; "Revitalization of the Sabbath," *The Torch* 11, no. 2 (Winter 1952): 3–4; "Reading Aloud from *The Sabbath:* Suggestions for a reading and discussion program," in AJHP, Box 163, File: Sabbath Jewish 1951–1952.

100. Emil Lehman, "National Sabbath Observance Effort," AJHP, Box 144, Folder: Sabbath 1951–1952.

101. United Synagogue of America, "Program of Exercises," November 1951 and "United Synagogue Sponsors New Book on Sabbath," *United Synagogue Review*, November 1951, in AJHP, Box 164, File: Sabbath (1 of 2), 1951–1953.

102. Joselit, *The Wonders of America*, 158–59.

103. Maurice Friedman, "The Thought of Abraham Heschel," *Congress Weekly* 222, no. 31 (November 1955): 18.

104. For the history of this modern notion of the synagogue, see David Kaufman, *Shul with a Pool: The 'Synagogue Center' in American Jewish History* (Waltham: Brandeis University Press, 1999).

105. Yakov Rozenberg, interview with Edward Kaplan, May-June 1999, EKP, Box 7, File: EK Interviews.

106. Irving Spiegel, "Religious Places Held Void of Spirit," *New York Times*, 24 June 1953. The speech is reprinted in *Moral Grandeur and Spiritual Audacity*, 100–126.

107. Abraham Joshua Heschel, *Man's Quest for God: Studies in Prayer and Symbolism*, rev. ed. (Santa Fe: Aurora Press, 1998), 49, 79–80.

108. For an analysis of the critics, see Arnold Eisen, "Re-Reading

Heschel on the Commandments," *Modern Judaism* 9, no. 1 (February 1989): 1–34.

109. Friedman, "The Thought of Abraham Heschel," 18.

110. Kaplan, *Spiritual Radical*, 129.

111. Friedman, "The Thought of Abraham Heschel," 18–19.

112. Baila R. Shargel, "The Texture of Seminary Life during the Finkelstein Era," in *Tradition Renewed*, 526, 544–45.

113. Arthur Green, *Judaism for the World: Reflections on God, Life and Love* (New Haven: Yale University Press, 2020), 312. Though in retrospect, Green realized that "I had learned a tremendous amount from him, and I have continued to do so, teaching him over and over again . . . respecting him greatly, and arguing with him (now unfortunately one-sidedly) for over half a century." See also Samuel Dresner, Comment, "Heschel: Roundtable Discussion with Samuel Dresner, Neil Gillman, Joe Lukinsky, David Novack, Fritz Rothschild, Sol Tannenzapf, Reuven Kimmelman, and Arthur Greene, August 1987, EKP, Box 25, Binder, 5.

114. Scult, *The Radical American Judaism of Mordecai M. Kaplan*, 217.

115. Harvey E. Goldberg, "Becoming History: Perspectives on the Seminary Faculty at Mid-Century," in *Tradition Renewed*, 380–86.

116. Numerous scholars have argued that Lieberman's animosity toward Heschel was more important than almost anything else in souring his position at JTS. However, the biographers Elijah Schochet and Solomon Spiro dispute this, arguing that the two had deep affection for one another. See Schochet and Spiro, *Saul Lieberman*, 191–95.

117. Kaplan, *Spiritual Radical*, 130, 367.

118. "Anecdotes," Notes from Sam Dresner Diary, EKP, Box 25, Binder.

119. Michael Marmur, *Abraham Joshua Heschel and the Sources of Wonder* (Toronto: University of Toronto Press, 2016), 37.

120. Abraham Joshua Heschel, *God in Search of Man: A Philosophy of Judaism* (New York: Farrar, Straus and Giroux, 1955), 3.

121. Ibid., 16.

122. Ibid., 3

123. Ibid., 137.

124. Ibid., 260.

125. Ibid., 33.

126. Ibid., 156.

127. Ibid., 49. Kirsch, *The Blessing and the Curse*, 239–40.

128. Arthur Green, "Abraham Joshua Heschel: Recasting Hasidism for Moderns," *Modern Judaism* 29, no. 1 (February 2009): 74.

129. Heschel, *God in Search of Man*, 402.

130. Ibid., 43.

131. Ibid., 338.

132. Ibid., 367–70, 420–21.

133. Ibid., 380; 384.

134. Dresner, *Heschel, Hasidism, and Halakha*, 42–43.

135. A. Powell Davies, "Revelation and the Needs of Man," *New York Times*, 12 February 1956.

136. Emanuel Rackman, "Dr. Heschel's Answer," *Jewish Horizon*, October 1956, 17.

137. Jack Riemer, "Review of God in Search of Man," *The Torch*, Summer 1956, 23–24.

138. "The Jew & God," *Time*, 19 March 1956, 64.

139. Rabbi William Feyer to Samuel Dresner, 25 June 1975, SDP, Box 1, File: Anecdotes.

140. Sylvia Heschel, Reminiscences about Abraham Joshua Heschel, AJHP, Box 42, File 3.

141. Susannah Heschel, interview with Rabbi Shmuly Yanklowitz, Valley Beit Midrash, youtube.com.

142. Susannah Heschel, "My Father," in *No Religion Is an Island: Abraham Joshua Heschel and Interreligious Dialogue*, eds. Harold Kasimow and Byron L. Sherwin (Eugene, OR: Wipf & Stock, 1991), 29.

143. Susannah Heschel, "Introduction," in *Moral Grandeur and Spiritual Audacity*, xxviii–xxix.

144. Susannah Heschel, "Introduction," in *The Sabbath*, xvii.

145. Ibid., x.

146. Elie Wiesel, *Memoirs: All Rivers Run to the Sea* (New York: Schocken, 1995), 353.

147. Susannah Heschel, "Introduction," in *The Sabbath*, xi.

148. Dov Peretz Elkins, 6 February 1973, AJHP, Box 38, File: Articles About Ab, 1972–1973.

149. Levy Kelman, interview with Edward Kaplan, 10 May 1992, SDP, Box 2, File: Kelman, Levy.

150. Susannah Heschel, "Introduction," in *The Sabbath*, xi.

151. Levi Kelman, interview with Edward Kaplan, N.D., EKP, Audiotape Collection.

152. Susannah Heschel, "My Father," 29; Victor and Ruth Goodhill, interview, 28 April 1988, EKP, Box 25, File: Binder.

153. Abraham Heschel to Wolfe Kelman, 7 August 1957, EKP, Box 11, File: Kelman Personal Files.

154. Eugene Borowitz, interview with Edward Kaplan, N.D., EKP, Box 25, Binder.

155. Kaplan, *Spiritual Radical*, 188–89.

156. Abraham Heschel, "Preamble for Constitution of World Council of Synagogues," 21 April 1959, AJHP, Box 10, File 6: Ben Gurion.

157. Kaplan, *Abraham Joshua Heschel*, 220.

158. "Summary of Discussion of American Participants in Jerusalem Ideological Conference and Members of New York Jewish Agency Executive," 6 January 1958, AJHP, Box 73, File: Least B, 1949–1958.

159. Eli Lederhendler, "The Ongoing Dialogue: The Seminary and the Challenge of Israel," in *Tradition Renewed*, 205–7.

160. Abraham Joshua Heschel, "Should the United Synagogue of America Join the World Zionist Organization?" *The Torch*, 1959, AJHP, Box 275, File: 1960, 1964, 32, 34.

161. Marshall Meyer, oral history interview, 13 January 1988, EKP, Box 25.

162. Ursula M. Niebuhr, "Notes on a Friendship: Abraham Joshua Heschel and Reinhold Niebuhr," in *Abraham Joshua Heschel: Exploring His Life and Thought*, ed. John C. Merkle (New York: Macmillan, 1985), 38.

163. Reinhold Niebuhr to Abraham Heschel, 9 July 1957, AJHP, Box 5, File 4: Niebuhr.

164. Ursula Niebuhr, recorded speech, N.D., EKP, Audiotape Collection.

165. George Kalinsky, *Rabbis: The Many Faces of Judaism* (New York: Universe, 2002).

166. Ikuru Teshima, "My Teacher's A Garden by the River's Side," 2 February 1973, AJHP, Box 38, File: 5 Articles About Ab, 1972–1973.

167. *Sixth Annual B'nai B'rith Institute of Judaism*, 18–21 August 1955, AJHP, Box 7, File 1: Symbolism (1 of 2).

168. For a lively history of these iconic elements of popular culture, see Ted Merwin, *Pastrami on Rye: An Overstuffed History of the Jewish Deli* (New York: New York University Press, 2015).

169. Dresner, *Heschel, Hasidism, and Halakha*, 92; Sachar, *A History of the Jews in America*, 687.

170. Leonard Dinnerstein, *Anti-Semitism in America* (New York: Oxford University Press, 1994), 150–74.

171. Henry L. Feingold, *Zion in America: The Jewish Experience from Colonial Times to the Present* (New York: Twayne, 1974), 308–9.

172. Fritz A. Rothschild, ed., *Between God and Man: An Interpretation of Judaism from the Writings of Abraham J. Heschel* (New York: Harper Brothers, 1959), 9.

173. Kaplan, *Spiritual Radical*, 201.

174. Cited in Yehudah Mirsky, "The Rhapsodist," *New Republic*, 19 April 1999, 41.

175. Wolfe Kelman, interview, N.D., EKP, Audiotapes.

176. Editor's Note, "The Call of the Hour," *Law and Order* 8, no. 5 (May 1960): 14–23.

177. Abraham Joshua Heschel, "The Older Person and the Family in The Perspective of Jewish Tradition," 9 January 1961, AJHP, Box 82, File: Age, 1961.

178. Kaplan, *Spiritual Radical*, 203.

179. "Way to Go," 1963, AJHP, Box 307, Reel: RL 10086-RR-0001.

180. Susannah Heschel, "Foreword," and Gordon Tucker, "Preface," in *Heavenly Torah: As Refracted Through the Generations*, ed. and trans. Gordon Tucker (New York: Continuum, 2006), xvii–xxxiii.

181. Ibid.

182. Reuven Kimelman, "Abraham Joshua Heschel's Theology of Judaism and the Rewriting of Jewish Intellectual History," *Journal of Jewish Thought and Philosophy* 17, no. 2 (January 2009): 207–38.

183. Kaplan, *Spiritual Radical*, 209.

184. Wolfe Kelman, oral interview, N.D., EKP, Audiotapes.

185. Paul Boyer, *When Time Shall Be No More: Prophecy Belief in Modern America* (Cambridge: Harvard University Press, 1992).

186. Arthur Green and Ariel Evan Mayse, eds., *A New Hasidism: Roots* (Philadelphia: Jewish Publication Society, 2019), 139.

187. Abraham Joshua Heschel, *The Prophets*, vol. 1 (Peabody, MA: Hendrickson Publishers, 1962), 9.

188. Ibid., 121.

189. Ibid., 5, 159, 181.

190. Ibid., 119.

191. Green and Mayse, *A New Hasidism*, 141.

192. Heschel, *The Prophets*, vol. 2, 64.

193. Heschel, *The Prophets*, vol. 1, 190.

194. Susannah Heschel, "Two Friends, Two Prophets," *Plough Quarterly* (Spring 2018); Andrew Young, interview with Edward Kaplan, EKP, Box 20, Audio Tapes; Taylor Branch, *Pillar of Fire: America in the King Years, 1963–65* (New York: Simon & Schuster, 1998), 31.

195. Branch, *Pillar of Fire*, 30–32; Gary Dorrien, *Breaking White Supremacy: Martin Luther King Jr. and the Black Social Gospel* (New Haven: Yale University Press, 2018).

196. Jonathan Rieder, *The Word of the Lord Is Upon Me: The Righteous Performance of Martin Luther King Jr.* (Cambridge: Harvard University Press, 2008), 145. On the longer tradition of Exodus in political mobilization, including civil rights, see John Coffey, *Exodus and Liberation: Deliverance Politics from John Calvin to Martin Luther King Jr.* (New York: Oxford University Press, 2013).

197. David L. Chappell, *A Stone of Hope: Prophetic Religion and the Death of Jim Crow* (Chapel Hill: University of North Carolina Press, 2004); David Blight, *Frederick Douglass: Prophet of Freedom* (New York: Simon & Schuster, 2018).

198. Robert Kirsch, "Reflections on Dimensions of Prophecy," *Los Angeles Times*, 27 January 1963.

199. Michael A. Chester, *Divine Pathos and Human Being: The Theology of Abraham Joshua Heschel* (London: Vallentine Mitchell, 2005), 20.

200. Heschel, "The Reasons for My Involvement in the Peace Movement," 1973, in *Moral Grandeur and Spiritual Audacity*, 224.

Chapter 5. Selma

1. Edward Kaplan, *Spiritual Radical: Abraham Joshua Heschel in America* (New Haven: Yale University Press, 2007), 215.

2. Lecture, Susannah Heschel, "Praying with Their Legs: Rabbi Abraham Heschel and Rev. Martin Luther King," YouTube; Susannah Heschel, "Reading Abraham Joshua Heschel Today," xxix.

3. Arthur Green, *Radical Judaism: Rethinking God and Tradition* (New Haven: Yale University Press, 2010), 158.

4. Marc Tanenbaum, oral history, October 1988, EKP, Box 25, Binder.

5. Conference Program, National Conference on Religion and Race, AJHP, Box 46, Folder: Chicago Conference 1963 (3 of 3).

6. Kaplan, *Spiritual Radical*, 215.

7. Abraham Joshua Heschel, "The Religious Basis of Equality and Opportunity," January 1963, AJHP, Box 101, File: The Religious Basis of Equality.

8. Jonathan Rieder, *Gospel of Freedom: Martin Luther King, Jr.'s Letter from Birmingham Jail and the Struggle that Changed the Nation* (New York: Bloomsbury, 2013), 19–20.

9. David L. Chappell, *A Stone of Hope: Prophetic Religion and the Death of Jim Crow* (Chapel Hill: University of North Carolina Press, 2004).

10. Richard H. Pells, *The Liberal Mind in a Conservative Age: American Intellectuals in the 1940s and 1950s* (New York: Harper & Row, 1985).

11. Daniel Bell, *The End of Ideology: On the Exhaustion of Political Ideas in the 1950s* (New York: Free Press, 1962).

12. Mrs. Theodore Krohn, "Conference on Religion and Race," 27 February 1963, AJHP, Box 9, File: Correspondence (2 of 2).

13. Carol Petegorsky, "Religion Fights Racism," *Congress Bi-Weekly*, 8.

14. "Religious Confab Hears Martin Luther King," *Austin Statesman*, 16 January 1963.

15. Kaplan, *Spiritual Radical*, 217–18.

16. Jonathan Sarna, *American Judaism* (New Haven: Yale University Press, 2004), 310–11.

17. Jonathan Rieder, *The Word of the Lord Is Upon Me: The Righteous Performance of Martin Luther King Jr.* (Cambridge: Harvard University Press, 2008), 282.

18. Martin Luther King Jr., "Statement to Freedom Riders Rally," 21 May 1961, MLK Papers Online.

19. Rieder, *The Word of the Lord Is Upon Me*, 290.

20. Marc Dollinger, *Quest for Inclusion: Jews and Liberalism in Modern America* (Princeton: Princeton University Press, 2000), 135–37, 164–213.

21. On the role of these organizations in the civil rights movement, see Cheryl Lynn Greenberg, *Troubling the Waters: Black–Jewish Relations in the American Century* (Princeton: Princeton University Press, 2010), 213.

22. "Relevance of the Prophets," *Time*, 25 January 1963, 66.

23. Abraham Heschel to President John F. Kennedy, 16 June 1963, Jewish Women's Archives, Living Legacy, Online Archives.

24. Abraham J. Heschel and Martin Luther King Jr., "What Happens to Them Happens to Me—and to You," *United Synagogue Review*, Special Issue (Winter 1964), 14–15.

25. "Inter-Faith Conference on Race," 2 March 1964, AJHP, Box 30, File: Correspondence 1958–1964 (1 of 2); Abraham Joshua Heschel, "Religion and Race: Reflections on Passover Eve," in *Jewish World*, March 1964, 40–41, 62; "Boston Conference on Religion and Race," 13 January 1964, AJHP, Box 10, File: 7 Correspondence 1963–1964; "Rochester Conference on Religion and Race," 30 October 1963, AJHP, Box 10, File: 7 Correspondence 1963–1964; Abraham Joshua Heschel, "Kaddish in Our Souls," 1963,

cited in "Meet the Family: Abraham Joshua Heschel: Susannah Heschel in Conversation with Barbara Kiershenblatt-Gimblett," 7 March 2021, Museum of History of Polish Jews.

26. Abraham Joshua Heschel, "Principal Address at Americana Hotel Dinner on Religion and Race," 25 February 1964, AJHP, Box 78: File: Addresses 1957/1964.

27. "Educators Join in Civil Rights Vigil," AJHP, Box 10, File: 5 Correspondence (2 of 2).

28. "Theological Students Vigil for Civil Rights: Statement at Lincoln Memorial, Washington, D.C. by Dr. Abraham J. Heschel," 1964, AJHP, Box 58, File: Paris, 1964–1966.

29. Heschel and King, "What Happens to Them Happens to Me—and to You," 14–15.

30. Elizabeth Borgwardt, *A New Deal for the World: America's Vision for Human Rights* (Cambridge: Harvard University Press, 2007); James Loeffler, *Rooted Cosmopolitans: Jews and Human Rights in the Twentieth Century* (New Haven: Yale University Press, 2018).

31. Gal Beckerman, *When They Come for Us, We'll Be Gone: The Epic Struggle to Save Soviet Jewry* (Boston: Mariner, 2010), 26–38.

32. Minutes, Executive Board Meeting, "The Situation of the Jews in the Soviet Union," 30 October 1963, AJHP, Box 65, File: Folder Russia 1963 (1 of 2).

33. Beckerman, *When They Come for Us, We'll Be Gone,* 56.

34. Moshe Decter, "The Status of the Jews in the Soviet Union," *Foreign Affairs,* January 1963, 420–30.

35. Beckerman, *When They Come for Us, We'll Be Gone,* 59.

36. Jerry Goodman, "American Response to Soviet Anti-Jewish Policies," *American Jewish Year Book,* vol. 66 (1965): 313.

37. Beckerman, *When They Come for Us, We'll Be Gone,* 67.

38. Minutes, "Dinner-Meeting, November 4, 1963 at JTSA," and Belfour Brickner to Abraham Heschel, 17 October 1963, both in AJHP, Box 65, File: 1963.

39. Abraham Heschel to Cardinal Cushing, 23 March 1963, AJHP, Box 55, Folder: Cushing 1964.

40. Abraham J. Heschel, "Jews in the Soviet Union," reprinted in Abraham J. Heschel, *The Insecurity of Freedom: Essays*

on Human Existence (New York: Farrar, Straus and Giroux, 1966), 262–69.

41. Marc Tanenbaum to Zachariah Shuster, 17 September 1963, AJHP, Box 53, File: AJC Bea, 1963.

42. Senator Abraham Ribicoff, "It Is Time for the Senate to Speak Up," and Joachim Prinz, "Cultural Genocide Continues in Russia," in *Jewish World*, March 1964, 28–29, 32, AJHP, Box 100, File: The Jewish World March 1964.

43. Miss D. McDonald to Bernard Segal, 6 November 1963, AJHP, Box 66, File: Russia 1963, 1966.

44. "1000 Students Picket Russ Mission in N.Y.," *Baltimore Sun*, 2 May 1964.

45. Irvin Spiegel, "2,000 Here March on Soviet Mission," *New York Times*, 29 October 1964.

46. "2,300 Jews March on Red HQ," *New York Daily News*, 29 October 1964. See also Fred Ferretti, "March by 2,500 Jews on UN Soviet Mission," *Herald Tribune*, 29 October 1964.

47. Photograph, *Milwaukee Journal*, 29 October 1964.

48. American Jewish Committee, "Anti-Jewish Elements in Catholic Liturgy: A Memorandum to the Secretariat for Christian Unity," 17 November 1961, AJHP, Box 48, File: Material 1960–1961.

49. John W. O'Malley, *When Bishops Met: An Essay Comparing Trent, Vatican I and Vatican II* (Cambridge: Harvard University Press, 2019), 164–65.

50. Zachariah Shuster to John Slawson, 18 October 1962, AJHP, Box 51, File: Schuster, 1962–1964 (1 of 2).

51. Kaplan, *Spiritual Radical*, 254.

52. David Hartman, "Foreword," in *Between God and Man: An Interpretation of Judaism*, ed. Fritz Rothchild, 2d ed. (New York: Free Press, 1997), 3.

53. "What God Thinks of Man," *Newsweek*, 31 January 1966, 57.

54. Reuven Kimmelman, "Rabbis Joseph B. Soloveitchik and Abraham Joshua Heschel on Jewish–Christian Relations," *Modern Judaism* 24, no. 3 (October 2004): 260.

55. Abraham Heschel, Unpublished Manuscript, AJHP, Box 61, File: Undated, 5.

56. Marc Tanenbaum to Abraham Heschel, 15 November 1961, MTP, Box 23, Folder 7.

57. Abraham Heschel, Unpublished Manuscript, AJHP, Box 61, File: Undated, 3–9.

58. Zachariah Shuster to John Slawson, 20 December 1960, MTP, Box 12, Folder 9.

59. Marc Tanenbaum, "Heschel and Vatican II—Jewish–Christian Relations," 21 February 1983, Paper Presented at the Memorial Symposium in Honor of Abraham Joshua Heschel, Jewish Theological Seminary.

60. Zachariah Shuster to Marc Tanenbaum, 1 December 1961, AJHP, Box 51, File: Vatican Rome, 1961–1962 (2 of 2).

61. Abraham Heschel, *On Improving Catholic–Jewish Relations*, 22 May 1962, Box 51, File: Vatican Rome, 1961–1962 (2 of 2).

62. Marc Tanenbaum, Memorandum of Meeting in Boston with Cardinal Bea, 5 April 1963, AJHP, Box 53, File: Boston, 1963.

63. Rabbi Abraham Heschel, "Dinner for Cardinal Bea," 1 April 1963, AJHP, Box 53, File: AJC Bea 1963.

64. Abraham Heschel to Martin Buber, 4 April 1963, SDP, Box 1, File: Buber.

65. Taylor Branch, *At Canaan's Edge: America in the King Years 1965–68* (New York: Simon & Schuster, 2006), 355–56.

66. AJC Memorandum, Paris Office to New York Office, 9 December 1963, MTP, Box 12, Folder 9.

67. Abraham Heschel to Father John Courtney Murray, 10 January 1964, AJHP, Box 55, File: Correspondence, 1964.

68. Arthur Hertzberg, "Church, State and the Jews," *Commentary*, April 1963, 280.

69. "Pope Receives Jewish Leaders," *Hartford Courant*, 17 March 1964.

70. "Jewish Leader Sees Interfaith Efforts Better," *Boston Globe*, 8 May 1964.

71. Abraham Heschel to Sylvia and Susannah Heschel, 12 September 1964, AJHP, Box 56, File: Tribune, 1964.

72. Abraham Heschel, Memorandum, 14 September 1964, AJHP, Box 55, File: Folder Paul VI Visit 1964 (2 of 2).

73. Abraham Heschel to Pope Paul VI, 30 September 1964, AJHP, Box 55, File: Paul VI Visit, 1964 (2 of 2).

74. "Lovingly Observant: An Interview with Susannah Heschel," *America*, 18 June 2007.

75. "What Happened on Yom-Kippur Eve at the Vatican?" *Jewish World*, October 1964, 23–24.

76. "Chief Israeli Rabbi Hails Vatican Action," *Chicago Tribune*, 23 November 1964.

77. "Council Declaration on Jews Praised by Rabbi," *Los Angeles Times*, 15 December 1964.

78. Kaplan, *Spiritual Radical*, 269–71.

79. Zachariah Shuster, Memorandum, 1965, AJHP, Box 50, File: Visit Rome, 1961–1972 (1 of 2).

80. Transcription, Telephone Conversation with Cardinal Bea, 31 December 1964, MTP, Box 12, Folder 10.

81. Abraham Heschel, Memorandum, 11 February 1965, AJHP, Box 50, File: Visit Rome, 1961–1972 (1 of 2). This entire story is recounted in Kaplan, *Spiritual Radical*, 238–76.

82. Ibid., 229–30.

83. Abraham J. Heschel, *Who Is Man?* (Palo Alto: Stanford University Press, 1965), 13–14.

84. Ibid., 57.

85. Ibid., 114.

86. "Seminary Honors Rev. Dr. King," *Democrat and Chronicle*, 8 June 1964.

87. "Rabbis Ordained by 2 Seminaries," *New York Times*, 8 June 1964.

88. Jewish Theological Seminary, *Commencement Exercises*, 6–7 June 1964. Program in the author's personal possession.

89. Heschel, "No Religion Is an Island," *Union Seminary Quarterly Review* 21, no. 2 (January 1966): 117–34.

90. Dresner, *Heschel, Hasidism, and Halakha*, 111; Heschel, "My Father," in *No Religion Is an Island: Abraham Joshua Heschel and Interreligious Dialogue*, ed. Harold Kasimow and Byron L. Sherwin (Eugene, OR: Wipf & Stock, 1991), 33.

91. Kaplan, *Spiritual Radical*, 280.

92. "Rabbi Proposes a Fund in Memory of Reeb," *Chicago Tribune*, 12 March 1965.

93. Cited in Lidia Jean Kott, "To One Jewish Professor, Martin Luther King Jr. Was a Mensch," North Carolina Public Radio, 16 January 2017.

94. Abraham Heschel, Notes, AJHP, Box 47, File 1: Race, 1963, 1965.

95. Ibid.

96. Ibid.

97. Online clips, Steven Brand, "Praying with My Legs," documentary in progress; "Abraham Joshua Heschel," *Religion and Ethics Newsweekly*, 19 January 2008.

98. Abraham Heschel, Notes, AJHP, Box 47, File 1: Race, 1963, 1965.

99. "Turning Point for the Church," *Look*, 18 May 1965, 32–37.

100. Eric Meyers, "Jewish Voices from the Selma-to-Montgomery March," 14 January 2015, *Freedom Forum Institute*.

101. Elon Green, "The Rabbis of Selma," *Tablet*, 26 December 2014.

102. "Southern Hospitality Not Extended, Say R.I. Rabbis Who Marched in Alabama," *Rhode Island Herald*, 2 April 1965.

103. Paul L. Montgomery, "The Marchers on Highway 80 Are of All Sorts and One Belief," *New York Times*, 22 March 1965.

104. "Selma Witness—the Rabbis Notebook," *Voice of Temple Beth Jacob*, April 1965.

105. Abraham Heschel, Notes, AJHP, Box 47, File 1: Race, 1963, 1965.

106. "Praying with My Legs," documentary in progress.

107. Rieder, *The Word of the Lord Is Upon Me*, 284.

108. John Lewis with Michael D'Orso, *Walking with the Wind: A Memoir of the Movement* (New York: Simon & Schuster, 1998), 357.

109. Abraham Heschel, Notes, AJHP, Box 47, File 1: Race, 1963, 1965.

110. Maurice Davis, oral history interview, 27 April 1988, EKP, Box 25, Binder.

111. Abraham Heschel, Notes, Box 47, File 1: Race, 1963, 1965.

112. Kaplan, *Spiritual Radical*, 223.

113. Ursula Niebuhr, recorded speech, N.D., EKP, Audiotape Collection.

114. "Rabbi Saul Leeman, Who Marched with Martin Luther King, Dies Age 100," *Haaretz*, 15 May 2017.

115. Abraham Heschel, Notes, AJHP, Box 47, File 1: Race, 1963, 1965.

116. Ibid.

117. Maurice Davis, oral history interview, 27 April 1988, EKP, Box 25, Binder.

118. Abraham Heschel, Notes, AJHP, Box 47, File 1: Race, 1963, 1965.

119. Andrew Young, interview with Rabbi Arnold Goodman, N.D. EKP, Box 20, Audio Tapes.

120. Abraham Heschel, Notes, AJHP, Box 47, File 1: Race, 1963, 1965.

121. Abraham Heschel to Martin Luther King Jr., 29 March 1965, AJHP, Box 47, File: Selma 1965.

122. Abraham Heschel to the Editors, 31 March 1965, AJHP, Box 47, File: Selma 1965.

123. "A.J.C. Head Hails Papal Act," *New York Times*, 29 October 1965.

Chapter 6. Washington

1. Abraham Joshua Heschel, *The Prophets*, vol. 1 (Peabody, MA: Hendrickson, 1962), 160.

2. Marshall Sahlins, "Teach-Ins Helped Galvanize Student Activism in the 1960s: They Can Do So Again Today," *The Nation*, 6 April 2017; McCandlish Phillips, "Now the Teach-In: U.S. Policy in Vietnam Criticized All Night," *New York Times*, 27 March 1965; "33 Hour Teach In Attracts 10,000," *New York Times*, 23 May 1965; Julian E. Zelizer, *Arsenal of Democracy: The Politics of National Security: From World War II to the War on Terror* (New York: Basic Books, 2010), 194.

3. Abraham Joshua Heschel, Notes, 1965, AJHP, Box 67, File: Vietnam 1965.

4. Harold Kasimow, *Interfaith Activism: Abraham Joshua Heschel and Religious Diversity* (Eugene, OR: Wipf & Stock, 2015), 47–48.

5. Barry Shrage, "Abraham Joshua Heschel and the Creation of the Jewish Renaissance," *Modern Judaism* 29, no. 1 (February 2009): 58.

6. Michael Friedland, *Lift Up Your Voice Like a Trumpet: White Clergy and the Civil Rights and Antiwar Movements, 1954–1973* (Chapel Hill: University of North Carolina Press, 1998), 8; Mitchell K. Hall, *Because of Their Faith: CALCAV and Religious Opposition to the Vietnam War* (New York: Columbia University Press, 1990), 5–7.

7. John Bennett, Francis Sayre, Abraham Heschel, and Thomas Merton, "Interfaith Statement on the Place of Morality in the Campaign," October 1964, AJHP.

8. Daniel and Philip Berrigan, Letter to the Editor, *The Post-Standard*, 8 September 1963.

9. Warren Goldstein, *William Sloane Coffin Jr.: A Holy Impatience* (New Haven: Yale University Press, 2004), 119.

10. Daniel Berrigan, *To Dwell in Peace: An Autobiography* (Eugene, OR: Wipf & Stock, 1987), 179.

11. Friedland, *Lift Up Your Voice Like a Trumpet*, 159.

12. Hall, *Because of Their Faith*, 14; Edward Kaplan, *Spiritual Radical: Abraham Joshua Heschel in America* (New Haven: Yale University Press, 2007), 300.

13. Richard Neuhaus, oral history with Sam Dresner, N.D., Box 25, Binder.

14. Daniel Berrigan, Abraham Heschel, and Richard Neuhaus to Fathers and Brothers, 30 October 1965, AJHP, Box 67, File: Vietnam 1965.

15. Hall, *Because of Their Faith*, 14–15. See also Clergy Concerned About Vietnam, *An Ecumenical Study Conference: The Moral Implications of the Viet Nam Conflict*," 28 November 1965, AJHP, Box 67, File: Vietnam 1965.

16. Telegram, National Emergency Committee of Clergy Concerned About Vietnam to President Johnson, 11 January 1966, AJHP, Box 68, File: Vietnam, 1965–1966.

17. Friedland, *Lift Up Your Voice Like a Trumpet*, 148.

18. Abraham Heschel to J. F. Andrews, 27 December 1965, AJHP, Box 67, File: Vietnam, 1965.

19. Reuven Kimmelman, Comment, "Heschel: Roundtable Discussion with Samuel Dresner, Neil Gillman, Joe Lukinsky, David Novack, Fritz Rothschild, Sol Tannenzapf, Reuven Kimmelman, and Arthur Greene, August 1987, EKP, Box 25, Binder, 20.

20. "2,000 Clerics Ask 3-Day Fast for Peace," *New York Times*, 2 February 1967.

21. Edward Kaplan to Abraham Heschel, 3 February 1966, AJHP, Box 69, File: Washington, 1966–1967.

22. Abraham Joshua Heschel, "There Still Is Time," *Long Island Jewish Press*, February 1966.

23. Richard Fernandez, Oral History Interview, N.D., EKP, Audiotape Collection.

24. Clergy Concerned About Vietnam, Executive Committee to Fathers and Brothers, 16 September 1966, AJHP, Box 68, File: Vietnam 1966.

25. "Vietnam Protests Erupt in Calcutta and Rome as Other Demonstrators March to City," *New York Times*, 6 July 1966.

26. Lawrence Roberts, *Mayday 1971: A White House at War, A Revolt in the Street, and the Untold History of America's Biggest Mass Arrest* (Boston: Houghton Mifflin, 2020).

27. Charles DeBenedetti, *An American Ordeal: The Antiwar Movement of the Vietnam Era* (Syracuse: Syracuse University Press 1990), 145.

28. John Bennett, Abraham Heschel, John McKenzie, and Philip Scharper to the Buddhist and Roman Catholic Leadership of Vietnam, 19 April 1966, AJHP, Box 68, File: Vietnam, Personal 1966.

29. Peter Novick, *The Holocaust in American Life* (Boston: Houghton Mifflin, 1999).

30. Abraham Heschel, Handwritten Notes, 1968, AJHP, Box 60, File: Material for B, Circa 1968.

31. Abraham Heschel, "What We Might Do Together," 23 November 1966, AJHP, Box 77, File: Miscellaneous.

32. Abraham Heschel, Notes, 1966, AJHP, Box 67, File: Russia 1966.

33. Irving Spiegel, "Inaction Charged to Western Jews on Soviet Issue," *New York Times*, 17 May 1966.

34. Kaplan, *Spiritual Radical*, 228.

35. Elie Wiesel, *All Rivers Run to the Sea: Memoirs* (New York: Knopf, 1995), 377.

36. Maurice Friedman, *Abraham Joshua Heschel and Elie Wiesel: You Are My Witness* (New York: Farrar, Straus and Giroux, 1987), 81.

37. Abraham Heschel to David Hunter, 6 June 1966, AJHP, Box 68, File: Vietnam, Personal 1966.

38. Abraham Heschel to Virginia Snitow, 9 September 1966, AJHP, Box 68, File: Vietnam, Personal 1966.

39. "Gallup Polls Shows Sharp Division Among U.S. Jews on Vietnam Issue," *Jewish Telegraphic Agency*, 22 September 1966.

40. Judith A. Klinghoffer, *Vietnam, Jews and the Middle East: Unintended Consequences* (London, Macmillan, 1999), 94.

41. Sol Linowitz to Abraham Heschel, 19 September 1966, AJHP, Box 68, File: Jewish Statement 1966 (1 of 2); Irving Bernstein to Abraham Heschel, 19 September 1966, AJHP, Box 68, Folder: Vietnam, Personal 1966; Rabbi Emanuel Rackman to Abraham Heschel, 11 September 1966, AJHP, Box 69, File: Jewish Statement 1966 (2 of 2).

42. Abraham Sachar to Abraham Heschel, 26 September 1966, AJHP, Box 68, File: Jewish Statement 1966 (2 of 2).

43. "Goldberg Sees Jewish Leaders in Effort to Mend Johnson Rift," *New York Times*, 14 September 1966. See also "Jewish War Plea Vexes Israel," *New York Times*, 11 September 1966.

44. "Jewish Leaders Discuss Rift with LBJ," *World Journal Tribune*, 15 September 1966.

45. Irvin Jay Fain to Rabbis, Commission on Social Action, Chairmen, Social Action Committee, UAHC Board of Trustees, UAHC Liaison Representatives, 23 September 1966, AJHP, Box 67, File: Vietnam–Johnson, 1953, 1966.

46. "Voices from the Community: Elie Wiesel," 1986, EKP, Box 20, File: Wiesel, Elie.

47. "Jewish Reform Leaders Denounce Viet Nam Statement by J. W. V. Head," *Jewish Telegraphic Agency*, 10 January 1966.

48. Jo-Ann Price, "Rabbi Balfour Brickner," *National Catholic Reporter*, 18 October 1967; "Eisendrath, 71, Dies Just Before Address," *New York Times*, 10 November 1973.

49. Philip Mendes, *Jews and the Left: The Rise and Fall of a Political Alliance* (New York: Palgrave, 2014), 249–50.

50. Rafael Medoff and Raymond A. Smith, *Jewish Americans and Political Participation* (New York: ABC-CLIO, 2002), 95.

51. William Lunch and Peter Sperlich, "American Public Opinion and the War in Vietnam," *Western Political Quarterly* 32, no. 1 (March 1979): 42.

52. Abraham J. Heschel, *The Insecurity of Freedom: Essays on Human Existence* (New York: Farrar, Straus and Giroux, 1967).

53. Donald Mintz, "How to Remain Human," *Washington Star*, 10 May 1966.

54. Friedland, *Lift Up Your Voice Like a Trumpet*, 177.

55. "VIET-NAM: The Clergyman's Dilemma," 1967, AJHP, Box 69, File: Washington, 1966–1967.

56. Executive Committee, Clergy and Laymen Concerned About Vietnam, "Vietnam–The Clergymen's Dilemma," 31 January 1967, AJHP, Box 69, File: Vietnam 1966–1967.

57. John Bennett, Abraham Heschel, John McKenzie, and Philip Scharper to Lyndon Johnson, January 1967, AJHP, Box 69, File: Washington, 1966–1967.

58. Hall, *Because of Their Faith*, 35.

59. "2,000 Clerics Ask 3-Day Peace Fast," *New York Times*, 2 February 1967.

60. Linda Case, "Clergymen at Capital Question Viet Policy," *Hartford Courant*, 1 February 1967.

61. Edward Kaplan, "Letter About the Clergy and Laymen Concerned About Vietnam," February 1967, AJHP, Box 69 File: Washington, 1966–1967.

62. Kaplan, "Letter About the Clergy and Laymen Concerned

About Vietnam"; William MacKaye, "Churchmen March to Protest the War," *Washington Post*, 1 February 1967.

63. CALCAV, Directions for Vigil and Walk to Capitol, January 1967, AJHP, Box 69, File: Washington, 1966–1967.

64. Willard Edwards, "Dirksen, War Foes Trade Verbal Jabs," *Chicago Tribune*, 2 February 1967.

65. Kaplan, "Letter About the Clergy and Laymen Concerned About Vietnam."

66. MacKaye, "Churchmen March to Protest the War."

67. "Address of Rabbi Abraham Heschel at the Worship service," 31 January 1967, AJHP, Box 69, File: Vietnam 1967.

68. Abraham J. Heschel, "Address of Rabbi Abraham Heschel," 31 July 1967, AJHP, Box 69, File: Vietnam 1967.

69. Schedule, 31 January–1 February 1967, AJHP, Box 69, File: Washington, 1966–1967.

70. William Sloan Coffin, interview with Sam Dresner, 9 December 1987, EKP, Box 25, Binder.

71. Taylor Branch, *At Canaan's Edge: America in the King Years 1965–68* (New York: Simon & Schuster, 2006), 578; Kaplan, *Spiritual Radical*, 308–11.

72. Goldstein, *William Sloane Coffin Jr.*, 180.

73. Kaplan, *Spiritual Radical*, 310–11; Friedland, *Lift Up Your Voice Like a Trumpet*, 181.

74. Gary Dorrien, *Breaking White Supremacy: Martin Luther King Jr. and the Black Social Gospel* (New Haven: Yale University Press, 2018), 410.

75. Linda Lyons, "The Gallup Brain: War and Peace Protests," *Gallup*, 25 March 2003.

76. Dorrien, *Breaking White Supremacy*, 415.

77. Andrew Young, interview with Edward Kaplan, EKP, Box 20, Audio Tapes.

78. Jervis Anderson, *Bayard Rustin: Troubles I've Seen* (Berkeley: University of California Press, 1998), 299–302.

79. Daniel S. Lucks, *Selma to Saigon: The Civil Rights Movement and the Vietnam War* (Lexington: University Press of Kentucky, 2014), 175.

80. Leroy F. Aarons, "King Urges Cease-Fire and End of Bombing, Denounces the U.S. Role," *Washington Post*, 5 April 1967.

81. Flyer, 1967, AJHP, Box 70, File: Vietnam 1967 (3 of 4).

82. "Comments by Abraham J. Heschel," 4 April 1967, AJHP, Box 70, File: Vietnam 1967 (3 of 4).

83. Peniel Joseph, *The Sword and the Shield: The Revolutionary Lives of Malcolm X and Martin Luther King Jr.* (New York: Basic Books, 2020), 268.

84. For a fantastic account of the Riverside speech, see Branch, *At Canaan's Edge*, 580–604.

85. Dorrien, *Breaking White Supremacy*, 414.

86. "Dr. King's Error," *New York Times*, 7 April 1967.

87. Anderson, *Bayard Rustin*, 300.

88. Robert Anglin, "400,000 March in N.Y. Against War," *Boston Globe*, 16 April 1967.

89. Richard Fernandez, Interview A, N.D., EKP, Box 10, File: Wonder.

90. Robert McAfee Brown, Abraham J. Heschel, and Michael Novak, *Vietnam: Crisis of Conscience* (New York: Association Press, 1967), 48–61.

91. Lawrence Brown, "Vietnam Viewed from Moral Standpoint," *Minneapolis Star*, 31 July 1967.

92. Rabbi Gerald Zelermyer to Samuel Dresner, 1 December 1987, SDP, Box 1, File: Anecdotes; Zelermyer to Sylvia and Susannah Heschel, 1 December 1997, SDP, Box 3, File: Letters of Students.

93. Daniel Berrigan, "My Friend," in *No Religion Is an Island: Abraham Joshua Heschel and Interreligious Dialogue*, ed. Harold Kasimow and Byron L. Sherwin (Eugene, OR: Wipf & Stock, 1991), 71.

94. Heschel published the comment in his book *Israel: An Echo of Eternity* (New York: Farrar, Straus and Giroux, 1969), 196–97.

95. "A Plea for Love Without Cause," *Time*, 14 March 1969, 63.

96. Press Release, "The U.N. Must Settle the Middle East War," 5 June 1967, AJHP, Box 64, File: Israel Crisis 1967.

97. Branch, *At Canaan's Edge*, 621.

98. Heschel, *Israel*, 113–15.

99. Ibid., 37.

100. Ibid., 186.

101. Levi Kelman, interview with Edward Kaplan, 10 May 1992, SDP, Box 2, File: Kelman, Levi.

102. "The United States and Southeast Asia," 11 October 1967, AJHP, Box 69, File: Correspondence (2 of 2).

103. Abraham Heschel, John Sheerin, and Richard Neuhaus to Friend, 4 December 1967, AJHP, Box 69, File: Correspondence (2 of 2).

104. Friedland, *Lift Up Your Voice Like a Trumpet*, 194–95.

105. William Berrigan, interview with Sam Dresner, 9 December 1987, EKP, Box 25, Binder.

106. Hall, *Because of Their Faith*, 56–57.

107. John Bennett and Abraham Heschel to Friend, November 1967, AJHP, Box 69, File: Correspondence (2 of 2).

108. *In the Name of America: A Study Commissioned and Published by Clergy and Laymen Concerned About Vietnam* (Annandale, VA: Turnpike Press, 1968), v, 1.

109. Edward Kaplan, "Report of a Participant," February 1968, AJHP, Box 70, File: Vietnam 1967–1968.

110. Ibid.; Abraham Heschel, Speech, February 1968, Box 70, File: Vietnam, Circa 1968.

111. "Silent March," *Newsweek*, 19 February 1968, 58; Ben A. Franklin, "Clerics Rebuffed on Protest Site," *New York Times*, 3 February 1968; William R. MacKaye, "Court Bars Arlington Service by Antiwar Clergy," *New York Times*, 6 February 1968.

112. Dorrien, *Breaking White Supremacy*, 416.

113. Kaplan "Report of a Participant."

114. Ibid.

115. Kaplan, *Spiritual Radical*, 323.

116. Peter Beinart, "'Thoughts and Prayers' Could Be Exactly What America Needs," *Atlantic*, 7 November 2017.

117. Richard Hernandez, Tape B, N.D. EKP, Audiotape Collection.

118. Reprinted in *Moral Grandeur and Spiritual Audacity*, ed. Susannah Heschel (New York: Farrar, Straus, and Giroux, 1996), 262–63.

119. Edward Feld, interview with author, November 2018; Jim Lebeau to Baila Shargel, 9 February 1988, SDP, Box 2, File: JTS.

120. Rabbi Joseph Brodie, interview with author, 2 November 2020.

121. Susannah Heschel, "Their Feet Were Praying," *New York Jewish Week*, 10 January 2012.

122. Kaplan, *Spiritual Radical*, 326; Friedland, *Lift Up Your Voice Like a Trumpet*, 203.

123. Abraham Heschel, Notes, 1968, AJHP, Box 48, File: King's Funeral 1968.

124. Kaplan, *Spiritual Radical*, 329.

125. "Group Begins a 3-Day Fast in 'Repentance' for the War," *New York Times*, 9 April 1968; "Clergy Will Widen a Fast for Dr. King," *New York Times*, 10 April 1968.

126. "Erie Religious Leaders Call for 3-Day Prayer Vigil," *Erie Pennsylvania Times*, 7 April 1968.

127. Operation Connection, Press Release, 1968, AJHP, Box 64, File: Connection 1968.

128. Hall, *Because of Their Faith*, 72.

129. John Bennett, Press Release, 23 October 1968, AJHP, Box 70, File: Vietnam, 1968.

130. Abraham Joshua Heschel, Handwritten Notes, 1968, AJHP, Box 60, File: Material for B, Circa 1968.

131. Susannah Heschel, "My Father," in *No Religion Is an Island*, 31.

132. Abraham Joshua Heschel, Handwritten Notes, 1971, Box 72, File: Amnesty, 1971–1972 (2 of 2).

133. Abraham Heschel, "Meditation," in Clergy and Laymen Concerned About Vietnam, *Vietnam and the Future of the American Empire* (New York: CALCAV, 1969).

134. Hall, *Because of Their Faith*, 78–79.

135. Richard Fernandez, interview, 2 June 1988, EKP, Box 25, Binder. The interview can be heard in the Audiotape Collection; Kaplan, *Spiritual Radical*, 333.

136. Friedland, *Lift Up Your Voice Like a Trumpet*, 215.

137. John Bennett, Abraham Heschel et al. to Richard Nixon, 20 February 1969, AJHP, Box 63, File: Correspondence, 1963–1969 (1 of 2); "Nixon Asked [to] Make 'Clear' Statement on US Viet Policy," *Providence Visitor*, 28 February 1969.

138. Thomas Dodd to Abraham Heschel, 18 June 1969, and Heschel to Dodd, 25 June 1969, AJHP, Box 71, File: Vietnam, 1969.

139. Friedland, *Lift Up Your Voice Like a Trumpet*, 227.

140. Transcript, "A Conversation with Rabbi Abraham J. Heschel," ABC Television Network, 21 November 1971, AJHP, Box 278, Folder: A Conversation with Rabbi Abraham J. Heschel, 20, 22.

141. Transcript, AJHP, Box 88, Folder: Dissent, 1971. See also "Heschel Sees Dissent as Vital to Judaism," *Times Herald Record*, 3 May 1971.

142. Josh Feigelson, "50 Years Ago, Upstart Rabbi Used Jewish Law to Tell Senate to End Vietnam War," *Times of Israel*, 7 May 2020.

143. "The Opposite of God Is Indifference: Interview with Arnold Eisen," *On Being*, 21 September 2017; Arnold Eisen, interview with author, 3 September 2020.

144. Abraham Heschel, Personal Notes, March 1971, AJHP, Box 61, File: Italy 1971 March.

145. "Religious Leaders for McGovern–Shriver," 1972, AJHP, Box 73, File: McGovern, 1972; "McGovern for President—Some Reasons Why," 1972, AJHP, Box 73, File: McGovern, 1972.

146. Abraham Heschel, "Jews and the Election," *New York Times*, 27 October 1972.

147. "An Open Letter to the President from a Group of Alarmed Businessmen, Law School Deans and Professors and Religious Leaders," *New York Times*, 29 October 1972.

148. Marcia Chambers, "Overreaction to Anti-Semitic Views Noted," 1968, *NJ News Tribune*.

149. "Heschel Says Jews Must Continue Their Fight to Attain Justice for Blacks," *Intermountain Jewish News*, 10 December 1971.

150. Marc Dollinger, *Black Power, Jewish Politics: Reinventing the Alliance in the 1960s* (Waltham: Brandeis University Press, 2018).

151. "The Jews: Next Year in Which Jerusalem?" *Time*, 10 April 1972, 57.

152. Byron L. Sherwin, Review, *Shofar* 26, no. 1 (Fall 2007): 184–85.

153. Abraham Joshua Heschel, *A Passion for Truth*, Sixth Printing (Woodstock, VT: Jewish Lights, 2013), 166, 242.

154. Ibid., 86.

155. Ibid., 318–19.

156. Ibid., 300–301.

157. Ibid., 321.

158. Ibid., 195.

159. Ibid., 310.

160. Samuel Dresner, Notes, "The Last Week," EKP, Box 10, File: Heschel's Last Days.

161. Yohanan Muffs, oral history interview, 12 May 1988, EKP, Binder.

162. Elie Wiesel, Memoirs: *All Rivers Run to the Sea* (New York: Schocken, 1995), 401.

163. Dov Peretz Elkins to Sylvia Heschel, 6 February 1973, AJHP, Box 38, File: 5.

164. Berrigan, "My Friend," in *No Religion Is an Island*, 74–75.

165. Stephen Wermiel, "Fr. Berrigan Has 'No Great Hopes' for Peace Movement Revival," *Boston Globe*, 24 December 1972.

166. Daniel Berrigan, interview with Edward Kaplan, 12 January 1988, EKP, Box 25, Binder.

167. Notes about Heschel's Passing, 31 December 1972, EKP, Box 10, File: Heschel's Last Days.

168. "Homage Paid to Rabbi Heschel by 500 at Traditional Service," *New York Times*, 25 December 1972.

169. Ibid.; Notes about Heschel's Passing, 31 December 1972, EKP, Box 10, File: Heschel's Last Days.

Chapter 7. Legacy

1. *Eternal Light*, NBC Television, 4 February 1973.

2. "Militant Mystic," *Time*, 8 January 1973, 43.

3. Martin Weil, "Rabbi Abraham Heschel Dies," *Washington Post*, 26 December 1972.

4. "Rabbi Heschel Eulogized as Fighter for Human Freedom," *Jewish Telegraphic Agency*, 23 January 1973.

5. Jimmy Carter to Senator Richard Stone, 15 December 1976, and Wolfe Kelman to Richard Stone, 6 January 1977 and 4 January 1977, EKP, Box 11, File: Jimmy Carter.

6. Jill Jacobs, "There Shall Be No Needy," in *American Jewish Thought Since 1934: Writings on Identity, Engagement, and Belief*, ed. Michael Marmur and David Ellenson (Waltham: Brandeis University Press, 2020), 158–59.

7. Marc Dollinger, *Black Power and Jewish Politics: Reinventing the Alliance in the 1960s* (Waltham: Brandeis University Press, 2018).

8. Jack Jenkins, *American Prophets: The Religious Roots of Progressive Politics and the Ongoing Fight for the Soul of the Country* (New York: Harper, 2020).

9. Michael Lerner, interview with Edward Kaplan, 2 January 1998, EKP, Box 7, File: EK Interviews I-L.

10. Michael Lerner, "Heschel's Legacy for the Politics of the Twenty-First Century," *Modern Judaism* 29, no. 1 (February 2009): 34.

11. Michael Lerner, "TIKKUN: To Mend, Repair and Transform the World," *Tikkun* 1, no. 1 (1986): 4.

12. Interview with Peter Geffen, American Jewish Peace Archive, 20 April 2016.

13. "Peter Geffen on Heschel as Social Activist," 2015, Vimeo.

14. Peter Geffen, "Covenant Award Acceptance Speech," November 2012, youtube.com.

15. Nadine Brozan, "Manhattan Day School Blends Diversity, Jewish Tradition," *New York Times*, 26 September 1985.

16. Samuel Dresner, *Heschel, Hasidism, and Halakha* (New York: Fordham University Press, 2001), 25.

17. Edward Kaplan and Samuel Dresner, *Abraham Joshua Heschel: Prophetic Witness* (New Haven: Yale University Press, 1998); Edward K. Kaplan, *Spiritual Radical: Abraham Joshua Heschel in America, 1940–1972* (New Haven: Yale University Press, 2007).

18. Held, *Abraham Joshua Heschel.*

19. Cornel West, "Black Intellectuals, Jewish Tensions: How to End the Impasse," *New York Times,* 14 April 1993.

20. Susannah Heschel, "Two Friends, Two Prophets: Abraham Joshua Heschel and Martin Luther King Jr.," *Plough Quarterly,* no. 16 (Spring 2018).

21. Richard Michelson, *As Good as Anybody: Martin Luther King Jr. and Abraham Joshua Heschel's Amazing March Toward Freedom* (New York: Dragonfly Books, 2008).

22. Pew Research Center, *A Portrait of American Jews,* 1 October 2013.

23. Abraham Joshua Heschel, "The Individual Jew and His Obligations," in *The Insecurity of Freedom: Essays on Human Existence* (New York: Farrar, Straus and Giroux, 1966), 191.

24. Arnold Eisen, interview with author, 3 September 2020.

25. Edward Feld, interview with author, 30 October 2018.

26. Leonard Felson, "Is the Conservative Movement's New Prayer Book a Step Towards Its Revitalization," *Tablet,* 19 February 2016.

27. Jeremy Gordon, "To Have Hold of a Tallit: Abraham Joshua Heschel's Rabbinic Scholarship," *European Judaism* 41, no. 1 (Spring 2008): 17.

28. Peter Steinfeld, "Beliefs," *New York Times,* 10 January 1998.

29. Rachel Zoll, "Jewish Life Addressed," *Associated Press,* 13 September 2007.

30. Arnold Eisen, interview with author, 3 September 2020.

31. Edward Kaplan, Notes, 13 May 1983, EKP, Box 11, File: Conference.

32. Eric J. Greenberg, "Reclaiming Heschel," *New York Jewish Week,* 9 January 1998.

33. Ibid. See also Elliot Resnick, "Abraham Joshua Heschel: An Orthodox Thinker?" *Jewish Press,* 4 December 2019.

34. Arthur Green, "A Neo-Hasidic Theology: Taking Jewish Monism Out of the Closet," Mordecai Kaplan Center for Jewish Peoplehood, September 2020.

35. Samuel G. Freedman, *Jew versus Jew: The Struggle for the Soul of American Jewry* (New York: Simon & Schuster, 2000).

36. "800 Rabbis and Cantors Sign Statement Supporting Peaceful Protest Against Racism," *Jewish Telegraphic Agency,* 9 June 2020.

37. https://www.jweekly.com/2020/12/15/raphael-warnock -lauds-black-jewish-alliance-in-video-amid-accusations-that-hes -hostile-to-israel/.

INDEX

Abernathy, Ralph, xvii
Abraham Joshua Heschel School (New York City), 228
Abram, Morris, 163
Abravanel, Isaac, 36
Adath Israel Synagogue (Cincinnati), 48
Adler, Cyrus, 43, 66, 67, 234
African Americans: anti-Semitism among, 214–15; antiwar movement and, 190; Jewish-African American alliance, 128–29, 205–6, 226–27, 229–30; military recruitment of, 190–91; social justice and, 229; Soviet Jews and, 138–39. *See also* civil rights movement
Agudas Yisroel (political party), 16, 59
Ali, Muhammad, 191
Altmann, Alexander, 90–91
American Jewish Committee, 46, 112, 130, 156, 163
American Jewish Congress (AJC):

antiwar movement and, 177, 181; civil rights movement and, 129–30, 141–45, 147, 150; founding of, 46; Madison Square Garden protest against Nazism (1942), 56–57; "Studies in Prejudice" series, 76
American Jewish Press, 93
American Jewish Yearbook on establishment of state of Israel, 77
American Oriental Society, 44
Anti-Defamation League, 45, 130, 197, 215
anti-Semitism: Catholic Church and, 142, 144, 147, 148, 162–63; in Germany, 24, 76; in Poland, 8–9, 12–13; racism's commonalities with, 130, 160; in Soviet Union, 136–37, 138; in United States, 44–45
antiwar activism, 165–213; African Americans and, 190; American

JEWISH LIVES is a prizewinning series of interpretative biography designed to explore the many facets of Jewish identity. Individual volumes illuminate the imprint of Jewish figures upon literature, religion, philosophy, politics, cultural and economic life, and the arts and sciences. Subjects are paired with authors to elicit lively, deeply informed books that explore the range and depth of the Jewish experience from antiquity to the present.

Jewish Lives is a partnership of Yale University Press and the Leon D. Black Foundation. Ileene Smith is editorial director. Anita Shapira and Steven J. Zipperstein are series editors.